Doing Science

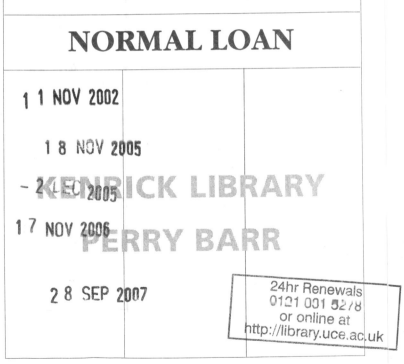

Doing Science:
Images of Science in
Science Education

Edited by
Robin Millar

The Falmer Press
(A member of the Taylor & Francis Group)
London • New York • Philadelphia

UK   The Falmer Press, Falmer House, Barcombe, Lewes, East Sussex,
            BN8 5DL

USA   The Falmer Press, Taylor & Francis Inc., 242 Cherry Street,
            Philadelphia, PA 19106-1906

First published 1989

British Library Cataloguing in Publication Data

Doing Science.
1. England. Schools. Curriculum subjects: Science. Science
teaching. I. Millar, Robin.
507'.1041
ISBN 1-85000-506-0
ISBN 1-85000-507-9 (pbk.)

Library of Congress Cataloging in Publication Data is available on request

Jacket design by Caroline Archer

Typeset in 10½/12 point California by
Chapterhouse Typesetting Ltd, Formby, Lancs

Printed in Great Britain by Taylor & Francis (Printers) Ltd, Basingstoke

Contents

List of Tables

List of Figures

Acknowledgments

The idea that I should edit a book which would relate science education and science studies was first suggested to me by Harry Collins, on board a boat on the River Avon near Bath on a pleasant summer evening in August 1985. The book seems to have come a long way since then! I am grateful to Harry for his initial encouragement and for his interest in this project as it has developed. I hope he will find the product as interesting as he said he would then.

My most significant debt, of course, is to the authors who have contributed chapters to the book. Many of them have fitted this writing into already busy schedules and all have tolerated my reminders about deadlines and responded positively to my editorial interventions and suggestions. In the process some have contributed significantly to my thinking about the overall shape of the book. I am grateful to all of them.

I also want to thank Trevor Pinch for reading and commenting on many of the draft chapters. Coming to science education material from the perspective of a sociologist of science, he provided me with an invaluable additional perspective, which I think has significantly improved the book.

I am grateful to Vivienne Taylor and Margaret Tull for typing parts of the manuscript.

Finally, to the customary acknowledgments of family support, I would like to add my thanks to Liz for contributions beyond the call of duty in helping my own chapter over one memorable 'block', and to Neil and Ruth for tolerating my recurrent absences 'at the computer' with good humour.

Robin Millar
February 1989

Introduction:
Science Education and Science Studies

Robin Millar

This book explores the areas of common interest between science education and science studies. These fields of study and their respective academic communities, whilst appearing to have many potential points of contact, remain surprisingly separate, with little apparent recognition of the relevance to the interests of each of work done within the other tradition. My aim in putting this book together has been to try to bridge the gap between the interests of these two groups.

As a field of study science education deals with the processes of passing on knowledge and understanding of science and its practices to new learners. That is, its concerns are with the induction of the next generation of scientists into scientific ways of thinking and working and with the wider dissemination of a 'public understanding of science' amongst the population at large, and with the issues which these concerns raise. Social studies of science (or science studies) is the collective term for a group of disciplinary interests in science, notably sociology, history and philosophy of science. Its concerns have centred on the institutions of science, the practices of scientists and the nature of scientific knowledge.

Science studies have produced an extensive body of work looking closely at scientific theory change, at the processes of development, negotiation and acceptance of new scientific knowledge. Sociologists of science, in particular, have rejected the older idealized accounts and reconstructions of scientific method, and have undertaken detailed studies of historical and contemporary episodes in science. The aim of these studies is to provide a 'scientific' account of science itself, grounded in empirical observations and matched to actual historical or contemporary practice. Although science studies has produced several very detailed studies of the scientific *research* laboratory, there have not yet been any comparable studies of the science *teaching* laboratory. This is surely surprising, as the science teaching laboratory is the locus of those processes by which the scientific community replicates itself, and by which public understanding (or misunderstanding) of science is promoted.

Conversely, although science educators have made studies of science learning and of social interaction within science classrooms and laboratories, they have rarely linked the two, to consider social factors in science concept learning. Perhaps more seriously, despite current enthusiasms for teaching about the social and economic implications of science and about the nature of science, there is little evidence that work in science studies is known to many science educators or has influenced syllabus prescriptions and recommendations. This apparent neglect of a large body of detailed scholarship which bears directly on these matters is, at the very least, a matter for concern.

In planning the book I have had a number of criteria in mind. The most obvious is that I have tried to include work which might show the significance of modern science studies for classroom practice and, conversely, the importance of the classroom and the teaching laboratory as a context for science studies. I have also tried, so far as possible, to make this a collection of work grounded in qualitative, empirical studies of science classrooms. In this regard the collection mirrors the emphasis in the 'new' sociology of science, whose impetus derives in large part from its insistence on studying scientists' *actual practice*, rather than on making retrospective reconstructions of that practice. This has ruled out review articles or 'position papers' arguing that this or that should be done. Some of the chapters *do* make recommendations or suggest changes to current practices, but these are always drawn from the empirical work which precedes them.

The thread which runs through the collection as a whole is children's experience of 'doing science' and the *image* of science which learners pick up along with the science knowledge, understanding and skills they acquire. So the book is about the 'hidden curriculum of science', the things students learn as unintended or, at least, unplanned outcomes, alongside the learning outcomes which the syllabus or the teacher intended to convey. Although school is not the only source of images of science, it plays a major role in forming most children's, and hence most adults', perceptions of what science is, what sort of knowledge it provides and why we should believe it.

Whilst the book was in preparation, the theme of the nature of science has become a particularly timely one, for UK readers at least. The Working Group set up by the Secretary of State to develop the framework for a National Curriculum in Science from ages 5 to 16 proposed as one attainment target that pupils should have some understanding of *The Nature of Science*. They recommended that: 'Pupils should develop an understanding that Science is a human activity, that scientific ideas change through time, and that the nature of scientific ideas and the uses to which they are put are affected by the social and cultural contexts in which they are developed' (DES, 1988: 70). This recommendation has survived the subsequent consultation process and is now part of the National Science Curriculum. Similar objectives have appeared in recent statements about science education in many countries; the general idea that science education should include some explicit treatment of the nature of science is widely acknow-ledged, at least at the level of science education rhetoric. This makes it all the more important to consider what ideas about science and scientific knowledge are transmitted *implicitly* during all science instruction. For these ideas may be very pervasive and durable. Piecemeal attempts to 'tag on' a few lessons or activities dealing overtly with the nature of science may achieve very little, if they ignore the implicit messages about the nature of science which are being communicated all the time.

Part of the task of opening up the hidden curriculum of science to scrutiny involves rendering problematic some taken-for-granted practices and approaches, for it is precisely those parts of a social enterprise which are the most taken-for-granted which are likely to embody its deepest assump-tions. In Chapter 1 Jane French looks at how a teacher and her pupils 'accomplish scientific instruction'. The context is children's first experiences of formal science lessons, and the chapter explores some of the aspects of early induction into science and the first steps towards becoming an 'insider'. By analyzing the teacher's reactions to intended and unintended outcomes of practical work, she shows the tacit dimension in science learning and indicates how 'errors' are useful if these tacit elements in 'doing science' are to be communicated.

Chapters 2 and 3 deal with *experiment*. In Chapter 2 I use a case study of teachers' reactions to an accepted textbook experiment which 'doesn't work' to explore the uses of experiment in science teaching more generally. The chapter provides a critique of the standard rhetoric of the 'method of science' in science education writings and, in particular, of the role this ascribes to experiment. It argues that the accounts of experiment arising from the empirical programme in sociology of science match rather better with the realities of classrooms. The case study is then used to explore the uneasy relationship between first-hand and second-hand information sources in science teaching — between personal enquiry and common knowledge — and to seek a more consistent integration of the two.

In Chapter 3 Colin Gauld considers the relationship between empirical data and espoused theory from another angle, comparing the reactions and strategies of students with those of research scientists. The chapter is a longi-tudinal study of the evolution of personal theories about electricity in simple circuits within a group of secondary school students. Gauld shows how em-pirical data may be incorporated in students' views or set aside, and explores the reasons for these reactions.

Gauld's work is rooted in the constructivist research programme, which has become very influential in science education research over the past decade. In the constructivist view of learning, children's ideas and understandings prior to instruction are seen as very important, as they may crucially facilitate or obstruct further learning. Teaching science from this point of view (Scott, Dyson and Gater, 1987) involves eliciting pupils' ideas at the outset and then using classroom experiences to develop these, by encouraging children to articulate their ideas more clearly to identify internal contradictions or deficiencies, or by challenging children's ideas using laboratory counterexamples. Group work, with an emphasis on language use and on the application of concepts and ideas, is used to consolidate learning. Within this approach there is an implicit issue about the 'weight' to be given to children's ideas compared with the accepted scientific view. The lack of consensus about this is reflected in the varieties of terminology used by researchers. Gauld (1987) has identified over twenty different combinations of 'basic terms' (such as ideas, meanings, conceptions, structures) and 'qualifiers' (for example, mis-, alternative, personal, children's). This vagueness in terminology has left the classroom implications of the constructivist programme open to a variety of interpretations. At the 'minimal' end of the spectrum it could simply be seen as providing the necessary information for teaching science concepts better; the more we know about children's *mis*conceptions the better we will be able to plan teaching strategies to eliminate them. On the other hand, some constructivist writing seems to invite a much more radical, relativist interpretation, where children's ideas are given the status of *alternative* constructions of meaning about the physical world, which can stand alongside scientists' ideas and be seen as *different* (because they are for different and usually more limited purposes), rather than necessarily *inferior*.

These issues underpin the discussion in Chapters 4 and 5. In Chapter 4 Rosalind Driver uses extracts from children's discussions in small groups whilst investigating scientific phenomena to reflect on the development of children's scientific ideas. She explores the relationship between the individual child's construction of meaning in relation to natural phenomena and events, and science as a body of public knowledge. Using extracts from classroom discussion, Driver shows how a commitment to listening to and exploring children's ideas, and a perception of science teaching as the restructuring of these ideas, can still have as its goal consensual public knowledge. There are clear parallels between this chapter and Chapter 2. Both explore the relationship between the personal, or first-hand, knowledge which the learner obtains directly from experience and the body of public, or second-hand, knowledge contained in books or provided by the teacher. Although the two chapters approach the issue from distinctively different angles, the conclusions they reach are mutually supportive.

In Chapter 5 Tom Russell and Hugh Munby explore the relationship between two sorts of knowledge held by science teachers: knowledge about the nature of science and professional knowledge — the knowledge expressed by particular teaching acts. They draw on Schön's idea of reflection-in-action to present parallel case studies of two teachers. For one teacher a view of science as a stable body of knowledge appears to parallel her professional knowledge and her understanding of how to think about her teaching. The constructivist position of the second teacher is shown both in how he speaks of science and in how his professional knowledge develops from his thinking about events in the classroom. Russell and Munby suggest that the contrast between the two signals the importance of teachers' professional knowledge and that the area merits more extensive and detailed study.

Science learning is, in a number of senses, a *social* activity. It involves groups of students and a teacher working together in classrooms; language and communication play a crucial role in allowing us to form, develop and consolidate our ideas and concepts. It can be argued that without an 'audience' for us to try out our ideas, we could never develop stable concepts at all. For research science the 'audience' is an essential part of the process of knowledge creation. A new knowledge-claim by an individual scientist or research group becomes a scientific 'fact' only when it is accepted as such by the scientific community. In Chapter 6 Joan Solomon considers the social aspects of science learning in the classroom. She looks at the function of pupil interaction in making learning in the laboratory possible and at the role of group discussion in concept formation. These glimpses of the social aspects of concept learning, often drawn from work originally undertaken for other purposes, again suggest an area where much useful work remains to be done, and where the parallels with studies of research science may suggest ways forward.

Learning science involves not only doing practical laboratory work but also reading and writing about science. For the pupil 'doing science' means doing it every week, at the desk as well as the laboratory bench. Here, too, many of the conventions and practices are taken-for-granted. Pupils become immersed in conventional formats for writing and in conventional styles of written and printed materials. These 'media' of science teaching may be conveying their own 'message' about the nature of the scientific enterprise. In Chapter 7 Clive Sutton explores the role of reading and writing about science in forming and sustaining children's images of science. He suggests that, as routines are powerful, the *general* ways of working might be more important than the content of particular lessons, giving the pupils tacit knowledge of what it means to 'do' science. Sutton uses examples to illustrate how certain writing styles may reinforce views of science as impersonal, objective knowledge. He proposes that other forms of text might be used to convey the idea of scientific knowledge as a human creation, and to give a flavour of the intellectual struggle involved in 'making sense' of nature.

The final two chapters deal with two specific attempts to modify the image of science presented to children through science education. Both use historical materials as their vehicle; importantly, both present an evaluation of the outcomes of actually using the materials they describe. The proposal that some history of science be included within science education in order to teach about the nature of science is a recurrent one. One widely recognized problem, however, is that it is difficult (for both students and teachers) to perform the mental leap to a time when a piece of scientific theory about which there is now consensus was open and problematic. It is hard to take seriously the views of those who 'lost' the argument; they look, with hindsight, to have been making 'obvious' mistakes. Nonetheless, it is difficult to see how we can give students a feel for the culture of science and the nature of scientific knowledge without making some use of historical case studies.

In Chapter 8 Ton van der Valk discusses the experiences of the PLON curriculum development group in The Netherlands with a teaching unit which sets out both to teach some physics and to introduce some ideas about theory change in science. The PLON group has been responsible for some very innovative curriculum development work over the past decade, which, because it is written in Dutch, may not yet have reached the audience it deserves. In his chapter van der Valk shows how the teaching unit evolved through various revisions, in the light of teachers' and pupils' experiences of using it. He explores the nature of the learning which it promotes, identifies the difficulties which remain and outlines some strategies for tackling these.

In Chapter 9 Patricia Burdett discusses the use of simulations of historical controversies in science through role-play. Using a simulation of the N ray affair of the early 1900s as an example, she presents and analyzes extracts from the dialogue produced by pupils in enacting the simulation and from the debriefing discussions which followed. She shows that 16-year-olds, having studied science to GCSE level, were able to enter imaginatively into a historical controversy and to appreciate, to some extent at least, many of the issues concerning scientific knowledge and theory change.

It is clear that these chapters do not cover all the areas of potential common interest between science education and science studies. They are a selection, the outcome of my approaching authors whose previous work I knew and working with those who responded positively to the framework of the book I was proposing. Indeed many of their responses modified and developed that framework as the collection took shape.

I am particularly aware of one topic which is not addressed by any chapter and which some might see as a significant omission. This is the image of science as *masculine*. We know that even at the primary school stage children already overwhelmingly perceive scientists as men (Chambers, 1983). A great number of other studies show that this perception of science as a male preserve is strong and persistent (see, for example, Kelly, 1981; Harding, 1986; Kelly, 1987). Kelly (1985) has written of the 'construction of masculine science', exploring four senses in which science might be labelled 'masculine'. First, she notes the numerical dominance of males in professional science, as science teachers and as science learners, particularly in the physical sciences. Then she comments on the dominance of male images used in 'packaging' science, in textbook illustrations and examples. Thirdly, she discusses how differences between girls' and boys' behaviours and self-perceptions, arising from out-of-school contexts, become recontextualized within school, so that different academic disciplines take on gender-differentiated associations. She notes differences in the classroom behaviours of boys and girls and in the reactions of teachers to them and identifies ways in which these sustain a gender-differentiated view of school subjects. Kelly's fourth sense is the argument that science is 'inherently masculine', a social construct which has developed in a patriarchal, male-dominated society. In this sense it is not only the image of science as an institution which is masculine; it is also the image of science-as-knowledge.

It is often unclear whether those who pursue this line intend a 'weak' or a 'strong' reading of their argument. The 'weak' position is that science is masculine in the sense that it has been dominated historically by males; its emphases and research directions reflect male interests and concerns. Its 'maleness' is a contingent feature of the historical and social context within which science happened to emerge. The sort of explanations which science provides are, however, independent of gender considerations; they are the only style of explanation which is possible if we are to pursue science's aims of explaining and making reliable predictions about the behaviour of the natural world. This 'weak' position would hold that had science developed in another culture at another time, then its emphases might well have been different, but its approach to understanding would be the same.

A 'strong' position, on the other hand, would argue that the analytic, reductionist approach to understanding is itself *essentially* masculine and represents only one, partial way of approaching and seeking to understand the natural world. Other ways of doing science are possible and would yield alternative accounts of nature. But if we are to label scientific knowledge 'masculine' in this sense, then it is important to recognize that we have no externally 'given' standard of 'masculinity' to use as a criterion. Like 'science', 'masculine' is a social construct; our image of 'the masculine' has evolved alongside our image of 'scientific knowledge'. This, as Keller observes, changes the questions we might ask:

> From the comparatively simple questions about women in science, or about the biology of women, grows a much larger set of questions about how our ideas of gender have helped shape our construction of science, and how our ideas about science have influenced our construction of gender — in short, it becomes a study of the simultaneous making of men, women and science (Keller, 1986: 173).

Keller (1985) and Sandra Harding (1986) argue that we have moved from the 'women question in science' to the 'science question in feminism'. It is, of course, much easier to ask these 'questions' than to provide evidence or answers. We can see readily enough that the language of science and technology is full of male imagery, from the general idea of the 'mastery of nature' to the distinction between 'hard' and 'soft' sciences, to the terminology of 'male' and 'female' connectors in electrical engineering (see, for example, Easlea, 1986). But it is harder to see what the effects of a non-patriarchal discourse might have been. As Keller notes: 'Modern science, as we know it, has arisen once and only once in cultural history. . .We cannot look to other cultures, with other gender systems, and ask how their science is or was different, for the simple reason that the knowledge practices of other cultures do not conform to what we call science' (Keller, 1986: 174). It is in this regard that Keller's detailed study of the work of the Nobel Prize winning biologist, Barbara McClintock, is so valuable (Keller, 1983). Keller shows how McClintock's 'feeling for the organism' she was studying led to a less analytic and more holistic approach to the problem.

This sort of work is necessarily limited in opportunity; few individuals practise science this way. But it offers the tantalizing thought that the context of 're-discovery' or 'personal construction of meaning' in the science classroom might be an easier locus for such an investigation than the scientific research laboratory. Can we observe gender-differentiated approaches to the understanding of ideas and concepts, or to tackling investigative problems in the classroom? Do male and female learners display different ways of trying to understand natural phenomena — different images of scientific knowledge? There is no chapter on the image of science as masculine in this book simply because I am aware of no work of this sort going on. Is it an area which might be worth developing?

Indeed, many chapters of the book open up areas of enquiry which the authors recognize they are merely beginning to explore. If the book can encourage a few science educators to explore the recent literature of science studies and consider its relevance to science education, and a few members of the science studies community to consider whether their neglect of the classroom is any longer justifiable, then these areas might begin to receive the attention they deserve — and this book would have achieved its aim.

References

CHAMBERS, D.W. (1983) 'Stereotypic images of the scientist: The draw-a-scientist test', *Science Education*, **67**, 2, pp. 255–65.

DEPARTMENT OF EDUCATION AND SCIENCE (1988) *National Curriculum: Science for Ages 5 to 16*, London, DES and Welsh Office.

EASLEA, B. (1986) 'The masculine image of science: How much does gender really matter?', in HARDING, J. (Ed.) *Perspectives on Gender and Science*, Lewes, Falmer Press, pp. 132–58.

GAULD, C. (1987) 'Student beliefs and cognitive structure', *Research in Science Education*, **17**, pp. 87–93.

HARDING, J. (Ed.) (1986) *Perspectives on Gender and Science*, Lewes, Falmer Press.

HARDING, S. (1986) *The Science Question in Feminism*, Milton Keynes, Open University Press.

KELLER, E. F. (1983) *A Feeling for the Organism: The Life and Work of Barbara McClintock*, New York, Freeman.

KELLER, E. F. (1985) *Reflections on Gender and Science*, New Haven and London, Yale University Press.

KELLER, E. F. (1986) 'How gender matters, or, why it's so hard for us to count past two', in HARDING, J. (Ed.), *Perspectives on Gender and Science*, Lewes, Falmer Press, pp. 168–83.

KELLY, A. (Ed.) (1981) *The Missing Half: Girls and Science Education*, Manchester, Manchester University Press.

KELLY, A. (1985) 'The construction of masculine science', *British Journal of Sociology of Education*, 6, pp. 133–54.

KELLY, A. (Ed.) (1987) *Science for Girls?*, Milton Keynes, Open University Press.

SCOTT, P., DYSON, T. and GATER, S. (1987) *A Constructivist View of Learning and Teaching in Science*. Children's Learning in Science Project, Centre for Studies in Science and Mathematics Education, University of Leeds.

Chapter 1

Accomplishing Scientific Instruction

Jane French

... classroom studies have typically overlooked — whilst at the
same time inevitably counting upon — what for the interested
parties in a given scene... are the characteristic, distinctive and
essential features of their activities, namely those of teaching and
learning about 'subjects' as incarnate in 'lessons'. This might be
termed 'education's essential work' (McHoul and Watson,
1984: 284).

Induction into Science

The first year of secondary schooling represents for many British school
children their first concentrated exposure to science as a subject discipline.
This is not to say that they are likely to be entirely ignorant of science, its
ways of working or areas of interest. With the growing policy emphasis on
curriculum continuity in science from age 5 to 16 (DES, 1985), the majority
of primary schools now include in their curricula elements of all the natural
sciences, frequently within the context of interdisciplinary project work
which encourages pupils to bring a variety of perspectives to bear upon a
particular topic or area of investigation. Within this sort of context pupils
may have carried out elementary experiments, absorbed the rudiments of
systematic observation and so on. In addition exposure to children's literature, toys and television is likely to have suggested to pupils a set of images
as to the work and nature of science and of scientists themselves. It is
probable, then, that first year secondary pupils come to the school laboratory with a certain informal knowledge of the subject gained from lay
contexts.

What is likely to be experienced as novel at this stage is the com-
partmentalizing of school subjects (including the eventual separating of
chemistry, physics and biology), and what might be termed the processes of
socialization into the modes of thought and practice pertaining to each

discrete area and which distinguish one subject from another. This chapter focuses on aspects of this induction into science, a theme which has long been of interest to sociologists, who have brought a range of different theoretical perspectives to bear on classroom interactional data. The chapter is based on research (French, 1987a) on the social organization of instruction in science in some first year secondary school lessons in practical chemistry.

The Study: Its Background and Aims

The aim of the study was to apply methods of analysis associated with the perspectives of ethnomethodology and conversation analysis to a database of video recorded lessons in practical science, in order to consider and to describe some of the interactional practices used by participants in accomplishing scientific instruction. The theoretical perspectives which underpinned the work may be of interest to some readers. However, the remainder of this section is not essential for an understanding of the chapter and some readers may prefer to go directly to the presentation and discussion of the data (pp. 15ff.).

Classroom Interaction Analysis: An Area of Study

The study belongs within a now established body of work on classroom interaction analysis. This is a multi-disciplinary area, with representation from psychology, sociology and linguistics, amongst others. The present study is sociological in orientation. Sociologists have brought a range of different theoretical perspectives to bear on classroom interactional data, with strong representation from symbolic interactionist and ethnographic approaches. From the late 1960s onwards an array of observational studies began to appear, beginning, in Britain at least, with the seminal contributions of Hargreaves (1967) and Lacey (1970). The area expanded rapidly, with analysts deploying a range of ethnographic research techniques, formerly more usually associated with the anthropological tradition.

A paramount aim of these studies was to provide a realistic, 'inside' account of schooling as a process, in welcome contrast to the previous tendency, noted, for example, by Delamont and Hamilton (1976) and Hammersley and Woods (1976), to treat the classroom as the unopened 'black box' between educational input and output. One noticeable divergence within the ethnographic–symbolic interactionist camp concerned the extent to which attention was paid to language. It was a difference of degree, but nonetheless significant in giving rise to issues concerning the presentation and status of data, and analytic description. Edwards and Westgate (1987), for example, describe some researchers as viewing language '. . . only as a more-or-less transparent medium through which to observe and record social interaction' (Edwards and Westgate, 1987: 11). They contrast this approach with one in which language is 'explicitly the focus of investigation'. Mehan (1974) similarly defines it as a question of 'looking at the window of language and not just through it' (Mehan, 1974: 181). Edwards and Westgate stress the primacy of language in the construction of the social world.

> It is largely through talk that we develop our concepts of self, as members of various social 'worlds' which can be brought into focus and in which we can locate ourselves and recognize the values, rights and obligations which permeate them. As we listen and as we talk, we learn what it is necessary to know, do and say in that area of social life or that setting, and can display the competence necessary to be accepted as a member (Edwards and Westgate, 1987: 12).

However, criticism of classroom ethnographic studies was also forthcoming from a small group of sociologists working from the ethnomethodological perspective developed by Harold Garfinkel (1967). Classroom studies undertaken within this tradition are relatively few in number, but include some significant contributions to our knowledge of the complex organization of teacher–pupil interaction. Perhaps the most *immediately* apparent difference between them and the more numerous ethnographic studies is one of focus. The general tendency within ethnography, notwithstanding those ethnographers who place a specific focus on language, is for the analyst to adopt a broad overall stance, surveying classes or, indeed, whole schools with the account then emerging on the basis of matters arising during the long period of observation generally undertaken. By contrast, the focus of ethnomethodological studies is narrower. Interest is centred on the organization of sequences of talk in the setting, which are generally recorded and transcribed for the purposes of detailed analysis, on procedures of sense-making, or other related aspects of the interactional structure and accomplishment of lessons. This study draws heavily on the ethnomethodological tradition, and on conversation analysis, an approach to the analysis of interactional data which developed in response to Garfinkel's work.

Ethnomethodology: Some Key Concepts and Their Implications

The principles of ethnomethodological analysis are by now well documented; introductory accounts may be found in Leiter (1980) and Benson and Hughes (1983). In the following the emphasis is on some central concepts and their implications for classroom interaction analysis.

(a) Indexicality The concept of indexicality arose from the observation

that the meaning of certain words is variable and dependent upon the circumstances surrounding their use. Such words were termed 'indexical signs'. Simple examples are adverbials of time, such as 'today', 'tomorrow', 'yesterday' and 'now', which have different meanings depending upon when they are used. Similarly the meanings of such place adverbials as 'here' and 'there' depend on the location of the speaker.

Garfinkel developed the concept of indexicality in two major ways. First, he proposed that it should be extended beyond narrowly defined linguistic phenomena to *all* social and behavioural forms. Non-verbal actions, in addition to all words and sentences, were also included; their actual significance on any particular occasion of performance could only be determined by reference to the stream or sequence of events in which they occurred, and by consulting culturally available background expectations and knowledge of social structure. Secondly, Garfinkel pointed out that this was not a one-directional phenomenon. Just as any form could potentially be assigned a wide array of meanings, so any meaning (i.e., object, event, idea) could be expressed or realized in a variety of ways. However, as Garfinkel observed, despite the absence of a fixed correspondence between form and meaning, persons engaged in interaction apparently experience few difficulties in assessing one another's meaning or intent. Their facility in this respect constituted a phenomenon for investigation.

(b) Reflexivity Like indexicality, reflexivity is an essential property of social setting. As meanings are inferred and accounts or descriptions produced by reference to the setting (indexicality), so these meanings, accounts and descriptions in turn constitute the setting (reflexivity): the acts of accounting, of describing, of behaving as though a particular occasion were an instance of *X* or *Y* actually construct the occasion as such. This mutual elaboration of account and setting leads analysts to speak of participants 'accomplishing' events such as classroom lessons.

(c) Implications of indexicality and reflexivity for sociology The pervasiveness of indexicality and reflexivity in relation to social settings leads to their having far-reaching consequences for sociology as traditionally conceived. The idea, implicit or otherwise, that sociology can provide scientific descriptions of social phenomena through the substitution of objective for indexical expressions, for example, is thrown into question. Such descriptions, which are themselves a product of the sociologist's cultural competence, constitute as well as describing aspects of the setting. Ethnographic studies thus become demonstrably identical in terms of their underlying mode of production to any other description. By the same token doubt is cast on studies which, in reducing behaviours to sets of variables and statistical correlations, aspire to the model of the natural sciences. Such accounts become understandable not as scientific descriptions of the social world but as the interpretive devices used by analysts to render the observed behaviours accountable.

(d) Recommendations for a departure from existing programmes   Because neither indexicality nor reflexivity is amenable to remediation through increasingly sophisticated or rigorous forms of analysis, Garfinkel advocated their acceptance as an essential feature in proposing an alternative programme for sociology. This was to run alongside rather than to replace existing programmes. The alternative programme was to be based, as in other sociologies, on the problem of social order, but to take as its starting point cultural members' facility in ascribing sense and meaning to the social world rather than taking this facility for granted. The term 'ethnomethodology' was adopted to refer to the study of the methods used.

Garfinkel proposed that in any social setting, members must engage in the practical repair of indexicality in order to make sense of the setting and to construct further meanings. In other words, the particular sense of any interactional component (e.g., utterances, gestures, activities) must appropriately be assessed and responded to in order for interaction meaningfully to proceed. The means by which this sense-making occurred were described by Garfinkel, after Mannheim, under the heading 'documentary reasoning'. Building upon the work of Schutz, Cicourel (1973) has summarized some of its components as follows:

(i) The reciprocity of perspectives
In order for interaction to take place, parties assume, until or unless indications to the contrary arise, that there is a fundamental reciprocity of perspectives between them. At its most basic, this consists in persons assuming that the utterances, gestures and activities used have roughly the same meaning for both parties.

(ii) The retrospective–prospective sense of occurrence
Interaction involves participants in a continuing process of forward and backward searching for meaning such that interpretations may be modified or refined, and ambiguities resolved by reference to what has previously occurred and what subsequently occurs.

(iii) The et-cetera principle
It is assumed between interactants that hearers will fill in the unstated but intended meanings of speakers' utterances.

(iv) Normal forms
Ambiguous behaviours are made rational by reference to normal forms. Puzzling aspects of observed behaviours are disregarded while readily comprehensible ones are foregrounded and fitted into a known scheme of rationality.

This summary is not exhaustive: further practices are detailed in both Garfinkel and Sacks (1970) and Sacks (1972, 1974). Garfinkel (1967) discusses them at length, together with elaborate demonstrations of their uses.

Leiter (1980) is helpful in both summarizing and comparing the different statements made on the subject, including the foundational contributions of Schutz. However, the summaries provided above are sufficient to demonstrate the sorts of observations on and interests in the social world initiated by some of the early ethnomethodological statements and studies.

(e) Conversation analysis: a development of ethnomethodology Conversation represents a rich area of investigation for anyone concerned with the issue of sense-making. In conversation, parties, usually unconsciously, monitor for meaning and rationality and, on the basis of their understandings, select appropriate courses of action. Conversation has the additional advantage of being relatively easily and accurately recorded, in contrast to some other forms of sociological data.

Introductory Science Lessons

Since the Nuffield science curriculum projects of the 1960s, science education in the UK has had a heavy practical bias, much of it based in the 'guided discovery' model. The database used in this study is an exemplar of this tradition. It comprises a set of six video tape recordings of science lessons, recorded and subsequently transcribed by the author.[1] All but one of the lessons were based in the laboratory. The main points of the lessons may briefly be summarized as follows:

> *Lesson 1* is taken up with heating the chemical potassium permanganate. Discussion of the procedure is followed by a practical demonstration performed by selected pupils. After further discussion, pupils disperse to carry out the experiment themselves in small groups.
> *Lesson 2* is a continuation. The results of the experiment are discussed as pupils prepare to write up their work, and discussion then moves on to the importance and the functions of oxygen gas.
> *Lesson 3* is short and non-laboratory-based. The teacher first goes over a homework assignment, and then discusses with the class the writing up of the potassium permanganate experiment.
> *Lesson 4* covers an experiment on 'Melting Ice and Boiling Water'. A pupil is selected to read the textbook instructions on the experiment to the class. Following discussion and elaboration of these instructions, pupils write out the method in their notebooks before splitting into groups to carry out the experiment.
> *Lesson 5* is a continuation. The teacher calls a halt to pupils' experiments on the grounds that some of them have failed to obtain accurate temperature readings. The reasons for this are extensively discussed. Pupils then resume the experiment.

Lesson 6 begins with further explanation of the reasons behind the previous lesson's temperature readings, and is followed by the teacher demonstrating correct procedure. Pupils are subsequently required to provide a written account of their results in light of the teacher's explanations. The reasons given are assembled in rank order of significance. The teacher goes on to explain procedure for the next experiment, the heating of iodine. Pupils list the method and disperse to carry out the experiment. They then gather to hear details of the final experiment in the series, that of finding the boiling point of methylated spirit, which is demonstrated by the teacher.

In this chapter some aspects of these practical activities are scrutinized, in particular the results of pupils' experiments, and the ways in which these are treated by the teacher, depending upon whether she deems them appropriate or otherwise. Her differential treatment of sought-after versus non-sought-after results can provide further insights into both the interactional organization of science teaching and the view of science being transmitted to pupils.

It is clear from the database as a whole that the teacher describes and rehearses the experimental procedures in great detail. Minimally, each experiment undertaken by pupils is described to them. More usually, it is both extensively described and rehearsed, potential pitfalls pointed out and solutions to problems formulated. However, all description is inevitably incomplete; no set of practical instructions can lie in an exact, one-to-one correspondence to the behaviours involved in their enactment. Assumptions of competence are thereby unavoidably contained within the descriptive instructions given to pupils. This may be problematic for them as novices, for, as Schrecker (1983) points out, the adequacy (or otherwise) of a set of descriptive instructions is accomplished through its translation into a set of physical activities.

Sometimes the degree of truncation embodied in the teacher's description is unimportant in the sense that pupils are able to make appropriate sense of the abbreviated instructions, and to carry them out to the teacher's satisfaction. On other occasions there are consequential descriptive inadequacies: pupils are unable to perform activities whose constituent parts have not been unpacked in greater detail, with the result that outcomes are not as predicted or expected by the teacher. These occasions prompt explanation as to why the infelicitous outcomes have occurred. It is in this environment that knowledge and skills assumed by and making up the repertoire of the socialized scientist, and which pupils must acquire if they are to attain socialized status, are made analytically (and for pupils) available. As Garfinkel (1967) has demonstrated, expected ways of behaving and perceiving are nowhere made more visible than in situations where they have first been breached.

Some Observations on Sought-After Results and Conclusions

As a first step in the analysis of data in which the teacher's responses to sought-after and non-sought-after results may be seen, some consideration should be given to the ways in which the teacher treats a sought-after result and conclusion. These are then contrasted in the subsequent two sections with her response to the (perceived) threatened failure of the experiment in question. Consider the following extracts of data, taken from the potassium permanganate lesson:

Extract 1, Lesson 1
```
1 T    what are you going to
2      make in this experiment?
3 A    oxygen
4 T    right (.) so we're going to make
5      oxygen aren't we? (.) so (that'll be)
6      the important thing (.) right we're
7      going to: (0.5) make oxygen
```

Extract 2, Lesson 1
```
1 T    so: our chemical would be in here
2      wouldn't it? (0.5) right? (.) now that's
3      the potassium permanganate (.) and the
4      gas is going to have to go down this tube
5      (.) and we're going to collect it in here
```

Extract 3, Lesson 1
```
1 T                     so (.) I'd like
2      you to (0.5) think (.) really (.) as you're
3      setting it up (.) er and if you concentrate
4      you can get it all perfectly right
```

Extract 4, Lesson 1
```
1 T                     now (.) when
2      it's nearly (.) full (.) you've got to try
3      and get the cork in quite quickly near the
4      (water's surface) haven't you? (.) now you'll
5      be able to tell when it's full of gas because
6      it (starts) as if it seems to be pushing itself
7      out
```

Extract 5, Lesson 1
```
1 T    now we're almost at the end here because (.) er
2      the next thing is that we're actually going to
3      collect the oxygen (0.5) and then afterwards we're
4      going to test it aren't we?
```

Extract 6, Lesson 3

1 T   when we heat potassium permanganate
2   (0.5) we get off a gas (2.0) that relights
3   (a) glowing splint (0.5) and the gas
4   is? (0.5) oxygen (0.5) now actually
5   (.) you don't *really* know if the gas is
6   oxygen *from* the results (.) I just
7   *told* you that it is (.) right? there's no
8   (way) really that you could actually
9   come to that conclusion (0.5) I'm afraid
10   it's a (0.5) rather a (.) helped
11   out conclusion (.) alright?

Extract 7, Lesson 3

1 T   when we heat potassium permanganate
2   (1.0) we:
3 P   it gives off oxygen
4   (1.0)
5 T   collect a gas (0.5) which relights a
6   glowing splint (0.5) and then actually
7   I (just told) you that the gas that (it gives)
8   off is oxygen

It is clear from these data that the teacher treats the experiment as *having* a particular outcome and conclusion; she specifically states that a gas will be produced and that the gas will be oxygen. It becomes equally apparent that pupils are involved in re-covering rather than discovering work: that their part in the lesson will consist in replicating a set of procedures to obtain the expected result. In this sense they are following a recipe ('we're going to make oxygen'), and, if they 'concentrate', they can get it 'perfectly right' (Extract 3, line 4). Stages and outcomes of the heating and gas production processes are outlined in advance ('the gas is going to have to go down this tube (.) and we're going to collect it in here', Extract 2, lines 3–5) and temporally ordered ('now (.) when it's nearly (.) full (.) you've got to try and get the cork in', Extract 4, lines 1–3), and hints offered as to how one may judge when one stage is completed and another about to begin ('it (starts) as if it seems to be pushing itself out', Extract 4, lines 6–7). In short, the teacher's talk here is reducible to a non-equivocal 'do x and y, and you will see z'.

In addition, and consonant with one's commonsense perceptions of the nature of science (Elliot, 1974), her grammatical and lexical selections in extracts such as 6 and 7 suggest the invariant and predictable nature of the results and conclusion. This non-equivocality is also apparent in some of the formulations used in Extracts 1–5: ('we're going to make oxygen', 'going to collect it in here', 'going to collect the oxygen'). Specifically, the adverbial 'when' and the simple present tense form of the verb, 'we heat', refer to time in generalized terms, and the pronoun 'we' to a generalized agency, thus divorcing the event referenced from any particular time, agent or context. The formulation used could be paraphrased as 'whenever one heats potassium permanganate, etc.', and confirms the 'scientizing' of the lesson's events in the formal, written account of the proceedings, presented to and recorded by pupils. The account can also be seen to act as confirmation and further constitution of the teacher as science-expert: her earlier predictions as to the experiment's outcomes are now confirmed and formalized.

It is noticable also that in these data and in these lessons as a whole the sought-after outcome is treated as the normal or unmarked case. In other words, we find no explanation as to *why* a particular form of heat applied to potassium permanganate should generate gas, or *how we know* from the test that this gas is oxygen. The production of gas is treated, simply, as a fact which is not explained, and the glowing splint test presented as a proof, a baseline where explanation actually ceases, a matter of fact (see Extract 6). (There are some parallels here with observations noted in respect of the professional scientific community by authors such as Mulkay and Gilbert (1982) and Latour and Woolgar (1979). These are discussed in a later section.) This is an important observation in view of the marked contrast in response when the experiment's outcome is perceived to be under threat during the pupil demonstration. Let us now consider Extract 8 from this point of view.

Accounting for an Infelicitous Outcome: The Potassium Permanganate Experiment

Extract 8, Lesson 1

```
 1 T    okay now then Neil you're
 2       going to move that tube onto the end now
 3       'cos we're going to (let all) the air out (.)
 4       so do you think you could move that into
 5       its place now? (0.5) right now you people need
 6       to give us a bit more space so could
 7       you move back again now?
 8                        (1.0) [Ps move]
 9 T    right now see that? (.) quite quick isn't
10       it? (1.0) right now when
11       you've got to the bottom (when you think it's
12       full) (.) you've got to whip the cork in the
13       (bottom) (1.0) oh!
         [A removes the tubing from the
         boiling tube, N delays corking it.]
14 Ps   [laughter]
15 T    now (.) would you like to stop giggling a
```

```
16          minute?
17 P18      (you missed it ****)
18 T        now (.) (that was too tricky that) wasn't it
19          really? (.) because er Neil wasn't quite ready
20          and (I wasn't going to remind you to get it in)
21 Ps       [laughter]
22 T        so he whipped it out (0.5) as fast as he could
23          now where's it gone where is it now?
24 Ps       in the air
25 T        well I don't think there's very much in the
26          tube however (.) shall we see if he's got any?
27 Ps       yes/no
28 N        [looking in tube] there's a little bit (**)
29 T                              alright well
30          let—let's just go through what we're going to do next
31 N        we're going to put the splint in
32 T        right now er Andrew let's give you the splint
33          then this time (.) now (.) what (.) Richard
34          what test are we going to do?
35                              (2.0)
36 R        er (****) = [indicates]
37 T        = I don't think this is going to work by the
38          way but you'll be just going to
39          be going through the procedure
40 P19      (perhaps we're going to light that and
41          put it in there) [indicates]
42 T        alright (.) right (then—then) Andrew
43          (.) light (the flame)
44                              (4.0)
45 P20      (I can't see anything)
46 P21      (it's going back in the bottle)
47 T        right
48                              (3.0)
49 P22      (you blowed it)
50 Ps       [laughter]
51                              (2.0)
52 A        just a minute
53                              (1.0)
54 A        go
55                              (1.0)
            [N takes finger off test tube, A places splint inside, a flame
            appears]
56 T        oh: I (well now) you *did* have some oxygen→
57 P23                          yea:h
58 T        → in it (0.5) well I misjudged you Neil (1.0)
```

59   alright (.) now (0.5) do you understand how
60   you'll be doing it?

In the extract the teacher predicts that the expected result (the splint re-lighting) will not be forthcoming, and explains its non-occurrence in advance. One of the pupil demonstrators is taken as having been slow in placing a cork in the mouth of a boiling tube full of gas, and the gas is presumed to have escaped as a result. The teacher's explanation contrasts with the *non-explanation* of the *occurrence* of the expected result in the earlier data extracts. The talk contained in lines 18–26 prepares pupils for the failure of the test by suggesting that the oxygen has escaped. This is attributed to the difficulties of the task, which is described as 'too tricky', Neil's unpreparedness for the specific moment of corking the tube ('Neil wasn't quite ready'), and the teacher's failing to remind pupils of the proper procedure. Each of these explanations implicates Neil or the teacher, suggesting that human error has intervened in the proceedings and thus interfered with the otherwise predictable arrival at the sought-after result. The production of oxygen gas on heating potassium permanganate is preserved as a fact of science, and the human element presented as the cause of the anticipated infelicitous outcome.

Thus the teacher's reading of the situation as potentially undermining to the sought-after result occasions an explanation which implicitly asserts the propriety of that result, and confirms its factual status. The teacher as socialized scientist makes available to the class of novice scientists simply that there are facts of science, and correct and incorrect ways of going about producing or seeing these facts for oneself. The science socialization of pupils involves their taking on the teacher's ways of seeing and doing, with the prospect of an infelicitous outcome providing a fruitful field for the dissemination of proper and appropriate modes of perception and behaviour. Similar patterning and more detailed transmission of knowledge and competencies are seen in respect of the data represented below, taken from the melting ice experiment.

Accounting for an Infelicitous Outcome: The Melting Ice Experiment

The melting ice experiment (Lessons 4 and 5) consists in pupils initially taking the temperature of a beakerful of crushed ice, and heating the beaker over a gentle bunsen flame until boiling point is reached. Temperature readings are to be taken and recorded at intervals. In the extract below, the teacher, circulating amongst the groups of pupils, has come across some untoward results. As the extract opens, she calls the lesson to a halt.

Extract 9, Lesson 5

1	T	right now (.) can you just stop for
2		a minute and let's er just think
3		through one or two ideas before we go
4		any further
5	T	now then (0.5) some of us have
6		difficulty in actually taking the
7		temperature of the ice (.) now (1.0)
8		perhaps er I didn't really point out
9		to you clearly enough at the start
10		(0.5) that em (.) the temperature of the
11		room (.) is quite a lot above
12		ice isn't it? (.) well now (if you
13		could) put your temperature in (0.5)
14		sorry put the thermometer in (a)
15		room for a minute and just see what
16		kind of temperature (0.5) the room's
17		at (0.5) right? (.) jus—just er
18		hold the: (.) thermometer in the: (.)
19		room (0.5) don't drop it just hold it
20		there not in your hand (.) at the bottom
21		(.) because of course then you're
22		taking your hand temperature aren't
23		you? (.) so just hold it like that
24		(.) right? (0.5) carefully of course (0.5)
25		so it won't drop through your fingers
26		that's right (.) now (*) find what
27		the: room temperature is
28		(4.0)
29	P6	oh
30	P7	(it's boiling)
31	Ps	[laughter]
32	P8	hey it's (started coming down)
33	T	well if you've had it in hot water it will
34		won't it?
35		(1.0)
36	P9	seventy-one
37	P10	it's going up
38	T	(******)
39	P11	(seventy-one)
40	T	seventy-one? (0.5) no I don't think it's
41		quite seventy-one
42	P12	twenty-four
43	P13	(***)

44	*P14*	twenty-four
45	*P15*	twenty-four
46		(1.0)
47	*T*	right now Catherine what do *you* think
48		it is?
49	*P16*	twenty-four
50	*C*	twenty-two
51	*P17*	twenty-one [at this point *Ps* all begin to call out numbers, ranging from 24 to 106]
52	*T*	I wonder if we perhaps waited a bit
53		longer (0.5) because er (.) as you're
54		all calling out different numbers it
55		suggests really (.) that (.) some of them
56		have been in er (1.0) rather a hot place
57		or perhaps have been (.) in the cold so
58		let's just leave them on the bench and
59		one of you keep your eye on the→
60	*P31*	( )
61	*T*	→thermometer
62	*P31*	( )
63		(0.5)
64	*T*	while (you are) keeping your eye on
65		the thermometer (.) if you're the one
66		( )
67		just put it on the bench (0.5) and
68		look again in a minute (0.5) right? (0.5)
69		Mary we don't want any more of those
70		(noises) thank you (.) right (.) now
71		let me go back to what I was (1.0)
72		saying a moment ago (2.0) it's a little
73		bit difficult to find the temperature
74		of the ice (0.5) if you don't leave
75		(0.5) long enough (0.5) for the: (0.5)
76		temperature (0.5) to drop (.) to the ice
77		temperature (0.5) right? (0.5) it's like
78		taking somebody's temperature ( ) and
79		not letting it go down (.) and adding on
80		(0.5) the person before's temperature
81		so you come out after (.) you know a
82		*hundred* and something or other (.)
83		rather a *big* number (.) right? (1.0)
84		so (1.5) really I think (.) that (.)
85		part of your trouble was (0.5) that
86		you didn't all wait long enough
87		(0.5) till it got to its lowest

```
88      temperature (.) right? (0.5) and then
89      (.) you were so eager to move on (0.5)
90      to the boiling temperature (0.5) that
91      we didn't really watch (.) the melting
92      temperature very carefully (.) right? (0.5)
93      now I'm going to say to you (.) that I
94      would've expected (.) allowing for the
95      inaccuracies (.) that there may be in
96      the thermometers (0.5) that our ice
97      (0.5) we would expect to melt (0.5) at
98      (.) nought degrees centigrade (.) right?
99      and before it melts (0.5) it's below that
100     temperature (.) (and you know) (.) some of
101     us have forgotten that temperatures below
102     nought are minus temperatures aren't they?
103     (0.5) right? (1.5) now (.) then (.) when
104     we move up from there (0.5) then er
105     (1.0) you'd find rises in temperature until
106     you got to boiling (.) when you got to
107     boiling (0.5) again em (0.5) the thermometers
108     aren't absolutely perfect so it mightn't—it
109     mightn't have been bang on a hundred (0.5)
110     but it (.) should've been pretty well on
111     a hundred degrees centigrade (.) right?

112 T   now (.) we
113     didn't really (0.5) (get on) very
114     successfully with the ice (0.5) so I
115     wonder whether perhaps (0.5) em before
116     (0.5) er (0.5) we go any further (0.5) perhaps
117     all of us that haven't—that—that haven't
118     really taken the temperature of melting
119     ice (.) could perhaps er (0.5) look at
120     this again.
```

Early in the extract the teacher identified a 'difficulty in actually taking the temperature of the ice' (lines 6–7). Pupils' readings of the initial ice temperature (in a subsequent lesson quoted as having included one at 13°C) and of the melting ice temperature are treated as inaccurate and in need of explanation. The teacher embarks upon this at line 10 where she describes the room temperature as being higher than that of ice, and suggests that pupils take a reading in order to see for themselves. The point of the comparison is then delayed as this procedure is carried out, and discrepancies between the teacher's and pupils' understandings of the instruction become apparent. One pupil, for example, is reminded to hold the thermometer at the top as opposed to the base, and thus to avoid taking a hand rather than room temperature (lines 19–23). Others call out widely discrepant figures which further delay the resolution of the teacher's point. The resolution occurs in lines 72–83, where it is suggested that thermometers were not left long enough in the ice for accurate readings to be obtained, and where an analogy is drawn between the present situation and that of improperly taken human temperatures.

As in 'documentary reasoning' more generally, pupils have to infer the underlying thrust of the teacher's explanation; that is, that thermometers register their surrounding temperature and that account must be taken of this in obtaining readings. As Wilson puts it, they must identify 'an underlying pattern behind a series of appearances such that each appearance is seen as referring to, an expression of, or a 'document of', the underlying pattern' (Wilson, 1971: 68). In this case an understanding of the principle at issue is dependent upon pupils either having grasped it already, or having generalized from the particular explanations given, for it is not made explicit. However, in the teacher's terms, future success in this procedure, as in the experiment where pupils have to find the boiling point of methylated spirit (i.e., to re-discover another 'fact of science'), requires that they have taken the general point.

As in the case of corking the boiling tube in the potassium permanganate experiment, pupils must also competently make a situated judgment. Phrases such as 'a bit longer' (lines 52–53) and 'long enough' (line 86), used here with reference to the time needed for accurate readings, are vague formulations, whose precise, occasion-relevant meaning can only be ascertained by pupils by their knowing that they are looking for a particular reading at a particular stage (e.g., 0°C as the ice melts, 100°C as the water boils). They must take cognizance of the amount of time needed to obtain these results, and generalize from there to the intervening readings, and, indeed, to future occasions on which they may be required to use thermometers. Their competence in this respect is also premised upon a common-sense recognition of the phenomena of melting and boiling, an assumption evident in the textbook account of the experiment and built upon by the teacher. (The textbook used states: 'You no doubt know that ice melts and water boils'; that is, it assumes that such knowledge is already contained within pupils' commonsense science repertoire.)

Again as in the case of the potassium permanganate experiment, the teacher's response to pupils' results rests upon the assumed facticity of the freezing and boiling points of water at 0° and 100°C respectively, and their realization in thermometer readings. Other results are treated as distortions in need of explanation: the outcome of human error, or of inaccuracies in the thermometer. Correct results are presented as facts which need no further explanation. The formulation 'our ice (0.5) we would expect to melt (0.5) at (.) nought degrees centigrade (.) right? and before it melts (0.5) it's below that temperature' (lines 96–100) is non-equivocal, suggesting 'that's the way it is'. Similarly, 'you'd find rises in temperature until you got to boiling (.) when you got to boiling . . . it should've been pretty well on a hundred degrees centigrade' embodies the notions of predictability and generalizability. There is an absence of explanation. Pupils are told nothing of the genesis of the concepts and their theoretical underpinnings and little of the thermometer, itself an item of reified theory. As with the earlier experiment, certain matters are presented as matters of scientific fact or proof, and used as a baseline for the lessons. Consider now Extract 10:

Extract 10, Lesson 6

```
 1 T   now (0.5) what I'd like to do first (.) is
 2     just e:r (.) think over (0.5) yesterday's
 3     experiment (0.5)
 4
 5 T   I'd like to (0.5) sort out really why we
 6     got the results that em (.) I wasn't really er
 7     (.) expecting that you'd get quite in the way
 8     that you did (0.5) alright? (0.5) now (.)
 9     first of all—first of all let's think er
10     (.) why some of us ended up (.) with rather high
11     starting temperatures = now one group that I
12     looked at (0.5) had down as their *first*
13     *temperature* (of this) *ice* (.) just ice (0.5)
14     they had down a temperature of thirteen
15     degrees centigrade (0.5) right? (1.0) now then
16     (2.0) can we suggest a reason why (0.5) we might
17     have got that temperature?
18                        (1.0) [hands go up]
19 T   Paul
20 P   'cos (.) at the beginning the: (.) room heat
21     was e:r (.) about that and (0.5) (he) hadn't
22     actually left it in long enough for it to go
23     down
24 T   that's right some of us (.) didn't (.) realize
25     (0.5) that we had to leave (.) the: thermometer
26     (0.5) right into the ice (3.0) long enough (.)
27     for it to get to the ice temperature (0.5) right
28     so actually we were (.) in part taking the air
29     temperature weren't we? (0.5) and then the second
30     thing (0.5) em (.) now (0.5) let's look at this
31     ice here (0.5) em and imagine (0.5) er (0.5)
32     packing them together in a beaker (0.5) right?
33     (0.5) now if you've got *big* chunks of ice (1.5)
34     can you think of any problems if you've got big
35     pieces of ice like this? (.) right can you see
```

36		(.) now? (.) shall I fill the beaker with (.)
37		pieces as big as that or bigger?
38	*P1*	the thermometer (
39	*T*	that's it the thermometer again is surrounded
40		by some air because we can't really pack the:
41		(.) thermometer well enough into the ice can
42		we? (.) right (.) (so) if you used big chunks
43		(.) then yes it *was* very difficult to get the
44		temperature (.) right? now (.) let's see if we
45		can sort out (.) any other problems

46	*T*	and the third problem (.) was (.) to do with
47		the bunsen (0.5) now I wonder if anybody can
48		work out what was the problem with the bunsen?
49		(1.5)
50	*T*	it's not a problem with the bunsen itself but
51		in the *use* of the bunsen can you suggest what
52		the matter was?
53		(1.0) [*D's* hand goes up]
54	*D*	it was on the wrong flame
55	*T*	some of you used too big a flame didn't you?
56		(.) and so er (.) yes it *did* shoot up (.) and
57		I think some of you were a bit surprised because
58		(0.5) when I said to you 'well (.) what kind of
59		temperature do you think ice melts at?' some of
60		you said (.) 'oh I think it's about forty' or
61		(0.5) any other number (0.5) right? (0.5) now
62		(1.5) this was partly because (.) you heated
63		it up rather quickly (0.5) right? (1.0) and
64		(.) yes you *can* end up with quite hot water in
65		one place (.) and lumps of ice in another place
66		in the beaker

67	*T*	it *was* quite a difficult experiment actually
68		(.) at the beginning (0.5) so (.) what we're
69		going to do is (.) I'm not going to ask you to
70		do it again (0.5) because (0.5) em if we were
71		(0.5) scientists (.) that this kind of result
72		depended on you know if the world's waiting for
73		your results (.) then perhaps you'd repeat it
74		many times (0.5) sometimes you actually *hear*
75		of experiments (0.5) that one set of people
76		have done (.) and they've got *one* set of
77		results (0.5) and then another set of people've
78		done it (.) and they've got different results

79		now who's right? (.) what've they got to do?
80		(1.5) [hands go up]
81	P	do it once again to =
82	T	= oh yes in fact lots more than perhaps er (.)
83		once again (.) you've got to repeat it (many
84		times) and then check it very carefully (.)
85		well (.) you know (if) every time we did an
86		experiment we did that what'd be the problem
87		Paul?
88		(1.0)
89	P	er take too much time up
90	T	it would (.) we wouldn't get on very far that's
91		right (.) so (1.0) let me explain to you (0.5)
92		what we *might've* got (0.5) if we'd had time (.)
93		to (sort the) problems (in every aspect) (.)
94		right? (.) if you read the textbook it says
95		'ice melts at nought degrees centigrade' (0.5)
96		right? (0.5) now sometimes even if you do it
97		very carefully it doesn't come out at quite
98		nought (.) so what might be another problem?
99	P2	the thermometer's not quite accurate
100	T	that's right (.) the thermometer might not be
101		quite as accurate (0.5) as we want it to be (.)
102		now often in science we think everything's perfect
103		don't we? (.) we think (.) it's going to be absolute
104		(.) well I'm afraid that's (.) it (isn't always so)
105		(.) you see (.) there's sometimes variations (0.5)
106		so (.) let's just jot down er (0.5) at the end of
107		this (.) experiment in rough (0.5) em something
108		(.) really to clarify (all) our ideas a bit (1.0)
109		right? (0.5) now I think we *will* have your results
110		as you got them (0.5) but er (0.5) where it's a
111		nought (0.5) you write what you actually found (*
112		******) a nought weren't they?
113	Ps	yes
114	T	so I want you to write here (0.5) as you found them
115		(.) now of course you're not going to be writing in
116		your book as you found them are you? (0.5) [T writes on board, Ps copy]
117	T	right (6.5) [T waits for Ps to catch up]
118	T	and then (.) we're not going to have a conclusion (0.5)
119		because (.) really (.) for some of you couldn't make
120		a very sensible conclusion (.) so (.) we're going
121		to have (.) 'Notes on Experiment' (.) alright?

122 T   now can we remember the problems? (.) Michael what
123   was a problem in being able to do this then?
124 M   the thermometer might be: faulty
125 T   yes (.) now (.) I'm not going to put that one
126   (under the) *major* problems (.) because it's only going
127   to be very slightly off (.) so (.) let's think of the
128   the bigger ones first although you're quite right that
129   may be the case
130   (1.0)
131 P3   the thermometer (ought) to (be**) to the end
132 T   that's right (.) you might not have packed it well
133   enough so (0.5) ice (1.0) may not
134   (4.0) [*T* begins to write on board]
135 T   have been well crushed
136   (13.0)
137 T   so that there were air spaces
138   (10.5) [*T* writing on board, *Ps* copying]
139   and can you remember any other problems? (.) that's
140   one (0.5) not crushing the ice
141 P4   the bunsen flame was high
142 T   that's right (.) the bunsen flame was too high
143   (13.5) [*T* writing on board, *Ps* copying]
144 D   people em (.) (didn't know) the room temperature
145   (.) was different than the ice and people weren't
146   leaving the thermometer (.) long enough in the ice
147   and so
148 T   that's right (.) yes (.) and three: (1.0)
149   thermometer (0.5) not left
150   (11.0) [*T* writing, *Ps* copying)
151 T   for long enough
152   (5.5)
153 T   okay and then we'll have as the last one (0.5)
154   er:m the thermometer (.) may not have been (.)
155   completely accurate
156   (18.0) [*T* writing, *Ps* copying]
157   now when I say completely accurate (1.0) it's (.) by
158   that I only mean that it's slightly out so (.) it's
159   when we're thinking about the difference between
160   ninety-nine and a hundred (.) not when we're
161   thinking about the difference between fifty and a
162   hundred or anything of that sort (.) alright?
163   (14.0) [*Ps* countinue to write]
164 T   well (.) now that we—we knew we had all these
165   problems but perhaps we'd better see what we
166   *did* find out from the experiment (.) because

167   I'd like you to compare what you found with
168   ice (.) with something else that you've not
169   not worked with before (.) em something called
170   iodine

As in the previous data extract, pupils' results are treated as incorrect, and as reflecting the intrusion of distorting external factors. However, on this occasion the teacher provides, and elicits from pupils, a more elaborate explanation, and assembles, again in collaboration with the class, a written record of significant deviations from the proper experimental procedures. In this sense an active alignment with the teacher's perspective is required on the part of pupils, its transformation into a permanent, written record acting to formalize the knowledge contained within it.

The mishandling of the thermometer is once more prominent in both the spoken and the written accounts. In the first place a pupil, Paul, demonstrates an understanding of one of its facets which is consonant with that of the teacher in his answer: 'at the beginning the: (.) room heat was e:r (.) about that and (he) hadn't actually left it in long enough for it to go down' (lines 20–23). This answer is positively evaluated by the teacher, reformulated, and has appended to it the general point being made: 'so actually we were (.) in part taking the air temperature weren't we?' (lines 24–29). Pupils are also invited to consider the possible consequences of using large as opposed to small pieces of ice: 'the thermometer again is surrounded by some air because we can't really pack the: (.) thermometer well enough into the ice can we? (.) (so) if you used big chunks (.) then yes it *was* very difficult to get the temperature' (lines 39–44).

The part played by pupils here is in contrast with that represented in the previous extract. On that occasion most of the talking was done by the teacher and pupils' spoken involvement limited to the statement of thermometer readings of the room temperature. Here, as mentioned above, they are required to recall the teacher's earlier explanations and to make further relevant inferences, thus demonstrating an awareness of and identification with the teacher's perspective. Similarly active participation is invited in relation to their misuse of the bunsen burner: 'I wonder if anybody can work out what was the problem with the bunsen?' (lines 47–48). Darren's characterization of the flame as 'wrong' is again accepted as appropriate, restated in more specific form, and followed by an explanation of results being obtained at one stage in the experiment's progress. In the case of possible inaccuracies in the thermometers, mentioned in the previous lesson, pupils are strongly cued in to the answer, but again required actively to participate in providing it, rather than being instructed by the teacher: ' "ice melts at nought degrees centigrade" . . . now sometimes even if you do it very carefully it doesn't come out at quite nought (.) so what might be another problem?' (lines 95–98).

The problems identified and discussed in the first part of the extract are restated in the second. Here the teacher is concerned to construct a written account of pupils' results, to be recorded in notebooks. It is noticeable that the first 'problem' suggested by a pupil (inaccuracies in the thermometers) meets with only qualified approval from the teacher: 'yes (.) now (.) I'm not going to put that one (under the) *major* problems (.) because (0.5) it's only going to be very slightly (off) (.) so (.) let's think of the bigger ones first although you're quite right that (.) may be the case' (lines 125–129). Air space around the packed ice, too fierce bunsen flames and the effects of room temperature are all given precedence in the order of priority: in effect, human error is presented as the more likely source of untoward results than faulty instrumentation. Here erroneous scientific theory is beyond serious consideration.

Summary of Observations

Sought-after Outcomes

The experiments carried out in the lessons have sought-after outcomes which are treated by the teacher as exemplifying facts of science. Their factual status is suggested in the teacher's use of formulations which signal generalizability and predictability through the absence of reference to specific time, place or agency. In addition, their occurrence is not explained, but presented simply as 'the way it is', and, in the case of the potassium permanganate experiment, as beyond pupils' power to comprehend.

Non-sought-after Outcomes

By contrast, results other than those sought by the teacher are treated as in need of explanation. Explanations given embody precisely the characteristics absent from talk about sought-after outcomes. So, for example, reference is made to (a) specific human agency (e.g., Neil did X, I forgot to do Y, some of you thought Z); (b) particular, contextualized problems (e.g., possible imperfections in equipment).

Achieving Reciprocity of Perspectives

The occurrence of results treated as incorrect by the teacher occasions the explication of hitherto taken-for-granted assumptions. In the case of the melting ice experiment, for example, the teacher has assumed pupils to be competent in the use of the thermometer, so that in the experiment's rehearsal instructions such as 'take the temperature' were not unpacked in terms of their precise constituent activities. The occurrence of infelicitous results prompts her to explain these in some detail. Consequential asymmetries in teacher-pupil perspective thus become visible, and the teacher works to establish alignment. Subsequent class participation, as in the second melting ice extract, can serve to demonstrate the achievement of reciprocity, and the incorporation by pupils of knowledge/skills contained within the socialized scientist's repertoire.

Discussion

This chapter has focused upon some aspects of the teacher's communication to pupils of scientific skills and knowledge. Although the focus has been limited, the observations made raise a number of issues and allow for some discussion of a more general nature.

The Inevitability and the Pedagogic Value of Mistakes by Pupils

Two points are perhaps obvious, but nonetheless important from the point of view of gaining insight into the processes of teaching and learning; they also bear on existing analyses in the field. The first concerns the making of procedural mistakes by pupils: one may expect mistakes to be made for two main reasons. As a competent, adult cultural member, and assuming oneself the teacher's categorization of the pupils as 'novice scientists', one may perceive mistakes as an expectable and inevitable feature of acquiring new knowledge and skills. Mistakes are also expectable from an analytic point of view. The lessons are organized so that experimental procedure is described to, and sometimes rehearsed by, pupils before they attempt to carry out the experiments for themselves. However, no description can be complete, nor always sufficient for all practical purposes. Thus the teacher's job of producing an *occasion-relevant description*, which matches the needs of her class at any one time, must be based on an estimate of their abilities vis-à-vis the tasks in hand and may not always work in practice. The combination of pupils' novice status, and consequent inability to fill in the unstated detail of instruction, and the potential descriptive incompleteness of even tailored instruction means that mistakes are 'doubly inevitable'.

The second point, however, concerns their *value* from the point of view of teaching/learning. As has been demonstrated in the present chapter, and as I have argued in the case of pupil participation more generally (French, 1987b), pupils' mistakes constitute active contributions to the lessons which allow the teacher some immediate insight into the state of their knowledge and competence. They act, in the terms of the study, as a ready index to areas of asymmetry between teacher and pupils, and prompt the teacher into establishing alignment.

The Accountability of Error and the Non-accountability of Fact

There are some similarities, at the level of surface features at least, between the ways in which the teacher explains infelicitous outcomes and the ways in which error and fact are treated among the professional scientific community as described by Mulkay and Gilbert (1982) and Latour and Woolgar (1979). Mulkay and Gilbert note that 'correct belief' is treated as the normal state of affairs, as relatively unproblematic and in need of no explanation. Error, on the other hand, is portrayed as due to the influence of intrusive, non-scientific variables which have a distorting effect on the phenomenon under investigation. Consequently scientists make use of a larger repertoire of interpretive resources when accounting for error than for correct belief.

Latour and Woolgar examine the ways in which a scientific fact takes on its factual status, suggesting that its facticity is only finally established when it is presented without temporal qualification and becomes part of a body of knowledge drawn upon by other scientists. Both of these sets of observations bear some obvious relation to the ways in which infelicitous outcomes and matters of scientific fact are treated in the present data. Pupils' results are treated not as candidate challenges to accepted scientific knowledge, but as erroneous and, like error in the Mulkay and Gilbert study, are explained by reference to a variety of external factors. By contrast, sought-after outcomes are presented as matters of fact, without, in Latour and Woolgar's terms, temporal qualification and as part of a body of knowledge used to instruct novice scientists.

It is reasonable to suppose, however, that these surface similarities have their bases in rather different sets of assumptions concerning the audiences for whom communication is designed. One might suggest, for example, that the reasoning informing the teacher's decision to explain or not to explain certain matters is again grounded in the science-novice categorization of pupils. For when experiments do fail, in the teacher's terms, the sorts of explanation offered have at least one characteristic in common: they are readily understandable to the layman, and are of the order of explanations encountered in relation to unfortunate occurrences in everyday, non-scientific life. Thus one might say, 'I was late because my watch was slow', or 'the cake failed to rise because Z didn't use the oven properly', and reasonably expect to be understood by cultural members, including children of 11 1Ω years.

The sort of explanation called for in respect of the occurrence of scientific experimental results, however, would seem to be of another order in the sense that the recipient may need to be a socialized scientist to understand it. To know why potassium permanganate produces oxygen when it is heated, for example, one would have to know something of the composition and structure of elements, and their behaviour under certain controlled conditions. In other words, one would have to be at least a partially socialized scientist. The same point applies in respect of the glowing splint test, the development of the thermometer, and the reactions of the chemicals pupils are subsequently required to heat. This is an issue of which the teacher demonstrates an awareness. In the case of the conclusion to the potassium permanganate experiment (Extract 6 above) she explicitly states that pupils cannot yet infer the conclusion that the gas produced is oxygen. She also draws a distinction (Extract 10, lines 70–93) between the class and 'real scientists', explaining that discrepant results within the professional scientific community call for further experimentation, while the same phenomenon within the context of the lessons can be resolved by reference to her own expertise. The teacher demonstrates an additional awareness of the distinction between school science and professional science in terms of the sense of certainty generated within the one and uncertainty within the other. Further on in Extract 10 she remarks, 'often in science we think everything's perfect don't we? (.) we think (.) it's going to be absolute (.) well I'm afraid that's (.) (it isn't always so) (.) you see (.) there's sometimes variations' (lines 102–105).

Science as a Craft

The observations arising here suggest that at this stage in pupils' careers science is being presented to them primarily as a craft: that is, as a practical subject where specified 'recipes' result in specified ends, and the body of theoretical knowledge informing their production is invisible, or at least not paramount. Delamont and Atkinson (1985) use the same analogy in their study of first year secondary school science. They also observe:

> What is striking in these early lessons is the absence of explanations or justifications for (the) activities and conventions . . . The disciplines of 'science' seem to be treated as self-evident and self-justificatory. The lessons on which we have information seem singularly devoid of any general introductions as to the nature of science or the rationale for the laboratory work to be undertaken by pupils (Delamont and Atkinson, 1985: 28–9).

Similarly in the present study pupils are taught, in the manner of craft apprentices, a variety of practical, manipulative skills which, if properly executed, produce given results. Explanations are mainly confined to the environment of their deviations from proper courses of action in terms which are readily comprehensible, rather than being presented in relation to the occurrence of phenomena and meaningful only to the already initiated. Bernstein (1971) describes science as a subject in which the revelation of what he terms the deep structures of its knowledge is considerably deferred, until its surface features have been presented to and accumulated by pupils. This is congruent with the analysis of the present database, where the transmission of practical skills for the controlled manipulation of selected variables is markedly more in evidence than the theoretical knowledge that informs them.

Thus, while pupils may well acquire a taste of what it is like to be a professional scientist, there is, in these data at least, no pretence that they are 'real scientists' engaged in real discovery. Indeed the distinction between themselves and 'real scientists' is quite explicitly stated by the teacher. There are, therefore, no grounds here for critically pointing to a discrepancy between the alleged preference for 'discovery' in school science and what actually happens in lessons. One would, rather, with the proponents of guided discovery science more generally, want to emphasize the extent to which school science may give an idea of what professional science is like, while not purporting to be real, discovering science. Within this context lack of competence or knowledge on the part of pupils may be viewed as an essential and beneficial component of the learning process: as in the acquisition of any other set of practical skills, one learns to perform in ways appropriate to the discipline by first making mistakes, which allow the instructor access to the state of one's knowledge and competence. In this sense environments where taken-for-granted forms of a discipline's behaviour are breached afford analytic access to some of the ways in which subject knowledge may be conveyed from initiate to novice members.

Note

1   Transcription of the extracts presented in this chapter was carried out using a simplified version of the system developed by Dr Gail Jefferson for use in conversation analysis. The main conventions are as follows:

   (i)   The text is laid out in the style of a dramatic text, with speakers' identities on the left. The lines are numbered for reference. Identities are shown as *T* for teacher, *P*, or *P1*, *P2*, etc. for pupils, and an initial if pupil's name is known.

   (ii)   Intervals between and within utterances are timed to the nearest half second and shown in brackets. A pause of less than half a second is shown as (.).

   (iii)   Characteristics of speech delivery: A colon : indicates extension of the sound it follows. A question mark ? is used where an utterance functions as a question and an exclamation mark ! as in normal usage. Dashes indicate hesitation or self-correction. Italics mark the placing of particular emphasis on a word or syllable.

   (iv)   Unclear utterances are enclosed in single brackets. Asterisks in brackets (***) represent unclear syllables, one asterisk per syllable. Empty brackets indicate that someone was speaking but that this was indecipherable.

   (v)   Details of the classroom scene are enclosed in square brackets [ ].

   (vi)   Overlapping speech is marked with a single bracket which links the utterances at the point of onset of overlap. Contiguous speech is indicated by = to show instances of immediate latching with no overlap.

(vii)   Arrows → and ← are used to link two or more parts of an utterance which has been interrupted by another speaker.

(viii) A blank line with a full stop indicates that the transcript has been edited and a section omitted at this point.

References

BENSON, D. and HUGHES, J. A. (1983) *The Perspective of Ethnomethodology*, London, Longman.

BERNSTEIN, B. (1971) 'On the classification and framing of educational knowledge', in YOUNG, M. F. D. (Ed.), *Knowledge and Control*, London, Collier Macmillan.

CICOUREL, A. V. (1973) *Cognitive Sociology: Language and Meaning in Social Interaction*, Harmondsworth, Penguin.

DELAMONT, S. and ATKINSON, P. (1985) 'In the beginning was the bunsen: The foundations of secondary school science,' Paper delivered at the British Society for the History of Science/British Sociological Association Science Studies Group conference, 'Experimentation in the Natural Sciences', Newton Park College, Bath, UK, August.

DELAMONT, S. and HAMILTON, D. (1976) 'Classroom research: A critique and a new approach', in STUBBS, M. and DELAMONT, S. (Eds), *Explorations in Classroom Observation*, London, John Wiley and Sons.

DEPARTMENT OF EDUCATION AND SCIENCE, (1985) *Science 5–16: A Statement of Policy*, London, HMSO.

EDWARDS, A. D. and WESTGATE, D. P. G. (1987) *Investigating Classroom Talk*, Lewes, Falmer Press.

ELLIOT, H. C. (1974) 'Similarities and differences between science and common sense', in TURNER, R. (Ed.), *Ethnomethodology*, Harmondsworth, Penguin.

FRENCH, J. (1987a) *Some Features of the Organisation of Instruction in Science*, PhD thesis, University of Manchester.

FRENCH, J. (1987b) 'Language in the primary classroom', in DELAMONT, S. (Ed.), *The Primary School Teacher*, Lewes, Falmer Press.

GARFINKEL, H. (1967) *Studies in Ethnomethodology*, Englewood Cliffs, N.J., Prentice-Hall.

GARFINKEL, H. and SACKS, H. (1970) 'On formal structures of practical action', in MCKINNEY, J. C. and TIRYAKIAN, E. A. (Eds), *Theoretical Sociology: Perspectives and Developments*, New York, Appleton Century Crofts.

HAMMERSLEY, M. and WOODS, P. (Eds) (1976) *The Process of Schooling: A Sociological Reader*, London, Routledge and Kegan Paul with Open University Press.

HARGREAVES, D. H. (1967) *Social Relations in a Secondary School*, London, Routledge and Kegan Paul.

LACEY, C. (1970) *Hightown Grammar*, Manchester, Manchester University Press.

LATOUR, B. and WOOLGAR, S. (1979) *Laboratory Life: The Social Construction of Scientific Facts*, London, Sage.

LEITER, K. (1980) *A Primer on Ethnomethodology*, Oxford, Oxford University Press.

MCHOUL, A. W. and WATSON, D. R. (1984) 'Two axes for the analysis of 'commonsense' and 'formal' geographical knowledge in classroom talk', *British Journal of Sociology of Education*, 5, 3, pp. 281–302.

MEHAN, H. (1974) 'Accomplishing classroom lessons', in CICOUREL, A. V. *et al.* (1974), *Language Use and School Performance*, New York, Academic Press.

MULKAY, M. and GILBERT, N. (1982) 'Accounting for error: How scientists construct their social world when they account for correct and incorrect belief', *Sociology*, 16, 2, pp. 165–83.

SACKS, H. (1972) 'An initial investigation of the usability of conversational data for doing sociology', in SUDNOW, D. (Ed.), *Studies in Social Interaction*, New York, Free Press.

SACKS, H. (1974) 'On the analysability of stories by children', in TURNER, R. (Ed.), *Ethnomethodology*, Harmondsworth, Penguin.

SCHRECKER, F. (1983) 'Doing a chemical experiment: The practices of chemistry students in a student laboratory in quantitative analysis', Department of Sociology, UCLA.

WILSON, T. P. (1971) 'Normative and interpretive paradigms in sociology', in DOUGLAS, J. (Ed.), *Understanding Everyday Life*, London, Routledge and Kegan Paul.

Chapter 2

Bending The Evidence:
The Relationship between Theory
and Experiment in Science Education

Robin Millar

Practical Work in Science

Perhaps the feature of school science which most clearly differentiates it from other subjects of the curriculum is that science classes take place in laboratories and involve students and teachers in carrying out practical investigations and demonstrations. In the UK, which has a long tradition of small-group practical work in school science, 11–13-year-olds typically spend over half of their science lesson time in practical activities (Beatty and Woolnough, 1982). For 16–18-year-olds the share of time allocated to practical work is still likely to be more than one-third (Thompson, 1975).

This practical emphasis — and the very substantial time allocation which it requires — can be traced back to the Nuffield curriculum projects of the 1960s and beyond. Nowadays it tends to be taken for granted and is seldom seen as requiring explicit justification. In the final report of the UK National Curriculum Science Working Party the section on practical activities is introduced simply by the statement that: 'Exploring and investigating is central to the work of scientists and to science education' (DES, 1988: 50, para. 4.23). In much the same way science teachers often informally justify the emphasis on practical work in the science classroom on the grounds that 'science is a practical subject'. The taken-for-granted idea here, that the processes of science education should in some sense mirror the work of scientists, echoes the Nuffield projects' view that pupils 'can acquire the feeling of doing science, of being a scientist — "a scientist for the day"' (Nuffield Physics, 1966: 3).

When more explicit and detailed statements about the role of practical work in school science are called for, these are likely to acknowledge the dual role of practical work in facilitating the learning and understanding of science concepts *and* in developing the skills and procedures of scientific enquiry. In more recent UK statements of this sort the procedural elements have tended to dominate. A recent influential example is the DES paper, *Science 5–16: A Statement of Policy*. It begins from the claim that 'the essential characteristic of education in science is that it introduces pupils to the methods of science' (DES, 1985: 3). In order to achieve this:

> the courses provided should . . . give pupils, at all stages, appro- priate opportunities to:
> — make observations;
> — select observations relevant to their investigations for further study;
> — seek and identify patterns and relate these to patterns per- ceived earlier;
> — suggest and evaluate explanations of the patterns;
> — design and carry out experiments, including appropriate forms of measurement, to test suggested explanations for the patterns of observations (DES, 1985: 3–4).

For convenience this view of science method will be referred to as the standard science education (SSE) view. It is a view which appears to conform to many science teachers' own perceptions of their work. UK science teachers appear to have welcomed the characterization of school science in the extract above, and courses and textbooks which claim to be grounded in this 'process' approach have been well received. In part this may be because it resonates well with the wider ideology of school science. An emphasis on science-as-a-method — a 'process' emphasis — is welcomed by many who see it as an alternative to the 'traditional' image of science education as the transmission of a given corpus of accepted knowledge. 'Skills' are seen as accessible to *all* pupils, not just the academic minority, and as being valuable in later life, even for those who will not continue to study science. On this view 'process science' provides the model for a viable 'science for all'.

The 'process' emphasis and the SSE view of science method in which it is embedded have, however, been criticized from a number of perspectives (Finlay, 1983; Millar and Driver, 1987; Millar, 1989; Woolnough, 1989). One important element of this critique is the mismatch between the SSE view and current philosophical and sociological accounts of science practice. This is reviewed briefly in the next section. This chapter, however, focuses on one specific aspect of the SSE model of science method, namely the role, within this model, of *experiment*, which is portrayed as a straight- forward means of testing suggested explanations of 'patterns' which have emerged from observational data.

The aim here is to show, through a case study of one particular set of experiments, that this understanding of the role of experiment in the class- room is an unhelpful one, which provides teachers with an inadequate resource for coping with the realities of practical investigation in the classroom and teaching laboratory. The science studies perspective appears to provide a better account of these experiments and of experiment in general. I will argue that the root cause of the problem lies in the long-standing failure of the science education community to acknowledge and to resolve the tension between first-hand and second-hand sources of information in science education. The final section of the chapter explores how this tension might be used more productively to develop a better rationale for experiment in science education.

Views of Science in Science Education and Science Studies

The standard view of science within science education (the SSE view) is strikingly at odds with that which is current within social studies of science — amongst historians, philosophers and sociologists of science. In the SSE view of 'science method', observation precedes theory. So too does the selection of 'relevant' observations. Data are independent of theory. These are elements of a *naive inductivist* view of science (Chalmers, 1982: 1–11). The subsequent steps of hypothesizing explanations of patterns and testing these by experiment might also be regarded as part of an inductive view, or as elements of a *hypothetico-deductive* view of science method.[1] The SSE model of science is perhaps best construed as a straightforward common-sense view, which claims no specific links with any particular philosophical view of science method.

From modern science studies, however, there emerges a much more complex picture of scientific method and, within it, of the role of experiment. Naive inductivism is, as Chalmers comments, 'too naive to be sympathetically dealt with by philosophers' (*ibid.*: 11). More sophisticated inductivist views are still put forward by some philosophers (van Fraassen, 1980) but these are far removed from the SSE version. The idea that observations are theory-laden is now generally accepted, clouding any clear distinction between data (observation) and theory; so, too, is the provisional and conjectural nature of theory.

Much philosophy of science has been concerned with the attempt to provide retrospectively a rational reconstruction of the grounds for accepting scientific knowledge. In contrast, a group of studies from the perspective which has become known as the sociology of scientific knowledge has focused attention on the actual practices of scientists through detailed case studies of both historical and contemporary scientific practice (see, for example, Kuhn, 1970; Mulkay, 1979; Barnes and Shapin, 1979; Collins, 1981; Barnes and Edge, 1982; Woolgar, 1988).[2] These studies seek to demonstrate that neither the inductivist nor hypothetico–deductivist view can provide an adequate account of what scientists do. They explore the consequences of the theory-ladenness of observation — the inevitability of theory intervening in every act of perception. They investigate the social factors in the assessment of knowledge claims. They point out that every theory has well recognized anomalies from the moment it is proposed. They note that scientists tend to celebrate experiments which have 'verified' theoretical predictions and not those which have falsified them.

Partly in response to this critique more sophisticated hypothetico–deductive views have been proposed (Lakatos, 1970), which accept that theories are never tested in isolation. Hence apparent falsification can, quite logically, lead to rejection or modification of some auxiliary hypothesis, rather than of the theory apparently under test. Lakatos argues that experiments can arbitrate only when we have two competing theories. Again empirical studies question the possibility of a clear-cut experimental decision between theories. The 'crucial experiment' may test theorists (and perhaps experimenters) rather than theory (Pinch, 1985). As Collins (1985a) has demonstrated, within controversial episodes in science, even the *replication* of experimental claims can become problematic. Pinch sums up one aspect of this particular problem in the following way: 'Scientists are reluctant to make a "me too" observation, and attempted replications will often be performed with different pieces of apparatus. This leaves open the possibility that the failure to replicate lies in some crucial difference between the experiments' (Pinch, 1986: 419). So the very act of agreeing that another experiment *is* a replication of a previous one is a matter of negotiation and consensus within the relevant expert community.

The net effect of this body of work is not, of course, to reduce the importance of experiment within science but rather to draw attention to the fact that the outcomes of experiments have to be *interpreted* and their significance *negotiated* within the community of scientists working in that field. Experiments do not involve a simple 'reading of the book of nature', or a ready touchstone to confirm or falsify a hypothesis or theory. The role of the scientific community is an active and important one; a knowledge claim becomes a 'fact' only when it is accepted as such by the relevant expert community (see, for example, Ziman, 1968). It is suggested in this chapter that these perspectives on science practice can provide a better account of what goes on when we do experiments in the science classroom than does the standard science education view.

Varieties of Practical Work

This chapter began by referring to 'practical work' in school science. The term which is used in the extract cited from the DES *Statement of Policy*, and which is central to the issues discussed in this chapter, is 'experiment'. Not all school science practical work can sensibly be termed 'experiment', and it is important to be more precise about this term and how it is being used. The UK National Curriculum Science Working Group (DES, 1988) makes the distinction along the following lines: 'Some investigations we describe as "experiments" in that they involve systematic change and control of variables in order to ensure that alternative hypotheses can be eliminated' (DES, 1988: 50, para. 4.25). Similarly Finch and Coyle (1988), in an attempt to work towards an agreed terminology within science education, recommend that 'experiment' be 'reserved . . . for true Popper-type experiments where an abstract high level theory, model or law is put to a cleverly devised check' (p. 45).

A common distinction within science practical activity is between experiment and observation. Harré (1983) comments: 'An observer stands outside the course of events in which he is interested. He waits for nature to induce the changes, to produce the phenomena and to create the substances he is studying. He records what he has been presented with' (pp. 14–15). By contrast, an experimenter *intervenes*, rearranging and manipulating a part of nature to produce the effects which she will then observe. Even this distinction, however, is not entirely without its problems; it would, for example, exclude the work of astronomers and geologists from the category of 'experiment'. Hacking (1983), in a detailed analysis of experimentation, plays down the significance of the distinction by arguing that: 'It is true that we cannot interfere very much in the distant reaches of space, but the skills employed . . . [are] identical to those used by laboratory experimenters' (p. 160). Rudwick, writing from the perspective of a geologist, argues a stronger case: 'The conventional dichotomy between experimental and "observational" sciences is highly misleading, unless it is recognised that the latter employ close analogues of experimentation, namely theory-guided strategies of selective observation' (Rudwick, 1985: 43). The *choice* of what to observe becomes, in this sense, the 'intervention'. From this viewpoint rather more of what we do as school science practical work might come under the heading of 'experiment'.

The term 'experiment' will be used here to mean specific planned intervention or structured observation intended as a check on the usefulness of a hypothesis or theory, or of a specific prediction deduced from a hypothesis or theory.

From a more specifically science education perspective, Woolnough and Allsop (1985) have proposed a three-fold classification of school science practical work: *exercises, investigations* and *experiences*. Their underlying theme is that a 'tight coupling of practical and theory can have a detrimental effect both on the quality of the practical work done and on the theoretical understandings gained by the students' (p. 8). They advocate a clearer separation of practical work from the demands of demonstrating and elucidating theory and set out to provide a rationale for practical work as an activity in its own right. *Exercises* are intended to develop specific skills and techniques, including the ability to use scientific apparatus and measuring instruments appropriately; *investigations* involve students working as 'problem-solving scientists' to tackle open-ended tasks; *experiences* are activities designed to give students a 'feel' for phenomena and some common experiences on which to draw in subsequent discussion and development. These are useful distinctions which are potentially of considerable help to teachers in clarifying the aims of their practical work.[3] Yet this model of school science practical work is, in an important respect, incomplete.

The missing component within this scheme is the place of experiments — practical work which is carried out specifically to provide grounds for acceptance of theory. Woolnough and Allsop's *investigations* avoid the problems of the practical/theory linkage by being drawn largely from applied science — dealing with *locally*, rather than *generally*, valid information. Students, for example, measure the efficiency of *this* bow and arrow, or *this* motor; they investigate the pollution of the *local* stream, or the distribution of 'minibeasts' in *their own* school grounds. They use general concepts and principles to measure and evaluate specific artifacts and contexts, and so the results of their investigations do not challenge or threaten established ideas and generalizations.

Yet a central characteristic of the scientific enterprise is its claim to provide *generalizable* knowledge about how the world behaves. By developing powerful conceptual tools, many of which are very far abstracted from everyday experience, science aims to provide generally reliable explanations and predictions about the behaviour of the natural world. Furthermore, experiment plays a key role in refining and checking theory and theoretical predictions. Woolnough and Allsop recognize that some school practical work must continue to have this role of providing a warrant for theory. Here they suggest that 'pre-eminently, demonstrations provide the ideal opportunity for the teacher to link the practical reality with the underlying theory' (p. 62). The nature of this linkage is explored in more detail through the case study which forms the central focus of this chapter. For whilst it is clearly true that teacher demonstrations may provide a means of avoiding some of the grosser sources of experimental error in students' practical work, it is not at all clear in the case study which follows that demonstrations can provide unproblematical access to 'the way things really are'. The difficulties of using first-hand experimental data in a teaching laboratory to provide a warrant for theory run deeper.

Using Scientific Controversy

As indicated above, the SSE view of experiment appears to have wide currency among teachers, possibly because of its congruence with their wider ideological commitments. A more compelling reason for its acceptability may be that it gives a recognizable account of what many teachers see themselves as *doing* in the laboratory. So despite the fact that it may be *epistemologically* suspect, it is *pedagogically* apposite. Science lessons often involve teachers in setting up situations in which students are asked to make careful observations. The materials and contexts provided will have been chosen so that the generalization (or 'pattern') which the teacher wishes the students to perceive will, indeed, emerge from the data. Teachers' perceptions of the quality and accuracy of students' observations and measurements are coloured by their (the teacher's) prior knowledge of what outcomes to expect. Data which do not conform to the required pattern can be relegated (by the teacher) to the category of 'error'. It can easily come to appear that the external world *compels* a certain interpretation of the evidence.

This is also, of course, a major difficulty for the researcher wishing to study how experiment is used within the teaching and learning situation. If, for example, one is observing a class investigating collisions between laboratory trolleys, it is difficult to 'see' the phenomenon other than from within the accepted framework of a defined quantity, *momentum*, which is conserved. Student results which corroborate this conservation rule are taken as evidence of good workmanship and accurate measurement; those which indicate non-conservation are explained away using contingent factors. In many respects this mirrors the situation in some versions of sociology of scientific knowledge, where distinctively different accounts are provided for accepted 'facts' and for 'anomalies' (Mulkay, 1979: Ch. 1).

More recently sociologists of science have argued that the study of contemporary scientific controversies provides a means of getting round this difficulty, and of seeing more clearly the (social) processes involved in the creation and validation of accepted scientific knowledge. Collins puts it like this:

> ... when we consider the grounds of knowledge, we do it within an environment filled with objects of knowledge which are already established. To speak figuratively, it is as though epistemologists are concerned with the characteristics of ships (knowledge) in bottles (validity) while living in a world where all ships are already in bottles with the glue dried and the strings cut.... My contention is that... it is possible to make a partial escape from the cultural determinism of current knowledge... by looking at [ideas and facts] while they are being formed, before they have become 'set' as part of anyone's natural (scientific) world. In short, the contemporaneous study of contemporary scientific developments... can provide an entry.... It should be expected that this will generate a picture of science in which the figurative 'ships' are still being built by human actors... (Collins, 1975: 205–6)

In much the same way some aspects of the uses of experiment in science classrooms can be perceived more clearly through a case study of a *problematic* topic within school science, that is, of a topic where the scientific knowledge has itself been rendered uncertain, yet where this uncertainty is not reflected in textbook accounts, nor widely recognized by teachers. The researcher can then approach the topic with an open mind about the phenomenon itself and without any clear external yardstick for distinguishing reliable experimental data from anomaly. As most school science deals with well attested science, there are not many topics which meet these rather special requirements! One which does (though this is not universally recognized within school science) is the biological topic of tropic responses in plants.

Plant Tropism

We all know that plants bend towards the light, and that their roots go down and shoots go up, sensing and responding in some way to gravity. These are not strange or unfamiliar effects! In biology the former is called *phototropism*, the latter *geotropism*. Experiments to demonstrate these tropic responses and to illustrate an explanatory theory — the Colodny-Went theory — are included in most school biology texts (see, for example, Mackean, 1973; Beckett, 1982; Roberts, 1986). Simplifying greatly, the theory proposes that tropic effects are due to the action on plant tissue of a plant hormone called indoleacetic acid, or IAA. This is one of a group of substances called *auxins*. The auxin, according to the Colodny-Went theory, is produced in the tip of a growing shoot or root and diffuses to other tissues. Its production is inhibited by light and its diffusion influenced by gravity. Complicated auxiliary hypotheses are called upon to explain, for instance, how it is that increased concentrations of the same hormone *inhibit* growth of root tissue but *promote* growth of shoot tissue in the geotropic response. This is explained by positing a high degree of sensitivity to precise concentrations of auxin in these tissues. A major attraction of the Colodny-Went theory is that it provides a single general theory of phototropic and geotropic responses, covering both roots and shoots in all plant species.

The school experiments used to investigate these tropic effects range from simple explorations of the phenomenon of bending itself to experiments of some complexity which seek to demonstrate aspects of the role of the apex and of IAA in tropic behaviour. These include experiments (originally reported by Darwin) where shoots are grown with and without foil caps placed over the apices, experiments involving the decapitation of shoots to remove the apex; experiments where IAA is applied externally to growing intact shoots or to the top of decapitated shoots; experiments where the decapitated tip is placed on an agar block to extract the IAA and the block is then replaced on the stump (possibly in an off-centre position). Many of these experiments are performed on a specialized organ, called the *coleoptile*, which first grows from oat, barley and grass seeds and from which the first leaves emerge (see Figures 1 and 2).

This theory was initially proposed in the 1930s and has subsequently entered school biology syllabuses — in simplified form in courses for

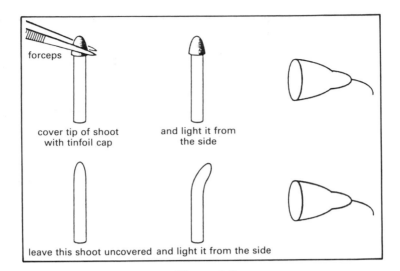

Figure 2.1
The Foil-Capping Experiment Used to Investigate the Role of the Tip in Phototropism

Source: M. B. V. Roberts (1981) *Biology for Life*, London, Nelson.

14–16-year-olds, more fully in pre-university courses. There is little in any of these accounts, even the most recent, to suggest that the information provided is in any sense uncertain. The standard textbook account has, however, recently been subjected to significant criticism in the biological literature. Since 1976 a number of plant physiologists have published articles, mostly in journals read by academic biologists, criticizing the Colodny-Went theory (Digby and Firn, 1976; Firn and Digby, 1980; Hall, Firn and Digby, 1980; Oxlade and Clifford, 1981). Newer investigations, some using the more sophisticated techniques available today, question various aspects of the theory. For example, plant shoots respond very quickly — within minutes — to lateral illumination. Yet the time for substances to diffuse from the tip to cells some centimetres further down the shoot is of the order of hours. Another problem concerns differential concentrations of auxin on either side of a shoot to produce a given amount of bending. If one uses externally applied auxin, this must be several orders of magnitude greater than is measured in growing plants. The uncertainties, however, are not confined to aspects of the theoretical model used to account for the tropic effects, but also include the observable surface features. Franssen, Firn and Digby (1982) report experiments showing that black-capped shoots bend towards the light when illuminated from the side, in much the same way as control specimens. As a review article in *New Scientist* (Weyers, 1984) makes clear, the whole area of plant hormones is now one of some controversy.

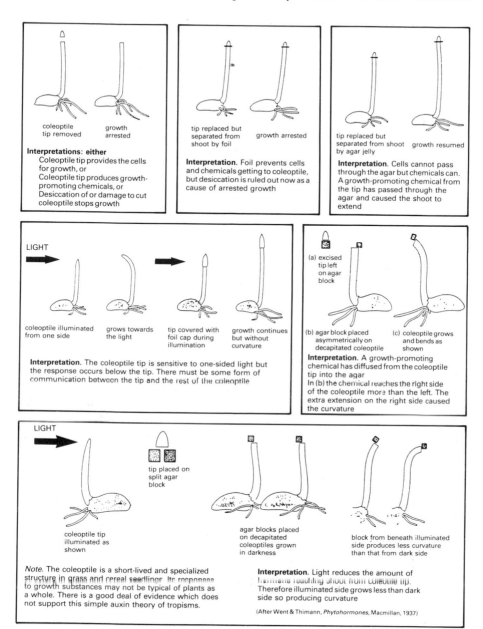

Figure 2.2
Some Classical Experiments to Test the Auxin Theory

Source: D. G. Mackean (1973) *Introduction to Biology*, 5th ed., London, John Murray.

Teachers' Perceptions of the Tropism Experiments

I conducted a series of individual interviews over three years with over twenty experienced school biology teachers. These teachers had attended an in-service course which included a lecture and practical session on plant tropism, in which the validity of the standard textbook information and explanations had been challenged. In the interviews I wanted to explore the teachers' views of classroom experiments on tropism, and the ways in which they reacted to the discovery that an area of scientific knowledge contained in all the textbooks is actually 'open' and still under negotiation.

At the heart of the SSE view of experiment is the idea that carefully conducted experiments yield reliable knowledge. None of the teachers I interviewed claimed to find the tropism experiments straightforward. Some said that they had suspected the experiments for some time and no longer attempted them. One teacher commented: '[there is] a general consensus that these experiments never have really worked properly and you were waiting for the wretched thing to bend when it should be and it wasn't and I think a lot of teachers have moved away from these experiments entirely.' Others saw the area as an attractive and coherent one, with a good interplay between theory and experiment: 'it's been quite a nice area in many ways ... because it was a nice concise thing. You could, in general, do the things, it had a nice sort of coherent theory behind it, you could get auxins reasonably cheaply, so it was quite a tidy area really.' The majority, however, painted a more equivocal picture, acknowledging that the influence of prior expectations was difficult to escape: ' ... [the experiments] don't always work very well, but we try it, yes. We try it with little silver paper, cooking foil, caps on ... you can convince yourself that it works if you want to, yes ... it's true to say that it works to some extent. That sounds a bit strange but, yes, it does seem to work.'

The variable response of biological materials is a particular difficulty which always faces the biological experimenter. Tropism experiments are carried out, not on one seedling, but on many. The variability of specimens is always liable to mask any anomaly: 'If you do a lot, you know, you say, well there's a lot here, you know, and some ... most of them seem to be looking all right, you know.' In such a situation the influence of prior expectations is difficult to escape. To the question, 'Do the experiments work?', one teacher replied: 'Well ... I ... thought ... they did. But I'm not sure if there isn't an element in this type of thing where even teachers almost read something into it, and ... um ... think they've worked when they perhaps haven't.' Many of the teachers quite spontaneously offered specific examples of other school biology experiments which also frequently failed to give the expected result, yet where the theory is not contested. Difficulties with the tropism experiments were not seen as in any sense a special case. Just as the textbooks do not flag tropism as in any way different from other topics on the syllabus, so too the experimental work does not reveal any special difficulties or uncertainties.

An important underlying assumption of the SSE view of science is that there is a congruence between the aims of teaching content and teaching a method — valid hypotheses can be identified by experimental testing. When experiments fail to produce the accepted results, however, this congruence breaks down and the situation becomes problematic. How do teachers respond when an experiment fails to 'work'? What account do they provide for their students and, indeed, for themselves?

> When you do experiments and they don't work, you tend to think it's your fault and that you can't be right and because you haven't got the facilities to investigate it in a different way or the time, then you don't . . . . Yes you've had results that are odd but you've felt, well, you don't know the whole picture.

It is scarcely surprising that both teachers and students in this situation tend to fall back on the textbook as a source of authority:

> If the experiment shows something different to what it says in the textbook, they'll tend to go with . . . the textbook . . . it's got to be somebody of very strong will to say something else.

> The bulk of teachers don't really question the textbooks too carefully . . . something as fundamental as the direct evidence for . . . the evidence for the apical dominance in this thing is rather fundamental and I don't really think that teachers are prepared to question those things too closely.

So despite the importance attached to experiment as a check on theory in the SSE view, anomalous experimental results in the tropism experiments are readily enough dismissed. Teachers commented on the minuteness of the systems under investigation, on the mechanical and technical difficulties of carrying out the experiments, on problems arising from dessication of specimens. Even recognizing whether particular specimens have bent gives rise to uncertainty:

> The capping experiment is possible, but it's so difficult to actually judge whether the things have moved because . . . you can't get them absolutely vertical. When they're sitting in the dish almost inevitably no matter where you grow them they tilt slightly one way or another, and they all tend to be slightly different particularly after students have moved them around a bit and put caps and things on them. When you come back, where did they start off?

> the difficulty [is] . . . the changing shape that takes place — the way that the thing appears to curve and then it straightens up, there's only the last bit that actually curves, you know, and this effectively changes the growth on one side and then readjusts.

In addition to these intrinsic difficulties of the experiments, teachers were aware of a range of extrinsic factors which prevented them undertaking a fuller investigation of tropism in the classroom. Timing was seen as crucial in the experiments: 'I've always felt it was very largely this time factor, that was the crucial thing . . . if the shoot had got beyond the stage when it was going to sensibly respond you'd had it.' The influence of external examinations was also seen by many teachers as a strong constraint, curtailing attempts to pursue anomaly at the expense of communicating the accepted picture. Recognizing this combination of examination pressures and the institutional constraints of schools is an important corrective to any over-simplistic drawing of parallels between school science and the professional practice of scientists. As one teacher commented: ' . . . [biology researchers] have the lengths of time that they can repeat things again serially whereas a teacher might say "That's strange, perhaps I'll come back to that next year and try again", and off to 3B down the corridor.' In summary, these experiments did not yield clear-cut results and their failure to 'work' did not pose a serious challenge to the textbook account, as many alternative explanations were available.

The interviews also explored teachers' reactions to finding that tropism was now an area of some controversy and uncertainty. The responses of many teachers indicate, in a variety of ways, the influence of the SSE rhetoric of experiment, in particular the primacy of first-hand experimental data over second-hand textbook accounts. One response is to switch immediately to accepting the new information as unproblematically correct. This is then perceived as a source of new ideas for experiments which will work better and hence resolve the uncertainty. Others who appeared to have changed their own interpretation of tropism still felt constrained to continue teaching the 'old' textbook account. Several seemed apologetic or defensive about this resolution:

> I tossed up what to do but decided that because all textbooks are still on the old idea I'm afraid I still stick to the old idea . . . . I think for O-level it's too confusing for them to have different views.

> . . . my tendency is . . . to teach it in a single lesson, to teach what the textbook says, particularly with the O-level candidates.

> . . . the sort of questions that they put on the examination are . . . . 'What's the name of the stuff that causes plants to bend?' So they just have to be aware that there's a substance called auxin, that the examiners think is involved.

For a few teachers the primacy of first-hand data was such that they were prepared to see experiment — even school experiment — as capable of conclusive falsification of established theory: 'If you got bending and the theory says that you shouldn't . . . well then the theory is wrong. I mean, that's the whole point — you disprove scientific theories. Obviously in that case you

actually disprove the theory and that could be a very useful teaching aid.'
Some, however, perceived that in the school context, as in academic biology
circles, the coherence and elegance of the Colodny-Went theory effectively
protect it from such ready rejection:

> [biologists] haven't actually put forward another theory they've
> just said it doesn't explain the facts as they see them, and so it's a bit
> difficult to put nothing in its place, you know, so what I'll do at the
> moment is continue with what we have been doing but point out
> that this has been contested . . . otherwise you're back to 'This
> bends but we don't know why'.

Many teachers wanted more time to reflect on how best to integrate the new
ideas with the standard textbook view; this was variously seen as leading to
the teaching of a hybrid approach or of a parallel presentation of conflicting
views. The latter approach was regarded by many as too sophisticated for
younger groups but appropriate for pre-university work. In general few felt
that their solution to the problem was an ideal one, but recognized that their
choices were limited by external constraints over which they had very little
direct control.

Some Conclusions from the Tropism Case Study

The general point which emerges from this account of teachers' experiences
of, and reactions to, the tropism topic is that the science studies perspective
on experiment matches more closely with teachers' experiences with the
tropism experiments than does the standard science education view. From
this one may draw two more general conclusions about experiment in
science teaching:

1   that a rationale for experiment grounded in a hypothetico–deduct-
    ive view of science is unsatisfactory. Experiment in the teaching
    laboratory cannot be used to confirm or falsify established theory;
2   that the outcomes of experiments cannot simply be regarded as
    revealing meaning but must instead be seen as the raw materials for
    the *negotiation* of meaning.

Experiment as a Test of Theory

Teachers' comments in the interviews showed that the SSE view of experiment as a test of theory does not provide an adequate account of the tropism
experiments. A teacher who is unaware that the standard textbook account
is contested will not discover, through these experiments, compelling
grounds for doubt. But the SSE view is of no more help to the teacher who

does know that the tropism topic is problematic. It is simply fanciful to suggest that she could use the tropism experiments as 'crucial experiments' in the school laboratory to arbitrate between the Colodny-Went theory and its critics.

This general point, that school experimentation cannot provide a serious test of theory, whether with a view to confirming or falsifying it, is not a new one. Koertge has similarly argued that it is doubtful whether a student can actively test the scientific structure he or she is learning.

> A major characteristic of the scientific enterprise is that it *severely* tests theories. This means, first of all, that one must have good experimental technique so that if a refutation appears, it is reasonable to claim that it is the theory which is in error, not the experimenter. However, this would rarely be a realistic judgment for a student to make. Secondly, to *severely* test a theory means to try it out in new areas in which it has not previously been tested or areas in which we have reason to believe it could fail. By definition, then, a *standard* laboratory experiment, one which 'works' and which has been replicated by thousands of people, is not a severe test of theory. The very laboratory experiments which are best for demonstrating a law, for making it easy to grasp, are typically *not* severe tests of that law (Koertge, 1969: 38–9, her emphases).

In the school context the authority of the textbook will always take priority over experimental data when general theoretical knowledge is at stake — a fact which students are often more prepared to acknowledge than their teachers! Questions like: 'What's supposed to happen, sir?' (Wellington, 1983) effectively recognize the authority of the textbook and of knowledge 'out there'. The problems which this poses for teachers following 'guided discovery' methods are well documented in the literature (Driver, 1975; Atkinson and Delamont, 1977; Solomon, 1980; Harris and Taylor, 1983). A particularly clear example is provided in a detailed account of one science lesson in a middle school by Edwards and Mercer (1987). This shows how even a teacher who sets out to frame a class investigation of the simple pendulum as an open-ended enquiry in fact curtails several lines of proposed pupil enquiry and arbitrates on the significance or non-significance of small differences between measured results, all on the basis of her (undeclared) prior knowledge of what *should* affect the period of swing. A more adequate view of experiment in the classroom will have to acknowledge that it cannot conclusively confirm or refute accepted theory.

Negotiating the Meaning of Experimental Outcomes

The evidence of the interviews is that the outcomes of experiments to demonstrate the 'facts' of tropism are equivocal. There is ambiguity about what conditions are needed to make shoots bend. The experiments fail to provide a convincing warrant for accepting the theory. Before attempting to draw more general conclusions from the tropism case study, however, we must first ask: is tropism a special case? In one obvious sense the answer is 'yes': tropism differs from almost all other school science topics in being currently controversial at the research level. But the important point is that it does not appear as a special case *from the learner's perspective*. It has no special conceptual difficulty, makes no excessive apparatus demands, and deals with a commonly known and recognized phenomenon. As we have seen, there is nothing in the textbook accounts to mark it out for special treatment.

Unless we are to argue that the tropism experiments are uniquely problematical (and the argument here is that there are no good grounds for doing so), then we must suppose that the experiments and demonstrations which we use as warrants for much textbook theory are similarly equivocal from the learner's point of view, and are open to varied interpretations. It is only our prior knowledge of what is 'supposed to happen' which normally prevents us seeing this. Indeed the value of the tropism case study is precisely that it may enable us to see this more clearly.

In general, then, we cannot simply assume that demonstrations demonstrate what we think they do. Instead we must see the demonstration as only a starting point. Its interpretation is unlikely to be obvious or compelling to a learner. A process of discussion and negotiation is required if students are to come to see the demonstration as demonstrating what we want it to. This has parallels with the process of negotiation which goes on within the scientific community before new knowledge-claims are accepted as 'facts'. It is worth noting that there is work to be done on how learners perceive and reinterpret practical demonstrations whose implications we (as 'insiders') regard as clear-cut and obvious.

First-hand and Second-hand Knowledge

We have seen in the previous section that 'demonstrations' do not demonstrate, and that the received rhetoric of experiment as a test of scientific theory in the classroom is unsatisfactory. I want to argue here that the root of these problems lies in the failure of science educators to resolve the relationship between the *first-hand knowledge* of practical experimentation and the *second-hand knowledge* contained in textbooks, which represents the store of accepted and accredited scientific knowledge.

Barnes, discussing Thomas Kuhn's account of scientific training, identifies as its most distinctive feature the extent to which it relies on textbooks. He goes on to write that, according to Kuhn: 'Scientific training is dogmatic and authoritarian.... [It] does not instruct students in the practice of research:... instead [it] concentrates on the transmission of existing knowledge and procedure'. (Barnes, 1982: 16). To explain how this transmission takes place, Kuhn introduces the concept of the scientific *paradigm*. A 'paradigm' is 'an existing scientific achievement, a specific concrete *problem-solution* which has gained universal acceptance through-out a scientific field as a valid procedure, and as a model of valid procedure for pedagogic use' (*ibid*.: 17). Kuhn's view is that:

> The culture of an established natural science is passed on in the form of paradigms. The central task of the teacher is to display them. Scientific training always requires that a paradigm or para-digms be recognised as the sole legitimate representation of, and mode of dealing with, an aspect of the physical environment. It demands acceptance of the existing orthodoxy in a given field . . . .
> It seeks to inculcate 'a deep commitment to a particular way of viewing the world and of practising science in it' (Kuhn, 1963: 349) (Barnes, 1982: 18–19).

Barnes finishes his account by noting that: 'This view of scientific training and its consequences was sometimes found startling when it first appeared, and was read as a critical account. It was offered, however, as an account of a well-ordered and effective regime, the existence of which helped to explain the 'success' of science' (*ibid*.: 19). This last point is important. Kuhn's account claims to be a *description* of what learning science is actually like, and not a *prescription* of how it ought to be. As a description it is readily recognizable in much current practice, whatever the rhetoric of science education might suggest.

Barnes' account of Kuhn has been cited at some length because it sets out very clearly a central problem (perhaps *the* central problem) of science education. The problem is this: if teaching science is really the transmission of a body of consensually accepted knowledge, what is its value as general education? Is there a role for personal enquiry and investigation?

Most science educators would, rightly, see significant potential dangers in teaching textbook science. In many ways science education rhetoric is the record of attempts to avoid these dangers. The *pedagogical* danger is that teaching becomes an arid business of rote learning of standard facts, theories and methods. The *epistemological* danger is that it makes science look like infallible, received knowledge. We need to find a way of avoiding these twin dangers, without returning to a distorted rhetoric of science as method. This *can* be done; the solution lies in accepting rather than ignoring Kuhn's insight that science is defined by paradigms. We can then find the means of avoiding both the epistemological and the pedagogical dangers.

The Role of Experiment in School Science

Experiments as Paradigms

Many school science 'experiments' are *paradigms*; their function (and it could be achieved in no other way) is to show what is involved in doing science. School experiments can work as paradigms on a number of levels. At the level of concepts it is *necessary* to see some experiments, perhaps even to handle them, in order to understand the theoretical ideas involved. For example, we learn something about *energy* by measuring inputs and outputs in a number of situations where energy is transferred. 'Understanding' the energy concept means coming to see these processes in energy terms. We become able to 'see' what is happening as a scientist sees it — from an energy point-of-view. The general principle of which this is a specific instance is that we learn abstract concepts *ostensively*, by being shown specific examples of a concept or idea, rather than from a definition (Kuhn, 1977).

On another level, paradigms demonstrate what counts as 'good practice' in a scientific field. The tropism experiments illustrated in Figures 1 and 2 are examples. They show what is an accepted way of *going about* investigations in practical botany. They display aspects of practical technique and of general strategies for investigating the phenomena. Indeed part of their hold on syllabus space, despite the current controversies about tropism, is that they exemplify 'scientific' botany — rather than 'mere' nature study. They show how one might go about investigating plant behaviour.

At a third and more general level still experiments are paradigms of what it means to conduct an investigation *scientifically*. Tackling a problem scientifically is *not* a matter of following a set of rules — the 'scientific method'. Rules could never help us in tackling a genuinely novel problem anyhow; the very term 'novel' implies that the problem differs from past problems whose solutions we know. We learn how to investigate scientifically through amassing experience of a wide range of paradigm approaches to problems which, taken together, embody the tacit aspects of 'working scientifically'.

So we *must* use experiment in teaching science, because it provides the only means of communicating many of its concepts and practices. Let us then see how we can avoid the attendant dangers of teaching through paradigms.

Avoiding the Pedagogical Danger: Pupils as Scientists

Recent work on how children learn science has shown an important sense in which experiment in the classroom remains epistemologically 'alive', even when acceptable outcomes are constrained by established textbook knowledge. The key to this is to perceive science, not as an algorithmic method for 'finding out', but as akin to the everyday processes of gaining commonsense knowledge. The way we learn science parallels the way we learn about common things. This insight forms the basis for a valuable piece of work carried out recently by a group of Leicestershire teachers. They suggest that:

> ... the learner is already, to some extent, a scientist. The difference between learner and scientist is one of degree rather than kind. They differ in:
> — the care with which they construct hypotheses;
> — the rigour with which they test hypotheses;
> — and the degree to which they can articulate their ideas and understanding (Crookes *et al.*, 1985: 7).

In everyday life we reach agreement with others about events and processes. We develop shared concepts and theories which allow us to talk and discuss situations with one another. We have varying degrees of confidence in how things will behave, ranging from those contexts about which we feel very certain to others where our knowledge is qualified with terms like 'maybe' and 'probably'. Science involves similar social processes in negotiating an accepted way of talking about phenomena, of making predictions and of assessing their reliability, and moves in a similar way between uncertainty and confidence as a field or an investigation develops.

As in everyday contexts, students in science classes construct their own meanings for events and phenomena through personal reflection and social encounter. The science teacher (and the textbook) have access to one preferred set of meanings which have been constructed by scientists and have been accepted as particularly powerful and useful. These necessarily carry greater weight than students' personal meanings and there may be a need to introduce them into the discussion at some point (Driver and Oldham, 1986: 119). But this does not negate the need to *discuss* and *negotiate* the meaning of observation and experiment in the science classroom. The teacher cannot ever be sure that the student's own construction of meaning during a teaching episode matches the accepted view. This view of learning, *constructivism*, is *not* the same as *discovery learning*. There is no ideological requirement here that the teacher wait until pupils 'discover' the scientific idea for themselves. She can legitimately introduce the accepted science view, but needs to be aware that it may be *reconstructed* by individual students as they make personal sense of it. Classroom activities are organized to maximize students' opportunities to articulate their personal constructions and teachers' opportunities to remain aware of these and to influence their development.

Avoiding the Epistemological Danger: Gaining Natural Knowledge

If we are to teach science as *common knowledge* without portraying it as infallible, received knowledge, then we may need to use some experiments in the classroom in a new way. We are familiar with the use of experiments to provide evidence for theoretical ideas. As Woolnough and Allsop (1985) have pointed out, some 'experiments' are best thought of as *exercises* in the use of specific techniques or as *experiences* to provide a 'feel' for phenomena. In addition to these uses, we need to design some experimental work specifically to give students some feeling for the real difficulty of wresting information from nature — in contexts where they cannot simply put this down to 'inferior' school science apparatus! Learning science should involve coming to appreciate that reliable knowledge of the natural world is not easy to obtain.

The tropism work could, for example, be used to explore with pupils the difficulty of obtaining knowledge which is reliable enough to convince others. For example, half the class might be asked to conduct an investigation of capped shoots to obtain evidence that the tip is the light sensor; the other half might be asked to obtain evidence that capped shoots also bend when illuminated from the side. In other words the two subgroups would be seeking data to support or refute a specific given hypothesis. These would, unknown to the groups, be mutually contradictory. Subsequent presentations to the whole class by the two subgroups might lead to useful discussion about the relationship between expectations, data and theory, and about the role of experiment in settling these matters.

Another contested topic (though one which is less central to a major field of science than tropism) is the so-called Mpemba effect — the suggestion that hot water freezes faster than cold (Mpemba and Osborne, 1969). This might be investigated along similar lines, But there is no need to limit the contexts to areas which are genuinely contested. Another category of potential contexts for this sort of work is suggested by Edwards and Mercer's account of the pendulum experiment. They note an instance where the teacher negotiates with pupils the 'conclusion' that two sets of timing results which differ slightly are 'really the same'; and on another occasion in the same lesson treats a smaller percentage difference between another pair of results as significant (Edwards and Mercer, 1987: 118–24). In science the attribution of significance or non-significance to differences between two measured results is always potentially problematic and a matter of skilled judgment. It would be difficult to argue that it could be encapsulated in a set of rules. We might again imagine two subgroups within a class, one given the hypothesis that altering the angle of swing does not affect the period and the other given the hypothesis that it *does* make a small difference. Both would collect data; and the teacher would then bring the groups together to present their findings to each other.

In all these approaches, which are offered here as tentative suggestions, the principle would be the same: to give students direct experience of the difficulties involved in reaching consensus about the interpretation of experimental data.

Summary

The central theme of this chapter has been the mismatch between the views of science within science education writings and in modern science studies. It has been suggested that the science studies perspective provides a better account of science as it is practised in the teaching laboratory and classroom. The tension within science education between science as method and science as consensual knowledge emerges most clearly in the uneasy relationship between first- and second-hand data sources in the classroom. The historical roots of this tension are deep and are intimately linked to the social contexts within which science evolved as a school subject (see, for example, Layton, 1973; Millar, 1985). The outcome is a rhetoric of school science which is an uneasy amalgam of naive inductive and hypothetico–deductive views of science; this overemphasizes ideas of science as a method of enquiry, and underemphasizes science as a body of consensually accepted knowledge. To say this is not to argue that science is other than a provisional body of knowledge, constructed by scientists, rather than revealed as 'truth'. It is rather to suggest that the rhetorical balance needs to swing back some way from science as *personal enquiry* towards science as *common knowledge*. This chapter has tried to outline how such a balance might be restored.

Acknowledgments

I am grateful to my colleague Bob Campbell for first drawing the tropism issue to my attention; to John Digby and Richard Firn for teaching me some biology and for many discussions about the tropism experiments; and to the teachers who agreed to be interviewed and who gave me some insight into the problems of using the tropism experiments in the classroom.

Notes

1   The hypothetico–deductive view, associated with the work of Karl Popper (1959), is that scientific theories are bold conjectures, which are then subjected to testing (including experimental tests) with a view to *falsifying* them. Popper argues that the criterion for a *scientific* theory is that it is stated sufficiently precisely to leave itself open to the possibility of falsification. In this view theory precedes observation and the theory-ladenness of observation is accepted. Popper's work is a reaction against the *positivism* of Carnap and others, in which it is argued that meaningful scientific theories are those which are *verifiable* (Hacking, 1983: 2–5).

2   The stimulus for this work came from Kuhn's seminal book, *The Structure of Scientific Revolutions* (1962, revised 1970). This opened up the possibility of a sociological account of scientific knowledge rather than merely of the institutions of science. It represents an articulation (and a vindication) of the sentiments expressed by Kuhn in his celebrated opening sentence: 'History, if viewed as a repository for more than anecdote or chronology, could produce a decisive transformation in the image of science by which we are now possessed' (Kuhn, 1970: 1).

3   The distinction between the three types of practical activity may, of course, be less clear than this simple classification suggests. Collins, writing of the Millikan oil-drop experiment, comments that in the teaching situation 'repetitions of Millikan's experiment are meant to train students in manipulative skills, and, perhaps, impress them with the perseverance of Millikan; they have almost nothing to do with the charge on the electron' (Collins, 1985b: 14). So even a classical 'experiment' when originally performed may become an 'exercise' or even an 'experience' when repeated in a teaching context.

References

ATKINSON, P. and DELAMONT, S. (1977) 'Mock-ups and cock-ups: The stage-management of guided discovery instruction', in WOODS, P. and HAMMERSLEY, M. (Eds), *School Experience: Explorations in the Sociology of Education*, London, Croom Helm.

BARNES, B. (1982) *T. S. Kuhn and Social Science*, London, Macmillan.

BARNES, B. and EDGE, D. (Eds), (1982) *Science in Context: Readings in the Sociology of Science*, Milton Keynes, Open University Press.

BARNES, B. and SHAPIN, S. (Eds), (1979) *Natural Order: Historical Studies of Scientific Culture*, London, Sage.

BEATTY, J. W. and WOOLNOUGH, B. E. (1982) 'Practical work in 11–13 Science', *British Educational Research Journal*, 8, pp. 23–30.

BECKETT, B. S. (1982) *Biology: A Modern Introduction*, 2nd. ed., Oxford, Oxford University Press.

CHALMERS, A. F. (1982) *What Is This Thing Called Science?*, 2nd. ed., Milton Keynes, Open University Press.

COLLINS, H. M. (1975) 'The seven sexes: A study in the sociology of a phenomenon, or the replication of experiments in physics', *Sociology*, 9, pp. 205–24.

COLLINS, H. M. (Ed.) (1981) 'Knowledge and controversy: Studies of modern natural science', Special Issue of *Social Studies of Science*, 11, 1.

COLLINS, H. M. (1985a) *Changing Order: Replication and Induction in Scientific Practice*, London, Sage.

COLLINS, H. M. (1985b) 'The consequences of experiments', in GOODING, D. (Ed.), *The Uses of Experiment*, Abstracts of papers prepared for the BSHS/BSA conference on 'Experimentation in the Natural Sciences', Newton Park College, Bath, Science Studies Centre, University of Bath, pp. 13–16.

CROOKES, J. et al. (1985) *Science as a Process: Encouraging the Scientific Activity of Children*, The Science Curriculum Review in Leicestershire, Leicester, Leicestershire Education Authority.

DEPARTMENT OF EDUCATION AND SCIENCE, (1985) *Science 5–16: A Statement of Policy*, London, HMSO.

DEPARTMENT OF EDUCATION AND SCIENCE, (1988) *Science for Ages 5 to 16*, London, DES/Welsh Office.

DIGBY, J. and FIRN, R. D. (1976) 'A critical assessment of the Cholodny-Went theory of shoot geotropism', *Current Advances in Plant Science*, 25, pp. 953–60.

DRIVER, R. (1975) 'The name of the game', *School Science Review*, 56, 197, pp. 800–4.

DRIVER, R. and OLDHAM, V. (1986) 'A constructivist approach to curriculum development in science', *Studies in Science Education*, 13, pp. 105–22.

EDWARDS, D. and MERCER, N. (1987) *Common Knowledge: The Development of Understanding in the Classroom*, London, Methuen.

FINCH, I. and COYLE, M. (1988) *BBC Teacher Education Project, INSET Secondary Science: Teachers' Notes*, London, BBC Education.

FINLAY, F. N. (1983) 'Science processes', *Journal of Research in Science Teaching*, 20, 1, pp. 47–54.

FIRN, R. D. and DIGBY, J., (1980) 'The establishment of tropic curvatures in plants', *Annual Review of Plant Physiology*, 31, pp. 131–48.

FRANSSEN, J. M., FIRN, R. D. and DIGBY, J. (1982) 'The role of the apex in the phototropic curvature of avena coleoptiles', *Planta*, 155, pp. 281–6.

HACKING, I. (1983) *Representing and Intervening*, Cambridge, Cambridge University Press.

HALL, A. B., FIRN, R. D. and DIGBY, J. (1980) 'Auxins and shoot tropisms — a tenuous connection?', *Journal of Biological Education*, 14, 3, pp. 195–9.

HARRÉ, R. (1983) *Great Scientific Experiments*, Oxford, Oxford University Press.

HARRIS, D. and TAYLOR, M. (1983) 'Discovery learning in school science: The myth and the reality', *Journal of Curriculum Studies*, 15, 3, pp. 277–89.

KOERTGE, N. (1969) 'Toward an integration of content and method in the science curriculum', *Curriculum Theory Network*, 4, 1, pp. 26–44.

KUHN, T. S. (1963) 'The function of dogma in scientific research,' in CROMBIE, A. C. (Ed.), *Scientific Change*, London, Heinemann, pp. 347–69.

KUHN, T. S. (1970) *The Structure of Scientific Revolutions*, 2nd Ed., Chicago, University of Chicago Press.

KUHN, T. S. (1977) 'Second thoughts on paradigms', in KUHN, T. S. *The Essential Tension*, Chicago, University of Chicago Press, pp. 293–319.

LAKATOS, I. (1970) 'Falsification and the methodology of scientific research programmes', in LAKATOS, I. and MUSGRAVE, A. (Eds), *Criticism and the Growth of Knowledge*, Cambridge, Cambridge University Press, pp. 91–196.

LAYTON, D. (1973) *Science for the People*, London, George Allen and Unwin.

MACKEAN, D. G. (1973) *Introduction to Biology*, 5th ed., London, John Murray.

MILLAR, R. (1985) 'Training the mind: Continuity and change in the rhetoric of school science', *Journal of Curriculum Studies*, 17, 4, pp. 369–82.

MILLAR, R. (1989) 'What is scientific method and can it be taught?' in WELLINGTON, J. J. (Ed.), *Skills and Processes in Science Education*, London, Routledge.

MILLAR, R. and DRIVER, R. (1987) 'Beyond processes', *Studies in Science Education*, 14, pp. 33–62.

MPEMBA, E. B. and OSBORNE, D. G. (1969) 'Cool?' *Physics Education*, 4, pp. 172–5.

MULKAY, M. (1979) *Science and the Sociology of Knowledge*, London, George Allen and Unwin.

NUFFIELD PHYSICS (1966) *Teachers' Guide I*, London/Harmondsworth, Longmans/Penguin.

OXLADE, E. L. and CLIFFORD, P. E. (1981) 'Experiments in geotropism', *Journal of Biological Education*, 15, 2, pp. 137–42.

PINCH, T. J. (1985) 'Theory testing in science — the case of solar neutrinos: Do crucial experiments test theories or theorists?' *Philosophy of the Social Sciences*, 15, pp. 167–87.

PINCH, T. J. (1986) 'Controversies in science', *Physics Bulletin*, 37, 10, pp. 417–20.

POPPER, K. R. (1959) *The Logic of Scientific Discovery*, London, Hutchinson.

ROBERTS, M. B. V. (1986) *Biology: A Functional Approach*, 4th ed., London, Nelson.

RUDWICK, M. (1985) 'Field observation as natural experiment', in GOODING, D. (Ed.), *The Uses of Experiment*, Abstracts of papers prepared for the BSHS/BSA conference on 'Experimentation in the Natural Sciences', Newton Park College, Bath, Science Studies Centre, University of Bath, pp. 43–6.

SOLOMON, J. (1980) *Teaching Children in the Laboratory*, London, Croom Helm.

THOMPSON, J. J. (Ed.) (1975) *Practical Work in Sixth Form Science*, Department of Educational Studies, University of Oxford.

VAN FRAASSEN, B. C. (1980) *The Scientific Image*, Oxford, Oxford University Press.

WELLINGTON, J. J. (1981), ' "What's supposed to happen, Sir?" — some problems with discovery learning', *School Science Review*, 63, 222, pp. 167–73.

WEYERS, J. (1984) 'Do plants really have hormones?', *New Scientist*, 17 May.

WOOLGAR, S. (1988) *Science: The Very Idea*, Chichester/London, Ellis Horwood/Tavistock.

WOOLNOUGH, B. E. (1989) 'Towards a holistic view of processes in science education', in WELLINGTON, J. J. (Ed.), *Skills and Processes in Science Education*, London, Routledge.

WOOLNOUGH, B. E. and ALLSOP, T. (1985) *Practical Work in Science*, Cambridge, Cambridge University Press.

ZIMAN, J. (1968) *Public Knowledge: The Social Dimension of Science*, Cambridge, Cambridge University Press.

Chapter 3

A Study of Pupils' Responses to Empirical Evidence

Colin Gauld

Teaching Science

Over the past ten years or so evidence has been produced to indicate that, while students may often show a grasp of the concepts taught in science classes, their interpretations of phenomena which they encounter in everyday life are guided by other beliefs than those presented by teachers (Driver, Guesne and Tiberghien, 1985). It has also been demonstrated that most pupils possess beliefs about areas covered in the science syllabus (such as motion, electricity, evolution, chemical change) before they are taught anything about these topics and that these beliefs are often substantially the same when they leave school (see Pfundt and Duit, 1988). They can also remain after university undergraduate and postgraduate study (Warren, 1971; Peters, 1982).

These findings point to the deep-rootedness of the beliefs which students have presumably developed from an early age and which help them to make sense of the world they find themselves in. They indicate a marked reluctance to abandon commitments which have proved so useful in their everyday life.

In coming to terms with this evidence and its implications for teaching science, a number of models of instruction have been proposed which are designed to make a greater impact on pupil beliefs (Cosgrove and Osborne, 1985a). Most of these models contain, among other things, two stages intended to challenge the ideas pupils have but which differ from the ideas being taught by the teacher. In the first stage the fact that pupils *have* preconceptions is acknowledged and they are invited to verbalize these and to discuss them with each other. Part of the rationale for this stage is that traditional teaching methods, by not requiring students to expose their prior conceptions, provide no opportunity for pupils to relate what they are being taught to what they already believe. Consequently the ideas being taught at school can be learnt and used in the school context without in any way being associated with ideas learnt and used in the context of everyday life. Another part of the rationale is that the ideas that other pupils present provide alternatives to those adopted by a particular pupil and arguments for and against various suggestions are able to be discussed.

The second stage is the presentation of empirical evidence which is designed to contradict implications of pupils' ideas and to be compatible with the syllabus notion being taught. The attempt by pupils to resolve this conflict between their ideas and the evidence is expected to cause them to alter their beliefs in the direction intended by the teacher.

However, studies have demonstrated that, even when such teaching strategies are used, pupils' beliefs are still very difficult to change or that they do not always change in the intended direction (Osborne, 1983; Cosgrove and Osborne, 1985b; Happs, 1985). In some cases pupils who admit that the empirical evidence conflicts with their ideas and supports the orthodox point of view are found at a later time to have given up the orthodox view and 'regressed' to their previous notion or to something like it (Happs, 1985).

Such a phenomenon immediately raises the issue of the reason pupils give to justify their ideas and leads one to ask what account they can give for their decision to reject ideas which they have admitted are more consistent with empirical evidence, in favour of ideas with which the empirical evidence is in conflict.

Teaching about Electricity

A teaching strategy based on the model outlined above was developed by Cosgrove and Osborne (1983, 1985b) to teach students basic notions about electricity in simple electric circuits.

Much research has been carried out to gain information about children's preconceptions in this topic area. This has shown that children learning about electricity for the first time possess a variety of models about the nature of electric current in a simple electric circuit consisting of a battery, a lamp and wires (Osborne, 1981; Shipstone, 1984, 1985). When talking about what happens in an electric circuit, students often use terms such as 'electricity', 'electric current', 'energy' and 'power' as though they were equivalent. The views that children adopt can be summarized as follows (see also Figure 3.1).

Model A: A *consumption* model in which 'electricity' emerges from one end of the battery and is all consumed by the lamp which lights up.

Model B: A *reaction* model in which two types of 'electricity' emerge from the battery — one from each end — and react in the lamp to make it glow.

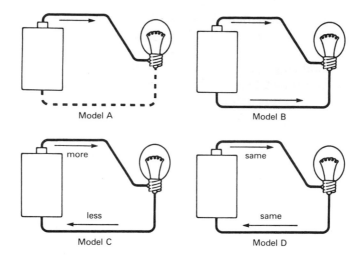

Figure 3.1
Pupils' Ideas about 'Electricity' in a Simple Electric Circuit

Model C: A *consumption* model in which some of the 'electricity' which emerges from one end of the battery is consumed in the lamp which lights up while the rest of the electricity returns to the other end of the battery.

Model D: A *squeezing* model in which all of the 'electricity' emerging from one end of the battery squeezes through the thin wire in the lamp filament causing it to glow and then returns to the other end of the battery.

Figure 3.1 about here

Model D is the one most closely resembling the scientist's view of electric current in a simple electric circuit.

During the first or focusing phase of the Cosgrove-Osborne strategy for teaching about electricity pupils construct electric circuits designed to perform different functions, use various systems for representing the circuits on paper, discuss with each other what they have done and begin to think about how they could explain what is happening in the circuits. During the second or challenge phase of the strategy, pupils are invited to identify which of the above four models they believe is the correct one and to debate with one another the advantages of their choice over those chosen by others. Out of the discussion arise reasons for and against the various models. Empirical evidence is then presented in the 'critical lesson' by placing ammeters

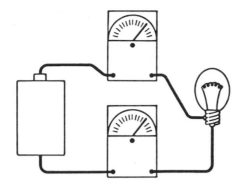

Figure 3.2
Positions of the Ammeters in the Circuit during the Critical Lesson

in the two arms of the circuit (see Figure 3.2). One meter is connected first to allow the current to be measured in that arm and pupils are encouraged to predict what the reading of the second meter would be when it is connected in the second arm. The four models above each lead to different expectations either for the size of the current or for its direction (or both). The meter is then connected and pupils are asked to respond to what they observe by selecting the model which is consistent with that evidence. In the third or application phase, pupils design circuits to solve practical problems outlined in the teacher's handbook (Cosgrove and Osborne, 1983).

Cosgrove and Osborne (1985b) have reported that, with a large sample, 11-year-old pupils tend to choose either model B or model C and that in some classes fewer than 10 per cent may choose model D. For pupils with no more experience of electricity than that provided by their everyday life, there is little evidence available for them to discriminate between models B and C. Table 3.1 shows the choices of models among a group of 11-year-old pupils at the beginning of such a lesson sequence, the views adopted as a result of the evidence from the meter presented during the critical lesson and the views adopted by the pupils one year after the sequence of lessons concluded (Cosgrove and Osborne, 1985b). Thirteen of the pupils adopted model C to begin with, while thirteen chose model D when confronted by the equal ammeter readings. However, with the passage of time a number of pupils have given up model D (the syllabus model) and 'regressed' to models C or B. It seems that the evidence which led to their assent to model D at the time of the critical lesson is no longer so compelling for them.

Another question which emerges from the data in Table 3.1 is: 'How can pupils, who have been confronted by the same empirical evidence and have largely agreed that it is consistent with only one particular model, end up at a later time adopting different models?'

Colin Gauld

Table 3.1

Numbers of Students Selecting Various Models of Electricity at Various Times

Period of survey	Model			
	A	B	C	D
Before teaching	0	1	13	1
After the critical lesson	0	0	2	13
After one year	0	2	6	7

Source: Cosgrove and Osborne (1985b).

The Response of Scientists to Empirical Evidence

A clue about why pupils' ideas are resistant to change and how sense can be made of evidence which clearly contradicts these ideas can be obtained from a study of the behaviour of scientists in similar situations. Similarities between scientists and pupils have provided the basis for the 'pupil-as-scientist' metaphor (Driver, 1983; Gauld, 1988) and for the notion of 'children's science' (Gilbert, Osborne and Fensham, 1982) widely found in current science education literature. The focus of these notions is not in the ideas which children hold but in the way in which these ideas are acquired and in the part they play in the pupils' cognitive functioning. Children's beliefs help them to make sense of the world in much the same way that scientists' theories assist scientists, and children's beliefs and scientists' theories are both acquired through much the same process of hypothesis formation and testing (Karmiloff-Smith and Inhelder, 1974; Rowell and Dawson, 1983). If these claims are true, there is some sense in looking at studies in the history, philosophy, psychology and sociology of science to indicate directions for investigating the course of development and change in children's ideas.

In 1961 Barber published a paper in which he provided evidence for the claim that scientists resist changing their ideas as long as they can, even though the arguments against them are thought by others to be convincing. Gruber (1974, 1981), in his study of the development of Darwin's ideas about man, was impressed by how slowly these ideas changed and how reluctant Darwin was to move from one position to another more consistent with the empirical evidence available to him. Gruber, who had studied with Piaget in Geneva, drew attention to the similarity between the stability of Darwin's ideas and those of children.

The controversy in the early decades of the twentieth century over whether nature was ultimately particulate or not provides a rich source of information about the way different scientists responded to the evidence that was available on this question (Holton, 1977, 1978; Gauld, 1985b). Anti-atomists, such as Ostwald, Helm and Lampa, were happy to accept the atomic hypothesis as a useful device while rejecting it as a description of reality. Mach and Duhem provided the philosophical foundations for this position. Rutherford, Thomson, Millikan and Perrin were amongst the best known atomists. Another atomist, Ehrenhaft, now almost forgotten, was a significant and respected figure in the international world of science at the time. In 1908, on the basis of the experimental results produced by people like Thomson and Perrin, Ostwald became an atomist although he did not find this change easy to undergo.

Between about 1905 and 1917 Millikan and Ehrenhaft were separately involved in major programmes to measure accurately the charge on the electron (e) using similar methods. In 1909 Millikan published a value for e together with criticisms of Ehrenhaft's procedure. Ehrenhaft modified his apparatus and obtained evidence of charges less than Millikan's minimum. He also reanalyzed Millikan's data to show that they were consistent with his own. By the end of 1910 Ehrenhaft concluded that there was no lower limit to the possible values for e and therefore electric charge was not atomic in nature. He had become an anti-atomist, at least where charge is concerned. Long after Millikan had received the Nobel prize for his work Ehrenhaft was still making similar claims, although few, if any, people continued to take any notice.

Since there was no definitive refutation of Ehrenhaft's results, many who were not directly engaged in this field of research accepted the discreteness of electric charge without being able to give good reasons for rejecting Ehrenhaft's data. Even in 1927, after the award of the Nobel prize to Millikan had substantially reduced public controversy over the matter, it was concluded by one writer that 'it cannot be claimed that it has been finally decided in favour of one side or the other, that is, that all researchers have adopted one or other of the two possible solutions of this problem. The state of affairs is rather strange' (Holton, 1978: 28). Holton's study of the laboratory notebooks containing the raw data from Millikan's famous oil-drop experiment published in 1913 demonstrates that, out of 140 drops studied, Millikan rejected the results of about 80 because he 'knew' something was wrong with the equipment, because he suspected something was wrong or simply because the results did not conform to what he considered to be reasonable.

This brief summary points to a number of ways in which scientists attempted to make sense of the empirical evidence available to them.

1　Data were accepted as confirming the currently held theory.
2　Discrepant evidence was accepted and resulted in conceptual change.
3　The same data were interpreted in quite different ways to support contradictory theories.

4 Discrepant data were rationalized without always applying rigid checks.

5 Discrepant data were tolerated but ignored while waiting for an explanation to turn up.

A number of writers have described strategies by which a theory can be maintained in the face of apparently contradictory evidence (see, for example, Lakatos, 1970; Pinch, 1985). In addition to rejecting or ignoring the evidence, it is possible to defend a theory by making modifications to less central auxiliary theories.

This repertoire of strategies gives some indication of how pupils might be able to maintain a range of different ideas in the face of the same empirical evidence.

Pupils' Ideas about Electricity

The investigation described below was part of an external evaluation of a series of lessons about electric circuits taught in a New Zealand secondary school to 14-year-old boys (Gauld, 1985a, 1986, in press). One of the major interests of the study was to determine the long-term effects of the lessons and the way the pupils supported their beliefs about electricity following instruction.

A comprehensive investigation of the way in which pupils justify their own ideas must also consider reasons they have for rejecting available alternatives. In this part of the study three types of information were sought and these corresponded to some extent to the conceptual context in which pupils' ideas about electricity were located. First, the ideas which pupils themselves adopt and believe to be important were investigated and information was available for individual pupils about the way these changed throughout the course of the lessons and beyond. Second, knowledge about other ideas which may be in competition with these beliefs provides a background of alternatives against which the beliefs are adopted. Third, knowledge of the reasons used by the pupils to justify their beliefs and to reject alternatives allows some assessment to be made of the extent to which the beliefs are held for sound reasons (Gauld, 1987).

The series of lessons was taught over three to four weeks by the class's normal physics teacher using the model and the material designed by Cosgrove and Osborne (1983, 1985b). The course of the lessons was monitored by Cosgrove who tape recorded them and produced a transcript (Cosgrove, 1984). The external evaluation took place eleven to fifteen weeks after the series of lessons had concluded. The present author carried out the external evaluation, had not been involved in earlier phases of the study and was not known to the pupils.

During the follow-up investigation, after asking the pupils to construct a circuit to light a lamp using a battery, lamp and a wire or wires, the following questions were used (along with subsequent subsidiary questions) to gather the types of information outlined above from fourteen pupils who made up about half the class.

1 *Present Beliefs*
   (a) What is happening in the circuit to make the light glow?
   (b) What would you expect the brightness of two lamps in series to be? Why?

2 *Alternative Understandings*
   (a) What was your original idea?
   (b) What other ideas did pupils have?
   (c) What did the teacher believe?
   (d) What do you think scientists believe?

3 *Reasons*
   (a) What made you change your mind?
   (b) Why do you believe other ideas are wrong?

Pupils' Beliefs

The effect of the critical lesson in the present study was much the same as that found in the investigation by Cosgrove and Osborne (1985b) and the results for the class are given in Table 3.2. In making their selection the pupils were asked to choose from the models A, B, C and D. In this class model B rather than model C (see Table 3.1) was initially the most attractive, and the movement to model D immediately after the critical lesson is again very evident.

In models A, B, C and D, the substance which flows in a particular wire consists of a single component (although in model B the 'electricity' emerging from the positive end is different from that coming out of the negative end of the battery). During the lessons one student introduced a two-component model in which the entity which caused the lamp to glow was transported from the battery by carriers which eventually returned to the opposite end of the battery with less or no load (see Figure 3.3). To some

Table 3.2
Models Adopted by Pupils at Various times (N = 29)

Period of survey	Model			
	A	B	C	D
Just before the critical lesson	0	18	7	4
Just after the critical lesson	0	?	?	25

extent this model caters for those pupils who wish to distinguish between the energy (the consumed substance) and the current (the carrier of that energy), although it can lead to a more materialistic view of energy than the one the scientist adopts (see Cosgrove and Osborne, 1983: WB19 TG31; 1985b).

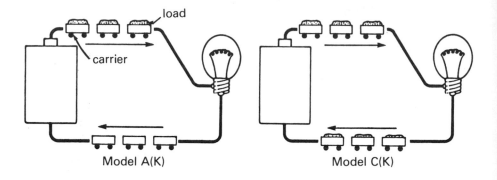

Figure 3.3
Two Carrier Models for 'Electricity' in a Simple Electric Circuit

While this carrier idea was not explicitly endorsed by the teacher, the pupil who initially introduced it was given further opportunities to talk to the class about its implications. Another pupil was also able to present his conception of what was happening in an electric circuit by referring to a river flowing past obstructions (a concrete representation of model D). Grouped data for the fourteen pupils who were interviewed are presented in Table 3.3, while data for each of the individuals are given in Table 3.4.

Although students were not identified individually when they were asked to indicate their choices immediately after the critical lesson, it can be concluded from the data in Table 3.2 that at least ten of the fourteen pupils interviewed chose model D when asked by their teacher. This is indicated in

Table 3.3
Models Adopted by Interviewed Pupils at Various Stages (N = 14)

Period of survey	Model					
	A (K)	B	C	C (K)	D	?
Just before the critical lesson	–	7	4	–	–	3
Just after the critical lesson	–	?	?	–	≥10	–
During the interview	7	2	1	3	1	–

Table 3.4
Changes in Pupils' Beliefs

Student	Model before critical lesson	Model during interview
P 1	B	B
P 2	B→C	B
P 3	B	C
P 4	C	B→C→C (K)
P 5	C	C (K)
P 6	B	D→C→C (K)
P 7	B	A (K)?
P 8	B→C	A (K)
P 9	B	A (K)
P10	B	A (K)
P11	B	A (K)
P12	?	D→A (K)
P13	?	D→A (K)
P14	?	D

the middle row of data in Table 3.3. Here A(K) refers to a carrier version of model A in which all of the 'load' is consumed in the lamp and the 'carrier' returns empty to the battery, while in C(K) some of the load is carried back to the battery (see Figure 3.3). In Table 3.4 the question marks indicate the absence of data or that the interpretation of the data is not certain. During the lessons and during the interview some students changed their minds and this is indicated by the arrows in the table.

Research into pupils' ideas about electricity (Osborne, 1981; Shipstone, 1984, 1985) indicates that pupils, without instruction, tend to adopt a one-component model in which batteries contain 'electricity' which can 'flow through wires' and 'make lamps glow'. After the series of lessons most of those interviewed adopted a two-component model. The most popular one was a carrier version of model A, a model which no one had chosen at the beginning of the series of lessons. In its new form the pupils expressed a confidence in it and were able to develop its implications.

Pupils' Awareness of Other Ideas

Spontaneously during the interview or in response to a question about ideas other people might have had, the students described a wide range of other possible models beyond the four basic one-component versions. Those mentioned are shown in Table 3.5.

Table 3.5
Models of Which Pupils Were Aware during the Interview

Model	A	A(K)	B	B(K)	C	−C	C(K)	D	−D
Number of pupils	6	9	7	2	10	1	3	9	1

A negative sign refers to electricity moving in the opposite direction to that which the student being interviewed considered to be normal. For Pupil P5, model B(K), which he did not hold but could discuss, was a compound of A(K) and − A(K).

> I   What were some of the other ideas in the class?
> P5   Electricity came out from both ends and round to the light.
> I   What happened in the light?
> P5   It just made it glow. It was like a two way road with [full ones] going that way, and empties going back that way . . . .
> I   Were there any other ideas?
> P5   Mm . . . there was the one I mentioned [C(K)] and that way with both of them coming round that way and there was also one that came out of the negative end and around.

Pupils' Justifications for Their Beliefs

During the interviews most students spoke confidently about their beliefs, about the implications of these for the behaviour of the components in electric circuits, and about those things which supported their ideas and were evidence against other points of view. Only a few students seemed uncertain, either because their ideas were not clear to them or because of a lack of confidence in speaking of them to an adult (and a stranger). Even the ideas which emerged from these students, however, possessed a similar coherence to those of other pupils.

Evidence Confirms the Original View

A small number of students were more firmly convinced about their original models by the evidence and experience encountered in the classroom. Pupils P1 and P2 adopted model B when they began the topic. As a result of the observation that the two meter readings were equal and two lamps in series were equally bright, P2's original belief was confirmed. Pupil P1 claimed not to have used the meters but he easily explained the equality of the lamp brightnesses (see Figure 3.4) by the symmetry of model B.

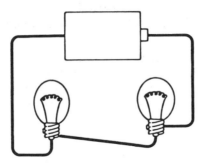

Figure 3.4
A Simple Electric Circuit with Two Lamps in Series

I   Now why would they be the same? What would be happening?

P1   Well, the power would be coming round from there and hitting that one first and vice versa there and it'd be splitting it up — just using more.

I   Right. And what would happen in this wire, between the two?

P1   There'd be some power coming back from here, to complete that circuit, and same from there.

I   Right. And what would happen to this little bit that went through there [the first lamp] after it got to there [the second lamp]?

P1   It'd be used up.

The difference in direction between the meters was apparently not something which was observed or remembered by any of the pupils and so was not a significant piece of evidence for anyone.

Evidence Refutes the Original View

The majority of pupils changed their minds as a result of the lessons and adopted a two component model with carriers and their load. In this model the load is the agent responsible for the lamp glowing and the carrier simply transports it around the circuit. During the interview Pupil P9 claimed that he originally believed model A (although there was evidence from the transcript that before the critical lesson he adopted model B). He gave the equal meter readings as the main reason for his present rejection of that model. For Pupil P12, a combination of previous knowledge that batteries go flat and that lights glow, together with the new information that the meter readings were equal, was convincing evidence that a two-component model was now required.

73

> *I* Why do you need to have two things? Do you need to have trucks and a load to understand what's happening in the circuit?
>
> *P12* Oh. Because we put ampmeters [sic] there and there and they read the same, so what came out also went back in but the bulb lit, 'cause if you just had whatever goes in and don't drop anything off the battery'd never go flat.

For this student (as for P9, P10 and P13), the carriers were necessary to make sense of equal meter readings when, at the same time, the electricity was being used up in the lamp. The auxiliary assumption that meters measure the flow of carriers and not load is essential in linking the empirical evidence to the model. Pupil P12 admitted that the above evidence was consistent with his original model (B), but he commented, 'we did something to prove it [that B was incorrect] but I can't remember what we did.' In rejecting a model in which electricity flowed from negative to positive, Pupil P3 said, 'we found the direction of it too; the direction of the electricity was this way — I can't remember how we did it.'

Other Memories of the Empirical Data

A number of students who adopted a carrier model 'remembered' that the two meter readings were different. In this case their auxiliary assumption was that meters measure the flow of load rather than of carriers.

Pupil P11 apparently accepted model D before the lessons although, immediately before the critical lesson, he indicated that he believed model B. However, he described his change of mind in the following segment of his interview:

> *I* What was probably the most important thing, that you think, that made you change your mind, and showed you that your old idea wasn't right but your new one now is?
>
> *P11* We tried our ideas, and we got those measuring instruments and measured the input through the light and measured coming out and there was nothing. Say that [the meter in one arm of the circuit] measured 500 watts, or whatever it is, and that [the meter in the other arm of the circuit] measured nothing.
>
> *I* On your old idea what would they have measured?
>
> *P11* Both 500. I also thought that if my other idea was right — with 500 and 500 — I thought again and thought the battery'd never get worn down so that made me sort of change my opinion too.

I   What other ideas did kids have, either before or after, that were different to the ones you've said so far?

P11   Most kids didn't agree with that opinion at first — how it went through and dropped off, and went back again.

I   What did you think?

P11   Some thought the same as me and some thought it was energy going straight through there but we didn't even need this wire here for it to go back. You just need one wire.

I   And how did they change their mind?

P11   They tried it on that with this circuit. They just got a positive and they didn't work.

In the case of this student the meter readings were presented as evidence that the load was all used up, but the fact that the lamp wouldn't glow if the second wire was absent supported a belief that the carriers must also be present.

Similar arguments were employed to support the carrier version of model C. All those who adopted this model 'remembered' that the reading on the second meter was less than that on the first (although it was not zero).

I   Was there anything else that you did in class which showed quite clearly to you that you were right?

P5   Oh. We stuck meters on wires here — measured the amount — and it was half the number that it was on this side.

I   So it's twice as much here and after it goes through the lamp it's only half. Do you remember what the numbers were on the meters?

P5   Two, I think — two on this side and it's about one to zero on that side.

I   What were the meters actually reading?

P5   The amount of electricity that was passing through the wires.

I   So this was what was being carried by the trucks?

P5   Yeah.

Only three students (P4, P5 and P6) indicated during the interview that they adopted model C(K), although this information only became available for P4 and P6 after all earlier evidence pointed to model C as their choice. In the interview Pupil P4 argued for model C on the basis that the meters 'showed' that there was less leaving the lamp than entered it. Unlike model A, model C needs the return wire to carry the unused electricity back to the battery, so there is no obvious indication that carriers are required to make sense of the observations. The following segment shows how P4 first introduced the notion of carriers.

I   I've heard of another view — that electricity comes out of this end here and it all gets used up in the light and none goes back to the battery. Have you heard of that one?

P4 Yeah. I think I've heard of it but some example uses trucks and they brought the electricity or energy around and the electricity was used up and the trucks went back into the battery and collected some more. They think all the electricity was used up in the bulb and just the trucks went back.

I Did anybody believe that in your class?

P4 I think one person did. I'm not sure.

I Does it make any sense to you?

P4 No. When it goes back into the bulb I don't think all of it would be used up. Some would have to go back.

I What if they had their trucks and thought that only some of the electricity got used up and the trucks carried the rest back?

P4 Yeah. Well, that's sort of my view.

I You haven't got any trucks in yours, have you?

P4 I didn't explain that I thought trucks — like trucks — brought them round.

I If you had that view with trucks dumping off some of the electricity here and then carrying whatever's [left] back and you put these meters in the circuit what would you expect the meters to read?

P4 This one would be less.

I Right. So the meters are measuring the electricity not the trucks?

P4 Yeah.

Up to the beginning of this segment of the interview P4 had not mentioned trucks and at no stage was the notion needed to account for any of the observations. However, nothing ruled out their existence and P4 was happy to accept the ideas of carriers as being consistent with his idea.

A Reconstruction of the Development of Ideas about Electricity

For most of the pupils interviewed, a reconstruction of the way in which these ideas may have developed in interaction with the expanding awareness of the empirical evidence during a pupil's lifetime can be illustrated in Figure 3.5, beginning with the widely accepted fact that lamps light and batteries go flat. If a carrier model had not been available, students would have been left with only two choices from the original range of four (unless others had been invented): B for those who remembered that the meter readings were equal, and C for those who remembered that they were unequal. The one component model A was probably eliminated by all pupils as soon as they began to construct circuits. The one component model D is discussed further below.

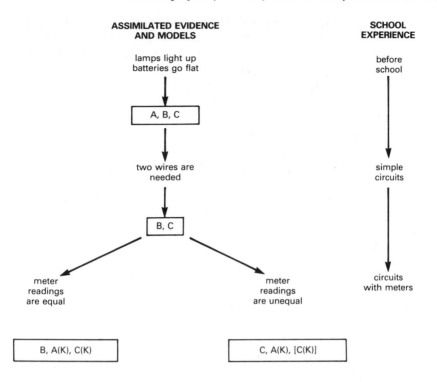

Figure 3.5
Reconstruction of the Development of Models of Electricity as Relevant Experience Changes

The Fate of the 'Scientific' Model

Model D, the preferred scientific model, does not feature in the above discussion as it would normally be eliminated in the early stages of the development. It is not easy to see how pupils would justify it because most (if not all) know that batteries eventually go flat. Confronted with only four models — A, B, C and D — during the critical lesson, there was general agreement that the evidence of equal meter readings supported Model D. The majority of pupils admitted this, but not without some reluctance as Cosgrove's transcript demonstrates (Cosgrove, 1984).

I   What do you think [P11]? Do you think D is wrong?

P11   No. I think it's all right now.

S1   It must be right . . . but I don't see how the battery gets flat though.

S2   It's strange, but it's true.

P11   Theoretically we agree . . . but it can't be right, because why does the battery go flat?

Only one pupil (P14) adopted model D unequivocally at the time of the interview, although three others (P6, P12 and P13) appeared to indicate at the beginning of their interviews that it was their preference. However, by the end they clearly adopted A(K). A number of pupils rejected model D on the grounds that the meter readings were unequal, while those for whom the meter readings were equal rejected it on the grounds that the battery eventually runs out. As P4 expressed it, 'if that idea was correct the battery'd never get flat. . . . Well, if it made it hot there wouldn't be as much, you know, energy with it, you know, and the power, to have the same amount coming out as well. Must've used some of it to light this.' These responses provide some indication that ideas which have developed as a result of everyday experience and have been used by pupils over a substantial period of time to make sense of everyday electrical phenomena are given greater weight than contrived laboratory experience which has little obvious relevance outside the classroom.

Pupil P14, the only one consistently to adopt model D throughout the interview, did so on the grounds that the meter readings were equal. He rejected carrier models although they helped him explain why the battery went flat.

> I   What happens to the battery when you've got a circuit like that connected up and you just leave it going?
>
> P14   It'll run down.
>
> I   Now, why does it run down?
>
> P14   [6 second delay] I dunno.
>
> I   What is it that makes the battery go flat?
>
> P14   Well, a boy in the class reckoned that there might be little trucks, or something, that drive along, and then they dump off some energy in there, and dump off more in each light but I don't believe that 'cause how are they going to know how much to take?
>
> I   Why don't you believe it?
>
> P14   'Cause if, say, the truck or whatever you want to call it starts there and comes driving along and say it's only got enough to run one light; it runs that light and then it comes round to the next one, and it won't have enough to run that one so that light does not work.
>
> I   Yeah. In fact you said they're both equally bright.
>
> P14   Yeah.

This pupil was aware that model A(K) was consistent with equal meter readings if the meter was 'measuring the amount of trucks — or whatever it was — going through and not the amount of energy that it was carrying.' But he rejected carriers because there was, for him, no reasonable way the load could be shared so that two lamps in series were equally bright.

The water circuit analogy is often used for teaching the one-component model D in the classroom and was mentioned in the teaching material (Cosgrove and Osborne, 1983). While this was referred to in the classroom discussion, there is some evidence that most students did not find it helpful and consequently preferred models A(K) or C(K). Little is known about what sense pupils make of a water circuit and this information is necessary before a judgment can be made about how it can be most effectively used in teaching.

Brightness of Two Lamps in Series

Except for models B and D which lead to the prediction that two lamps in series will be equally bright (although they may differ about their implications for three lamps in series), other models require an auxiliary assumption before such an inference can be made. If the brightness depended on how much was consumed by each light and each light used the same amount of 'electricity', then the lamps would be equally bright. If the first lamp encountered by the 'electricity' always took the larger amount, it would always be the brightest. On the other hand, if the brightness depended on how much *entered* the light, then the first would always be the brightest. In no case did any pupil 'remember' that the second lamp was the brightest. Although he recalled that the meter readings were equal, P10's memory that the lamps were *not* equally bright was used by him as evidence that model B was not correct.

Discussion

In a number of ways the responses of pupils to the information presented in the lessons bear close resemblance to some of the methods and attitudes of scientists outlined earlier. Pupils usually demonstrated a high regard for empirical data as a standard against which their ideas should be assessed. During the interview most students sought to demonstrate the consistency between the model they adopted and the evidence they remembered. In only one case did an inference from the current belief conflict with a memory of the experiments in the lessons (Gauld, 1985a: 20). Caution must be exercised here as it may be possible to interpret this consistency as an artifact of the interview rather than as something which the pupil would demonstrate in other less formal contexts.

In spite of embarrassment with the terms 'trucks' and 'load', they were happy to work with an analogy to assist them in making sense of the behaviour of electric circuits in much the same way that scientists make use of analogies, metaphors and models to help understand the phenomena they investigate.

As with the 'normal science' of scientists, items of taken-for-granted knowledge and a number of underlying and unexamined assumptions about the nature of electricity remained unchallenged by the experiences encountered during the lessons. These included the ideas that circuits need to be complete, that batteries go flat and that electricity is a 'substance' which is consumed in lamps.

Auxiliary assumptions or hypotheses were introduced where necessary to help to relate the various models to the observations being explained, a strategy which has been noted by Lakatos (1970) and Pinch (1985) as one of the ways scientists protect a theory from refutation by experimental data.

There is evidence that a great deal of consolidation in pupils' ideas has taken place over the months between the lessons and the interviews. The uncertainty about model D following the critical lesson was replaced by a general confidence in some kind of carrier model set in a coherent cognitive network of 'remembered' empirical data, rejected alternatives and relationships between these various components of this network. It is not at all certain how long this consolidation took but it is clear that the initial response to the meter readings in the class was just that — an initial response — and a great deal more time was required to sort out inconsistencies, some of which the students discussed at the time of the critical lesson.

Gruber (1974, 1981) has described the struggle Darwin underwent as his own ideas developed and refers to the parallel between the slowness of that development and that of the growth of children's ideas. There is, however, one crucial difference between the consolidation of pupils' ideas about electricity in this study and Darwin's or Ostwald's or Ehrenhaft's movement towards confidence in their new ideas. The public nature of science demands that scientific ideas develop with due regard being taken of what others say about them, of criticisms of arguments used to support them and of the defences provided by others for alternative views. The development, although internal to the mind of the particular scientist, is nevertheless carried out with continuing awareness of the constraints imposed by other people and by the external world. Unlike some of the pupils described above, a scientist would not be allowed to base his or her ideas on memories of results which, if checked, could easily be shown to be in error.

For most of the pupils such public pressures and incentives existed only during the three weeks of lessons. Discussion and experimentation ended after that and further development of the ideas took place internally, as inconsistencies between the elements of the cognitive network were removed, probably unconsciously, and without external control as there was no further external interaction. The above investigation illustrates the way in which, in these circumstances, memories can be reconstructed under the action of dominant beliefs (see Bartlett, 1961; Piaget and Inhelder, 1973).

Millar (1987) has recently drawn attention to the notion that scientific knowledge is negotiated through the interaction between scientists, and has suggested that greater emphasis on discussing and evaluating experimental outcomes and results could assist this dimension of learning in the science classroom. The evidence presented above demonstrates the importance of such activity but also the limitations which occur when these activities are confined to the brief period during which the topic is dealt with in school. The main new and valuable product from a series of lessons such as those whose effects have been outlined above is that the coherence achieved now extends further than it did at first and incorporates many more alternatives, a wider range of empirical evidence and new types of arguments. It is not difficult to imagine that if the series of lessons (appropriately adapted) were repeated, the outcome may then encompass even more of the empirical data, suitably interpreted by the pupils, actually available at the time of the lessons.

References

BARBER, B, (1961) 'Resistance by scientists to scientific discovery', *Science*, 134, pp. 596–602.

BARTLETT, F. C. (1961) *Remembering: A Study in Experimental and Social Psychology*, Cambridge, Cambridge University Press, (originally published 1932).

COSGROVE, M. (1984) 'Observing the teaching', unpublished transcript of lessons and interviews, 2 April–12 April, Hamilton, New Zealand, Science Education Research Unit, University of Waikato.

COSGROVE, M. and OSBORNE, R. (1983) *Electric Current — Developing the Concept: Teacher's Guide*, Working Paper No. 207, Hamilton, New Zealand, Science Education Research Unit, University of Waikato.

COSGROVE, M. and OSBORNE, R. (1985a) 'Lesson frameworks for changing children's ideas', in OSBORNE, R. and FREYBERG, P. (Eds), *Learning in Science: The Implications of Children's Science*, London, Heinemann, pp. 101–11.

COSGROVE, M. and OSBORNE, R. (1985b) 'A teaching sequence in electric current', in OSBORNE, R. and FREYBERG, P. (Eds), *Learning in Science: The Implications of Children's Science*, London, Heinemann, pp. 112–23.

DRIVER, R. (1983) *The Pupil as Scientist?* Milton Keynes, Open University Press.

DRIVER, R., GUESNE, E. and TIBERGHIEN, A. (1985) *Children's Ideas in Science*, Milton Keynes, Open University Press.

GAULD, C. F. (1985a) *Teaching about Electric Circuits*, Working Paper No. 209, Hamilton, New Zealand, Science Education Research Unit, University of Waikato.

GAULD, C. F. (1985b) 'Empirical evidence and conceptual change', in OSBORNE, R. and GILBERT, J. (Eds), *Some Issues of Theory in Science Education*, Hamilton, New Zealand, Science Education Research Unit, University of Waikato, pp. 66–80.

GAULD, C. F. (1986) 'Models, meters and memory', *Research in Science Education*, 16, pp. 49–54.

GAULD,, C. F. (1987) 'Student beliefs and cognitive structure', *Research in Science Education*, 17, pp. 87–93.

GAULD, C. F. (1988) 'The "pupil-as-scientist" metaphor in science education', Paper presented at the 19th Annual Conference of the Australian Science Education Research Association, 9–11 July, Sydney, Australia, University of New South Wales.

GAULD, C. F. (in press) 'The cognitive context of pupils' alternative frameworks', *International Journal of Science Education*.

GILBERT, J. K., OSBORNE, R. J. and FENSHAM, P. J. (1982) 'Children's science and its consequences for science teaching', *Science Education*, 66, pp. 623–33.

GRUBER, H. E. (1974) 'Courage, and cognitive growth in children and scientists', in SCHWEBEL, M. and RALPH, J. (Eds), *Piaget in the Classroom*, London, Routlege and Kegan Paul, pp. 73–105.

GRUBER, H. E. (1981) *Darwin on Man: A Psychological Study of Scientific Creativity*, 2nd ed., Chicago, University of Chicago Press.

HAPPS, J. C. (1985) 'Regression in learning outcomes: Some examples from the earth sciences', *European Journal of Science Education*, 7, pp. 431–43.

HOLTON, G. (1977) 'Electrons or subelectrons? Millikan, Ehrenhaft and the role of preconceptions', in WEINER, C. (Ed.), *History of Twentieth Century Physics*, New York, Academic Press, pp. 266–89.

HOLTON, G. (1978) 'Subelectrons, presuppositions, and the Millikan–Ehrenhaft dispute', in HOLTON, G. *The Scientific Imagination: Case Studies*. Cambridge, Cambridge University Press, pp. 25–83.

KARMILOFF-SMITH, A. and INHELDER, B. (1974) 'If you want to get ahead, get a theory', *Cognition*, 3, pp. 195–212.

LAKATOS, I. (1970) 'Falsification and the methodology of scientific research programmes', in LAKATOS, I. and MUSGRAVE, A. (Eds), *Criticism and the Growth of Knowledge*, Cambridge, Cambridge University Press, pp. 91–196.

MILLAR, R. (1987) 'Towards a role for experiment in the science teaching laboratory', *Studies in Science Education*, 14, pp. 109–18.

OSBORNE, R. (1981) 'Children's ideas about electric current', *New Zealand Science Teacher*, 29, June, pp. 12–19.

OSBORNE, R. J. (1983) 'Towards modifying children's ideas about electric current', *Research in Science and Technological Education*, 1, pp. 73–82.

OSBORNE, R. and FREYBERG, P. (1985) *Learning in Science: The Implications of Children's Science*, London, Heinemann.

PETERS, P. C. (1982) 'Even honors students have conceptual difficulties with physics', *American Journal of Physics*, 50, pp. 501–8.

PFUNDT, H. and DUIT, R. (1988) *Bibliography: Students' Alternative Frameworks and Science Education*, Kiel, FRG, Institute for Science Education (IPN), University of Kiel.

PIAGET, J. and INHELDER, B. (1973) *Memory and Intelligence*, New York, Basic Books.

PINCH, T. J. (1985) 'Theory testing in science — the case of solar neutrinos: Do crucial experiments test theories or theorists?' *Philosophy of the Social Sciences*, 15, pp. 167–87.

ROWELL, J. A. and DAWSON, C. J. (1983) 'Laboratory counter-examples and the growth of understanding in science', *European Journal of Science Education*, 5, pp. 203–15.

SHIPSTONE, D. (1984) 'A study of children's understanding of electricity in simple DC circuits', *European Journal of Science Education*, 6, pp. 185–98.

SHIPSTONE, D. (1985) 'Electricity in simple circuits,' in DRIVER, R., GUESNE, E. and TIBERGHIEN, A. (Eds), *Children's Ideas in Science*, Milton Keynes, Open University Press, pp. 33–51.

WARREN, J. (1971) 'Circular motion', *Physics Education*, 6, pp. 74–7.

Chapter 4

The Construction of Scientific Knowledge in School Classrooms

Rosalind Driver

... at the heart of any good teaching and learning experience is a critical relationship, that is, a relationship in which teachers and learners alike seek to question each other's ideas, to reinterpret them, to adapt them and even to reject them, but not to discount them. To be critical in this sense, we need to know something of the origins of those ideas, their roots, the frameworks in which they are embedded (Rowland 1984: 1).

This chapter presents a constructivist perspective on learning in science and discusses the implications of this perspective for teaching and learning in classrooms.

Epistemological Issues

Children's Knowledge Schemes

From the earliest days of their lives children have developed ideas or schemes about the natural world around them. They have experiences of what happens when they drop, push, pull and throw objects, and in this way they build up ideas and expectations relating to the way objects feel and move. Similarly ideas about other aspects of the world around them develop through experiences, for example, with animals, plants, water play, light and shadows, fires and toys. A 9-year-old boy noticed that it took a few seconds after a record player was turned off for the sound to die away. 'There must be miles and miles of wire in there,' he said, 'for the electricity to go through for the sound to take so long to stop.' This boy had received no formal teaching in science and yet had developed the notion that electricity was involved in making the sound, that it flows through wires and it flows very fast!

There is now an extensive literature which documents the ideas children develop about the natural world (Driver, Guesne and Tiberghien, 1985; Osborne and Freyberg, 1985; Gentner and Stevens, 1983) and the way these progress through childhood (Carey, 1985; Strauss and Stavy, 1982). Work in this field has drawn attention to the fact that when they come to science lessons, pupils already have knowledge schemes which can be drawn on in a learning situation. What pupils learn from lesson activities, whether these involve talk, written text or practical work, depends not only on the nature of the tasks set but on the knowledge schemes that pupils bring to these tasks (Driver and Bell, 1986); learning thus involves an interaction between the schemes in pupils' heads and the experiences provided. The experiences may fit with pupils' expectations in which case little change is required in the pupils' schemes. On the other hand, the experience may be novel and pupils may change or adapt their knowledge schemes as a result. This process of using and testing current ideas in new situations requires active involvement of learners in drawing on their present schemes, relating them to new tasks and perhaps reorganizing them. In this way learning science is seen to entail the progressive development and restructuring of learners' knowledge schemes.

Social Factors in Learning

Learning about the world does not take place in a social vacuum. Children have available to them through language and culture ways of thinking and imaging. Phrases such as, 'shut the door and keep the cold out', or 'dew is falling', provide, through metaphor, ways of representing aspects of the physical world. This dynamic relationship between children's personal knowledge schemes and the schemes available through the culture has been commented on and explored by science educators (Sutton, 1980), psychologists and anthropologists (Rogoff and Lave, 1984). Drawing on the work of Schutz and Luckmann, Solomon presents a theory of the social construction of meaning in which it is argued that 'objects of common sense' only exist through social communication whereby ideas are exchanged, explored and reinforced.

> In what Schutz and Luckmann refer to as 'life world knowing' the essential criterion is no longer the internal logic of the explanation but that it should be recognised and shared with others. We take it for granted that those who are close to us see the world as we do, but, through social exchanges, we seek always to have this reconfirmed. This continual reaffirmation of social notions makes them very durable and resistant to change (Solomon, 1987: 67).

Whether an individual's ideas are affirmed and shared by others in classroom exchanges has a part to play in shaping the knowledge construction process.

Science as Socially Constructed

The perspective presented here, whereby individuals through their own mental activity, experience with the environment and social interactions progressively build up and restructure their schemes of the world around them, has been broadly termed *constructivist*.

So far I have sketched how such a perspective portrays the development of children' knowledge about the natural world. However, science as public knowledge is also personally and socially constructed. Scientific ideas and theories not only result from the interaction of individuals with phenomena but also pass through a complex process involving communication and checking through major social institutions of science before being validated by the scientific community. This social dimension to the construction of scientific knowledge has resulted in the scientific community sharing a view of the world involving concepts, models, conventions and procedures. This world is inhabited by entities such as atoms, electrons, ions, fields and fluxes, genes and chromosomes; it is helpfully organized by ideas such as evolution and procedures of measurement and experimentation. These ideas, which are constructed and transmitted through the culture and social institutions of science, will not be discovered by individuals through their own empirical enquiry; learning science involves being initiated into the culture of science.

There is an important point at issue here for science education. If knowledge construction is seen solely as a personal process, then this is similar to what has traditionally been identified as discovery learning. If, however, learners are to be given access to the knowledge systems of science, the process of knowledge construction must go beyond personal empirical enquiry. Learners need to be given access not only to physical experiences but also to the concepts and models of conventional science. The challenge lies in helping learners to construct these models for themselves, to appreciate their domains of applicability and, within such domains, to be able to use them.

Towards a Constructivist Pedagogy

What might teaching and learning science be like if such a perspective on knowledge construction were to be adopted in classrooms? This question has been explored during the last few years by various groups of science teachers and researchers. These groups have identified a number of features of science teaching which derive from a constructivist perspective and have explored the implications of putting them into practice in classrooms. Important features which have been identified include:

> identifying and building on the knowledge schemes that learners bring to lessons;

> developing and restructuring those knowledge schemes through experiences with phenomena, through exploratory talk and teacher intervention;

> enabling pupils to construct for themselves and use appropriately conventional science schemes;

> encouraging pupils to take responsibility for their own learning;

> helping pupils develop an understanding of the nature and status of scientific knowledge itself, the claims it makes and the way these are validated and may change over time.

It has also been recognized that such approaches may require teachers to reconstruct their ideas about the teaching/learning process and to modify their teaching accordingly.

How do these ideas work in practice? This section identifies and documents aspects of pedagogy which take account of children's current understandings while encouraging the development of conventional science ideas. The examples are taken from the reports of two action research projects, the Children's Learning in Science Project based at the University of Leeds (Driver and Oldham, 1986) and the Students' Intuitions and Scientific Instruction (SI)[2] Project (Kuhn and Aguirre, 1987), based at the University of British Columbia and directed by Gaalen Erickson. Both projects have been working collaboratively with teachers for a number of years, exploring the implications of a constructivist approach for work in classrooms.

Listening to and Exploring Children's Ideas

Opportunities for pupils to talk through their existing ideas can invite further learning as pupils clarify and compare ideas. In the following extract 13-year-old pupils were presented with a range of simple phenomena and in each case were asked to describe their observations and to explain them in their own way. In one task pupils were presented with a block of perspex and a block of granite of identical size and shape. They focused their attention on the obvious difference in weight:

> *Darren*: So, what we're really saying is we think the particles are spread out in one and bunched together in another.
>
> *Clive*: Yeah. So it's obvious, they're different weights and the only way they can be different weights is different

materials — and particles — all t'particles could be bunched up or spread out.

Darren: I think if they're bunched up they could be more heavy so that would be the heavier one and the lighter one . . . .

Clive: Yeah, well — what do you think, Daniel?

Daniel: Er, they both could be plastic but the darker one could be more bunched up but they don't have to be different substances, they could both just be plastic.

This notion that the difference in the weight of the two blocks is due solely to the difference in packing of the component particles, while the component particles themselves are the same, is further explored:

Darren: Yeah, they *could* be, but they both look like different materials.

Daniel: But it wouldn't make any difference if they were the same material, say like paper, paper might be all spread out, all the particles in it might be spread out but *wood* they're all bunched together.

Darren: Yeah, and when they make . . .

Daniel: They make paper from pulp and wood and that.

Darren: And they might be — it becomes lighter, obviously.

Daniel: Oh yeah. 'Cos all t'particles are spreading out. So that's what I think's happening (Johnston, 1989: 43).

Here the pupils introduced the notion that density could be explained in terms of particulate ideas. They explored the idea that the differences in the densities of the two blocks could be due to the packing of constituent particles, and they checked these ideas against other experiences such as their knowledge of wood and wood pulp. For these pupils such an initial discussion enabled them to share ideas and to make some progress in their thinking.

Such discussions also reveal to pupils where their thinking is confused. Towards the end of a topic on plant nutrition 13-year-old pupils were asked to review in small groups the part played by a number of substances in the process of photosynthesis:

Anna: I don't know about chlorophyll.

Kate: I don't know what it is.

Dianne: It's a green substance in plants.

Kate: It breathes out carbon dioxide.

Anna: No, it doesn't, it breathes out oxygen and breathes in carbon dioxide.

Dianne: It takes in carbon dioxide and breathes out oxygen.

Kate: But it needs oxygen at night (Oldham, 1989: 159).

The confusion about the gas exchange processes in plants is beginning to emerge and the teacher is asked to help.

Taking a little time to find out how children may think about a particular topic or problem provides indications of their initial knowledge schemes. In an exploratory discussion in small groups some 13-year-old pupils were considering what 'food' is for plants:

I:	Do you think food for plants is similar to food for animals?
John:	No.
Jason:	Er, no, I don't think so.
David:	Flies. Plant eating animals they get the same sort of things out of the plants probably.
I:	As . . . .
David:	Well, the plants could take it in and . . . .
John:	Like with cows, when they eat the grass they get the minerals out of the grass.
I:	I see, whereas you're saying that the plant gets the minerals . . . .
John:	From the ground.
I:	From outside itself.
John:	Yeah.
I:	And what does it need food for, anyway?
Steven:	For growth.
Jason:	To make it grow.
John:	And repair.
David:	All the cells.
I:	So, if you wanted to 'starve' a plant, could you starve a plant in some way?
Steven:	Yeah, just take it out of the soil (Oldham, 1989: 67).

The way animals feed appears to be extended by the children to plant feeding, and hence they are identifying the substances that plants take in from their environment to support life processes as food. This notion differs substantially from the biological idea that the starch and sugars that provide energy to support life processes in plants are manufactured by the plant.

Although the children are using their present knowledge in an intelligent way and are relating this to plants, .they are using a different knowledge scheme from that of conventional science. Such a difference in meaning often persists through lessons and can cause problems for children's learning unless it is identified and addressed. Experience from classrooms shows that simply pointing out such differences in meaning to pupils is not enough for them to construct alternative meanings for themselves. The process of restructuring ideas can be lengthy and can take unforeseen paths. (Scott, 1987).

Restructuring Ideas

One of the most commonly recommended strategies for promoting change in pupils' ideas is to show pupils the limitations of their notions through a discrepant event. As part of their work on the topic of 'air' a class of 13-year-olds was considering whether or not air has weight. They were presented with a simple equal arm balance with a deflated balloon on each end and asked to predict what would happen to the balance if one of the balloons were inflated. One group of four pupils differed among themselves about the outcome:

Daniel: Air's heavy, right. It's heavier, isn't it?
Joanne: No.
Daniel: It is, it is.
Ann: It's the same, air weighs nothing.
Daniel: Look, it'll go down — air's heavy.
Jaspal: Look, listen! When we blow the balloon up it's gonna come down, isn't it, 'cos the air in the balloon's heavier and gravity pulls it down.
Joanne: Yes, but air's light, so how can it come down?
Ann: It floats so it'll stay the same.

They then inflate one of the balloons and see that the side of the balance with the inflated balloon hanging on it does go down. Although they acknowledge the event, the two girls are still not convinced that air has weight.

Ann: Hey, it's gone down.
Joanne: But what makes it go down?
Jaspal: Look, we're doing about air, right? It's heavier than normal air outside — gravity pulls the balloon down.
Ann: Air's light, it'll make the balloon float.
Daniel: How come it came down then?
Ann: I dunno. I thought it'd stay the same.
Joanne: If it were light it would go up wouldn't it.
Jaspal: Look, gravity pulls it down — it pulls the air down.
Daniel: Only when it is in the balloon (Brook, Driver and Johnston, 1989: 70).

As this example illustrates, observational evidence (in this case that the side of the balance with the inflated balloon went down) is not enough by itself for pupils to reconstruct their ideas. They need not only the evidence but a new theory which the discrepant event by itself does not provide. In this example about air and weight the problem appears to be in the way the girls are conceptualizing weight. Their notion that air has no weight — it floats — tells us not only about their knowledge about air but about their conception of weight. Results from further investigations (Brook and

Driver, 1989) indicate that pupils' notion of weight is that it is a property of solid objects, it is what makes them fall down when released and press down when resting on surfaces. Everyday experience of air tends to indicate that it does not have these properties. To promote change in the ideas these children hold about air one may need to recognize that the conceptual structure within which their ideas and concepts are embedded differs from that of conventional science. Learning involves children in the process of theory change, not the mere acceptance of empirical evidence.

In some cases when discrepant events are presented, children's observations are influenced by what they expect to see so as to avoid conflict with their existing ideas (Nussbaum, 1985; Gunstone and White, 1981). Sometimes discrepant events may occur in the course of conventional lessons. In a lesson on change of state and boiling points a class of 13-year-olds was undertaking the familiar activity of heating a beaker of water over a burner and taking the temperature of the water at regular intervals of time.

T: What are you expecting to happen to the temperature?

P1: To rise as it gets hotter. It should be about 100 when it evaporates.

P2: Water should evaporate at 100 degrees centigrade, so it might shoot off this gauge. It should be about 100 degrees centigrade for the water to evaporate.
[A little later:]

T: Well, what happened?

P2: It stayed at 103, the last er two goes (referring to two earlier trials). We haven't marked it in for them two.

I: Is that what you'd expect?

P3: I would have thought it would keep going up, but it stayed at 103. It isn't going up.

I: Why do you think it would still keep going up?

P2: 'Cos it would, the bunsen burner's still er, heating up the water but it isn't getting any hotter.

I: Well, how do you explain that?

P2: I don't know.

P1: I don't know. It's evaporating with steam, er.

P2: And that could be taking out the heat.

P1: 'Cos when you feel steam it is hot.

I: What do you mean when you say taking out the heat?

P2: Well, the steam there holds in er so much heat and it, and it's taking out just enough to keep it at the same constant temperature once it starts boiling (Wightman, 1986: 237).

This familiar class activity presented the pupils with what was for them a discrepant event based on their lack of distinction between temperature and the process of heating. Discussion with an adult in this case enabled them to go beyond their surprising observation to construct a possible interpretation.

Children in secondary school classes seem to expect explanations and generalizations to be offered or at least 'orchestrated' by the teacher. It is interesting that in the above example the pupils repeated their observations three times as a check rather than stopping to consider whether the thermometer 'getting stuck' could 'make sense'. It was only when the adult invited them to consider this observation that they entertained an interpretation. If pupils are explicitly invited to consider explanations for the observations they make, then small groups are often able to make useful progress in theorizing and explaining events.

After a number of initial activities relating to change of state, a class of 13-year-olds was invited to develop their model to explain the properties of ice, water and steam. After an initial discussion in which the idea of molecules was introduced by pupils and adopted, a group started paying attention to the question of bonding.

P1: Water turned to ice? I think it probably strengthens the bonding.

P2: Yeah, that one's not too clear really.

P1: 'Cos we didn't really do an experiment similar to that today. We were just on about melting.

P2: We weren't sure, I mean we are more or less clear how things go from solids to liquids to gases, but not from gases to liquids to solids.

P1: The point is in the gas the bonding has totally gone.

P2: So how does it happen that bonding comes back?

P1: I suppose it works vice versa, when it's heated, it destroys the bonding, when it's cold it, you know, remakes it.

P3: But how does it remake it? What does it remake it with though?

[The question of where the re-made bonds come from continues to exercise the group.]

P2: If atoms are bonded an atom can't change into a bond to hold the other atoms together, can it?

[At this point an observer in the classroom intervenes:]

I: How do you imagine bonding?

P4: Sort of like a string between the atoms.

P1: No, it isn't. He [referring to the teacher] explained to us about magnetic, magnetism. Some sort of force.

P4: Static electricity or something like that.

P2: Yeah. That kept them together. And I suppose if it was hot, then it wasn't magnetised as much or something and when it was cold it — magnetised more.

The group seems to have adopted the idea of bonds being due to a kind of magnetic force, and they return to considering how this can account for bonding apparently changing when a substance is heated.

> *P4*: When they are hot they vibrate more, so that the static isn't as strong.
> *P2*: Yeah, I know, but they vibrate more, and break the bonding and then they finally get to a gas and that's as far as they go . . . but how does it get the bonding back!? [emphatically]
> *P4*: When it starts to cool down, they don't vibrate as much.
> *P1*: Ah, yeah. When they cool down, the bonding will be increased so they won't be able to move around as much, that fits in doesn't it?
> [Note the obvious checking for consistency here. The idea being checked appears to be that due to the greater strength of the bonding at lower temperatures the molecules will not be able to vibrate so much due to being constrained. This idea, however, still begs the issue of how the bonding becomes stronger at lower temperatures as the next pupil's comment indicates.]
> *P2*: Yeah, but the point is, how do we get the bonding back?
> *P4*: Slow down the vibrating . . . .
> *P2*: Slow down the vibrations.
> [One of the pupils at this point has a different insight. He suggests that the force is present all the time].
> *P4*: I suppose it's ever present *there* but . . . yeah it hasn't got a chance to like grip, grip them, you know and keep them together. Well, where it slows down, you know, it might get to grips with the . . . .
> *P3*: A bit easier to keep slower things together (Wightman, 1986: 292).

This outcome of the discussion is a considerable achievement. The pupils have brought together their knowledge that particles are in constant motion and that this motion increases with temperature with the idea of the force between particles being present all the time to explain the apparent 'making and breaking' of bonds.

This example clearly illustrates that pupils, if motivated and if given the opportunity, can bring ideas and prior experiences together to take their thinking forward. However, it would be misleading to give the impression that pupils can essentially teach themselves from experience and discussion. If the teaching is to lead pupils towards conventional science ideas, then the teacher's intervention, both through providing appropriate experiential evidence and making the theoretical ideas and conventions of the science community available to pupils, is essential. This is illustrated in the next example. A grade 10 class (16–17-year-olds) in Vancouver, Canada is studying the topic of radiation and nuclear energy. The teacher has set up a Geiger counter and before bringing a radioactive source near the tube he calls students' attention to the fact that the counter was already counting.

T:	Why is it counting now?
Terry:	From the environment?
T:	Yeah. Somewhere and from different sources, radiation is coming to us all the time. What are the sources for this radiation?
Ann:	The sun, the stars.
Others:	From space.
T:	Is it coming from any object around us? [no response] Yeah, from buildings, rocks, even your bodies. All these put together produce the so-called background radiation — and it happens everywhere. As a matter of fact North Vancouver is higher than normal.
Susan:	And the clicks happen at uneven intervals. Is that supposed to happen?
T:	Well, what do you think? Has anyone else noticed what Susan has heard? [Several students agree by nodding.]
Stan:	Yeah — clicks happen at random.
T:	What do you mean by random?
Stan:	Well, you can't predict when it's going to happen.
T:	Now, I would like to measure background radiation and I'm not sure how to do it. Dave, what sort of measurement, will you do it? [pause] How am I going to assign a number to tell the background radiation?
Gary:	Just count.
T:	If we do it we can get 1000. What does it mean? [no response] What else do we have to measure?
Student:	Measure how many per second or per minute.
T:	And then get the average?
Student:	Yeah.
T:	Well, let's do that. O.K., how long should we use?
Students:	One minute!
T:	Let's try that. Craig, tell me when to start — and how many in one minute [pause] nine — [most agree on 9].
T:	If we take the measurement again, what is your prediction?

Students:	9.
	8.
	10.
	11.
T:	Ann will time this time. Tell me when to start [pause] and what is the count? It's eleven this time. If I do it again what am I going to get?
Students:	13.
	11.
	9.
T:	Let's do it again. Are you ready, Ann? [pause] Now it's twelve.
T:	If we do it again, can we get twelve? [majority of students say no]
T:	What we have been measuring is the radiation intensity. It's the number of counts per unit of time — the unit is in seconds — then — it's the number of counts per second — and this unit is called the becquerel. [The teacher writes on the board:

$$\text{Becquerel} = \frac{\text{counts}}{\text{t in sec.}}]$$

T:	What was the last radiation intensity? It is twelve over sixty equals point two becquerels. [On board: $\frac{12}{60} = .2$ Becquerel.]

(Aguirre and Kuhn, 1987)

In this sequence the teacher first gives students direct experience of counting background radiation. A student observes that it appears to be random and this observation is checked with measurements and confirmed. Finally, after students have some informal experience of measuring the rate at which the Geiger counter is recording, the teacher introduces the term 'radiation intensity' and the unit 'the becquerel'; both are conventional aspects of knowledge that pupils could not discover from experience but which needed to be introduced through an authoritative source.

In a simple way this example illustrates a common feature of science classes: the introduction of concepts, models, measurements, conventions of the scientific community. In this case these were introduced after students had gained familiarity with the phenomenon, and so the terms 'radiation intensity' and 'becquerel' were linked to the students' experience and readily adopted and used.

Ideas that teachers suggest may not always be readily adopted however. This is often the case when pupils have strongly held conceptions which differ from conventional science ideas. As the earlier example about weighing air illustrated, it may take time, a range of experiences and opportunities to think things through for pupils to begin to adopt a different conception. The following example illustrates the subtle conceptual problems which are encountered by children when they are introduced to the idea of gravitational potential energy. The class of 12-year-olds was considering the question of energy transfer when a heavy object was pulled up using a pulley system. The class readily agreed that energy was used by the person who pulled the object up, but they were not able to make sense of the idea that this energy was transferred to the lifted object. The teacher tried to make this notion reasonable by asking them to think about what happens when the lifted object is released.

> *T*: Why should the weight fall, then?
> *Matthew*: Because gravity pulls it down.
> *T*: Gravity pulls it down . . . you need energy to push up, but not fall down.
> *Matthew*: You do. You need energy for lifting, but when you let go it's only gravity pulling it down.

Here the idea of energy being 'stored' in the lifted object is not accepted by the pupil because for him the subsequent movement of the falling object is due to the external influence of gravity and this is seen as different from the energy being 'stored' in the object.

After further activities in the lesson, the class returns to discuss the question of energy transfer in the case of raising a brick. The brick was pulled up and was secured near the ceiling of the laboratory.

> *Mark*: Sir, it can't be getting energy, because it's not a living object.
> *T*: So you are saying that only living objects have energy?
> *Matthew*: No, Sir — electricity.
> *Andrew*: Cars have energy.
> *T*: Yes, he's got a point. Well, if a car can have energy, why can't a brick have energy?
> *Andrew*: A car's moving, though — gets energy from petrol.
> *T*: But you're going to tell me that that brick has got no energy.
> *Steven*: Ah, but it's gravity what's coming down on it.
> *T*: I'm asking about energy — not force. Does that brick [pointing to the brick near the ceiling] have energy?
> *Steven*: No.
> *T*: If I take that brick and I hold it high up and then I drop it, has it got energy?
> *Steven*: Yes, it's moving (Brook, 1987: 57).

Children can reflect on experiences in and out of lessons. Ideas can be reorganized in unpredictable ways and at unpredictable times. However carefully a teacher may plan a particular activity to introduce an idea, in the end it is the pupils who have to think through and make sense of the experiences for themselves. Sometimes this can happen quite quickly, in other cases pupils may be reorganizing their ideas and trying to make sense of a new topic over months or even years.

From early days in school, children's ways of seeing the world are being shaped by adults. Much of the interactive teaching that occurs in secondary science practical classes reflects an often patient shaping and selection by teachers of the aspects of experience which pupils need to pay attention to in order to construct the conventional scientific interpretation. This process, which has much in common with what Vygotsky refers to as 'scaffolding', can be carried out in ways which vary in their sensitivity to learners' perspectives. In some cases, as in the following example, the teaching is not negotiating the meaning of the activity with pupils. In a review of energy transfer in simple devices with a class of 13-year-olds attention turns to an electric bell.

T: Do you remember the electric bell?
Ss: Yes.
T: Did any of you notice, did any of you actually hold on to the bell after it had been working? What did you notice?
S: Vibration.
T: Well, the arm vibrated, yes. Sound. What else did you notice? Anything? — If you held on to this bit here, where the wires were, did you notice anything there?
S: There were sparks there.
T: Heat. Did you notice some heat?
S: There were sparks from there.
T: There were?
S: Sparks. I don't know about....
T: There were some sparks, yes. Let's just ignore the sparks a minute, but we can come back to those. Some heat. There was a little bit of heat there with that one (Brook and Driver, 1986: 48–9).

In this case it was clear that the teacher was looking for a particular observation. He did not consider the observations offered about vibrations and sparks to be relevant and in the end he introduced the answer he was looking for. This game of 'guess what the teacher has in mind' is commonly played in classes. Through it the teacher manages to keep what appears to be a clear line of reasoning leading to the point to be made. Pupils play the game to provide the answer the teacher wants. In the process the engagement necessary for knowledge construction by the pupil is short-circuited. This structuring of the discourse by teachers is not confined to secondary school classrooms. In a study of discourse in 'child-centred' primary classrooms Edwards and Mercer (1987) commented:

While maintaining a tight control over activity and discourse, the teacher nevertheless overtly espoused and attempted to act upon the educational principle of pupil-centred experiential learning, and the importance of pupils' engagement in practical activity and discovery. This led to the pupils' grasp of certain important concepts being essentially 'ritual', a matter of what to do or say, rather than 'principled' i.e. based on conceptual understanding (p. 157).

One of the features of this 'ritual' procedural knowledge which the authors identified is that of 'cued elicitation'.

This distinction between pupils' responses being based on ritual or principled understanding is of critical importance if classroom talk is to lead to meaningful knowledge on the part of pupils. Doing this successfully, however, means listening to what the pupils are contributing and assessing the degree of shared understanding. This process of collective negotiation about what pupils could see when looking down a microscope at Brownian motion in a smoke cell illustrates some features of this process.

T: Right, well, let's have somebody else come to have a look, just keep to yourself what you've seen. Have a look. Now, have a look and tell me what else you can see. You've got the circular field of view, can you see anything else?

P: Little white bits.

T: Little white bits, all right. Let's have somebody else come and have a look, come and have a look. Little white bits. I'll just sort of make some notes as we go along of some of the things that you see. White bits. Can you see anything else? Would you agree about the colour, would you call them white?

P: Yes.

T: You would, right. Can you tell me anything else about those bits? Are they doing anything? [laughter] They're moving, yes. O.K. Let's have somebody else to have a look. Come on keep coming round because I want everybody to have a look. [children chattering] So, we've got some white bits that are moving. Would you agree about the white bits? What can you tell me about the movements?

P: Jumping.

T: Jumping. All right. Let's, come on, keep coming and having a look. . . . How would you describe the movement apart from being jumpy?

P: Sir, they look, they're all bump . . . they're all dodging. They're all dodging . . . Sir, they go along straight next minute when they get dead near to each other they shoot away from each other.

> *T*: How would you describe the movement?
>
> *P*: They are like dodges.
>
> *P*: Two magnets going for each other.
>
> *P*: Like if there's two magnets. But when they get near to each other they shoot away to the sides. Is that the way they charge? Like you said they charged.

Pupils have noticed that the 'white bits' are moving, that they change direction without touching each other and there is speculation about how this might happen.

> *T*: Is there a simpler explanation? I did give you a clue . . . .
>
> *P*: Are they just not attracted to each other?
> [chattering]
>
> *P*: Sir, is it something to do with cohesion being reversed and they are pushing each other away?
>
> *T*: Right, let's have your attention again then. Now, let's try to piece together all the observations that people have made.

> *T*: Um, perhaps we ought to ask ourselves, first of all, what it is you're actually seeing, when you see these white bits, gold bits, call them what you will, what do you think it is you're actually seeing?
>
> *P*: Particles.
>
> *T*: What of?
>
> *P*: Smoke.
>
> *T*: Alright, what is smoke?
>
> *P*: Gas.
>
> *T*: Alright, it's the debris, isn't it, that's left over when you burn the string.
>
> *T*: How do you describe some . . . the movement of something that you can't predict where it's going to go, what sort of word?
>
> *P*: Irregular.
>
> *P*: Random.
>
> *T*: Go on.
>
> *P*: Random.
>
> *T*: Yes, that's the best word, all right. It's a random movement which means you don't know quite where it's going to go next. So we've got a rapid, random motion.

Having established through feedback from pupils what they are seeing, the teacher then moves to consider how the rapid random motion of the 'white bits' is caused.

> *T*: Now the question is, what causes it? What makes those particles of dust in the smoke move about? Now, I gave you the clue at the beginning because *you* told *me* that there was

something else in the tube. What was it?

P: Air.

T: Yes, there's air. Now suppose that we think about air as being made up of particles just the same as everything else that we've been talking about. The particles are very tiny. Much too tiny even to catch the light and reflect them up through the tube of the microscope, but they're not too tiny perhaps to do something to the smoke — what do you think they might be doing to the dust particles? Can you think of what might happen? Suppose that at half-past twelve you try to go out through that door and everybody's all turned out at the same time and you're trying to get down the corridor, and you know you want to go straight down the corridor, what path are you likely to follow?

P: Zig zag.

T: Right, a zig zag path. Why, what makes you follow a zig zag path?

P: You're bumping into them.

T: Right, you're bumping into people. Somebody pushes you from one side, somebody shoves you from the other side, and you've got a zig zag path. So what might the air particles be doing to the smoke particles?

P: A zig zag path.

P: Deflection.

T: How?

P: Well, they're . . . they're moving as well, and they're hitting them as well and bouncing off.

T: All right, the air particles might be moving about, bumping into the smoke particles and making them move completely at random, and that's the process that we think is taking place. And it's called Brownian motion, um, this chap Robert Brown first discovered, I think with pollen grains, on the surface of water and he found that *they* did exactly the same thing (Wightman, 1986: 95–100).

The direction and initiative in this sequence clearly came from the teacher. However, the questions and ready answers from the class gave continuous feedback as to the extent to which the pupils shared in the observations and interpretation. Edwards and Mercer (1987) comment on this process of negotiation as follows:

The overriding impression from our studies is that classroom discourse functions to establish joint understandings between teacher and pupils, shared frames of reference and conceptions, in which the basic process . . . is one of introducing pupils into the conceptual world of the teacher and, through her, of the educational community. To the extent that the process of education can be observed taking place in the situated discourse of classrooms, it is on our evidence essentially a process of cognitive socialization through language (p. 157).

This seems to be a truism when we consider science classes; moreover, it is of the nature of scientific knowledge as socially constructed that this process is essential to learning science. What is problematic is to enable individual pupils to engage in the negotiation so that the socialization process enables them to develop principled understanding rather than giving ritualized responses. This requires teachers to be prepared to listen to the suggestions and ideas of pupils as a check on their understanding.

Reviewing and Checking Understandings

Listening to pupils' contributions in a diagnostic way means going beyond an immediate judgment of whether the contribution is 'right' or 'wrong'. It means attempting to understand how the pupil comes to the answer that is given. In the grade 10 class in Vancouver the teacher gave the class a series of simple exercises to calculate the activity of different radioactive substances. He then checked the answers round the class:

Tom: 125 Bq.
Tammy: 113 Bq.
T: What is she doing incorrectly?
Nancy: She is putting the time over the counting. She should put the counting over the time.
T: If you do that, Tammy, what do you get?
          [no response]
T: The number of counts is . . . ? And the time?
Tammy: Oh, I see, it's 50.
T: I think you just misread before . . . emissions mean the same as counts (Aguirre and Kuhn, 1987: 58).

Here the teacher has not only identified the problem with Tammy's response but encouraged others as well as Tammy to do so and to correct it.

At the end of a topic on photosynthesis with 13-year-olds the teacher has given groups the chance to discuss their answers to a number of questions and these are being shared with the rest of the class. Rachael is called to explain her group's task.

Rachael: 'You are provided with the following meal: potatoes, carrots, beef and milk. Describe how the energy you get from this meal may be traced back to the sun.' Potatoes: the sun goes into the leaves which is the chlorophyll and then makes it into sugar and starch and the starch builds up into spuds — I mean, potatoes [laughter]. It's the same with the carrots. It goes into the leaves of the carrots and it's all built up. And the beef — it gets in through the grass which is the chlorophyll and then it goes into the cow which eats it and then the milk is done the same but it's all sort of processed.

T:	Did you all get that?
Class:	Yes, yes. No.
T:	Who just said no?
Class:	Christopher.
T:	Right, Chris. What did you miss?
Christopher:	How is all this light getting into the leaves, then?
Michael:	From the sun.
Rachael:	The sun's light just gets into the leaves and it makes sugar and starch.
Susan:	Through them holes.
Michael:	The rays.
Rachael:	You're just trying to complicate it all and get me muddled up.
Susan:	He is — he does that in English.
T:	No, I think he's asked a good question. How does the sunlight get into the leaves? How does the leaf grab hold of the sunlight? Sh! I'm asking Rachael.
Rachael:	Through them holes?
T:	Through the holes in the leaf?
Susan:	Yes, it just falls upon them and it all sort of absorbs it.
T:	Do we all agree?
Michael:	No . . . .
T:	Hands up if you agree. Hands up if you disagree. Hands up those who don't know. Right, who said they disagree? Right, what do you think happens?
Michael:	The chlorophyll — it lets all the light through . . . .
T:	Right, it's the chlorophyll which catches some of the light. Right, do you remember looking through those spectra shining through chlorophyll and there were bits missing? O.K., that's how the plant catches the light. What does go through the holes?
Michael:	Water. I mean — yeah — rain.
T:	Do we agree with that one?
Susan:	No.
T:	Any volunteers as to what does go through the holes? Brendan?
Brendan:	Oxygen and carbon dioxide (Oldham, 1989: 211–2).

Here again the teacher is giving time to sort out a problem and to check understandings with the whole class. He also makes links to previous class activities (such as shining white light through chlorophyll extracted from leaves to show that some of it was absorbed).

Concluding Remarks

Teachers as Diagnosticians

Classrooms are places where children are in the business of constructing and reconstructing meanings as a result of learning experiences. However, in a classroom where the teacher is adopting constructivist approaches, that teacher is also constructing meanings — identifying the sense that children are making of the learning experiences presented. The Vancouver case study makes this point clearly:

> Mr. Kuhn [the teacher] mentioned how crucial it was to *listen* to what students had to say. He expanded this by saying that this 'listening' meant that the teacher must open her/his ears and mind when listening to students' ideas. He added that many teachers say that they listen to students but they really don't, for they have prepared their lessons step by step, not allowing room for possible changes; they can pretend they are listening, they can even make a remark such as 'that's interesting', but after this they will proceed as planned without considering the students' ideas. Mr. Kuhn was positive that listening is a skill that can be learned, but teachers have to be willing to do so. Part of this listening is to reflect back on what a student has said or done; one must address what lies behind a response or question (Aguirre and Kuhn, 1987: 78).

If teachers are familiar with some of the more common features of children's ideas, then this diagnostic process is more easily undertaken. In the last analysis, however, although it is possible to learn about what to expect, the analysis has to be undertaken for each class afresh.

The Interactive Process of Teaching

Some pedagogical thinking has been influenced by an oversimplistic dichotomy: either children discover things for themselves or they are told the answers by the teacher (or by some surrogate authority such as a book, worksheet or computer program). The analysis in this chapter has indicated the fallacy in this dichotomy. On the one hand, there are things which children cannot be expected to 'discover' for themselves because of the conventional nature of science. Moreover, if given the opportunities, children will make discoveries but these will not necessarily be what was intended. On the other hand, even when pupils are told something they still have to make sense of it for themselves. Edwards and Mercer (1987) comment on this dichotomy:

> ... we shall not be using any critique of progressive education to argue for a return to traditional didactic methods. The progressive movement was right to argue for the importance of children's active engagement in their own education. What we shall advocate is a third step, towards a cultural-communicative model of education . . . . The traditional ideology was all about teaching, and the progressive ideology is all about learning. What is needed is a new synthesis, in which education is seen as the development of joint understanding (p. 36).

Authority and Belief

If learning science is essentially a process of a culturation into the ideas and models of conventional science, the danger from the point of view of learners is that they accept what they are presented with through books, teacher talk and guided experimental work because of its authoritative status. This can and does get in the way of pupils making sense of the ideas for themselves and results in the 'real world' and 'school science' being kept as distinct systems.

Within a constructivist perspective there are two aspects to the issue of authority. One is whether an idea is accepted within conventional science — that information can be obtained from external authorities. The other is whether the idea makes sense to the learner, whether it has the authority of his or her own experience and knowledge schemes behind it (in other words, whether it is believed). After a unit of work on particle theory a 14-year-old was addressing this problem:

P: I can't really explain, but there's summat where you think, well this table it's made up of particles — I think it's too, well you can't see any particles or owt, so it's just — just can't believe it. You know, that this table's made out of particles — hundreds of millions.

T: You don't believe it?

P: Well, I do in me own way, you know, but well wood's wood, I mean it grows from trees — you know more or less — well — sometimes — if a teacher tells you that it's made out of particles you think — well fair enough it's made out of particles, but it's, you can't really believe that this table's made out of particles.

T: What about the atmosphere in this room? Can you accept that that is made of particles?

P: Not really because — 'cos you can't really see 'em. I mean, for all we know there could be particles, but in another way, for all we know it could be scientists saying that there's particles in the air and making us believe it. Well it could just be normal sky you know, because there is sky coming all the way down — it could be sky — you know in t'buildings and that (Wightman, 1986: 69).

Learning as the Progressive Reconstruction of Conceptual Schemes

Learning in science can involve learners in changing the knowledge schemes they use. Such changes are not trivial and can, as illustrated in the example of air and weight given earlier, involve learners in radically changing the meanings of component elements in their schemes and the way they are organized. A number of areas have been identified as requiring learners to make significant changes in their conceptual schemes; for example, moving from impetus notions of mechanics to Newtonian ideas or changing from a thermal theory in which heat and temperature are undifferentiated to one in which they are distinguished as separate entities.

Making these changes is not a trivial matter. We know that despite some carefully structured teaching, learners may continue to use their prior ideas. The question of how to design teaching approaches which promote conceptual change in learners is currently a focus of research interest. An important starting point is to recognize this as a significant problem. It requires an adequate description of the prior conceptual schemes of learners, a description which indicates how the learners' concepts are related within their way of seeing (and goes beyond a superficial identification of 'misconceptions'). Further, it requires learning tasks which specifically address the changes that learners need to make in their conceptual schemes. Lastly, such changes also require time and opportunities for revisiting the ideas in a range of contexts.

The Responsibility of the Learner

Within a constructivist perspective teachers have an important role to play in diagnosing the pupils' current understandings, making decisions about what could be useful learning activities and interacting with pupils to help them interpret those activities appropriately. Pupils too have their part to play. Only they can make the links between their current knowledge schemes and presented learning experiences. There will always be the questions of judgment for teachers about how far a pupil may be helped to progress in his or her understanding, about when and how to intervene. In suggesting a guiding principle for teachers on this matter, Osborne and Freyberg (1985) comment:

> The problem, however, is to decide just when a pupil will be able to benefit from visual and verbal input which deliberately encourages the scientifically acceptable viewpoint . . . if we wish to avoid alienating many pupils from science, we must take care not to insist upon conceptual change at the expense of children's self-confidence, their enthusiasm and curiosity about the world, and their feeling for what constitutes a sensible explanation (pp. 89–90).

It is maintaining learners' confidence in themselves as capable of making sense of their experience and the will and interest to continue to do so which is essential to the learning process.

References

AGUIRRE, J. and KUHN, K. (1987) *An Interpretive Approach to Learning Science: A Case Study on Teaching Radiation and Nuclear Energy in Junior High School*, monograph available from (SI)[2] Project, Gaalen Erickson, University of British Columbia, Vancouver, B.C.

BROOK, A. (1987) 'Designing experiences to take account of the development of children's ideas: An example from the teaching and learning of energy', in NOVAK J. (Ed.), *Proceedings of the Second International Seminar: Misconceptions and Educational Strategies in Science and Mathematics*, Vol. 2, Ithaca, N.Y., Cornell University, pp. 49–64.

BROOK, A. and DRIVER, R. (1986) *The Construction of Meaning and Conceptual Change in Classroom Settings: Case Studies in the Learning of Energy*, Children's Learning in Science Project, Centre for Studies in Science and Mathematics Education, University of Leeds.

BROOK, A. and DRIVER, R. (1989) *Progression in Science: The Development of Pupils' Understanding of Physical Characteristics of Air Across the Age Range 5–16 Years*, Children's Learning in Science Project, Centre for Studies in Science and Mathematics Education, University of Leeds.

BROOK, A., DRIVER, R. and JOHNSTON, K. (1989) 'Learning processes in science: A classroom perspective', in WELLINGTON J. J. (Ed.), *Skills and Processes in Science Education*, London, Routledge.

CAREY, S. (1985) *Conceptual Change in Childhood*, Cambridge, Mass., MIT Press.

DRIVER, R. and BELL, B. (1986) 'Students' thinking and the learning of science: A constructivist view', *School Science Review*, 67, 240, pp. 443–56.

DRIVER, R. and OLDHAM, V. (1986) 'A constructivist approach to curriculum development in science', *Studies in Science Education*, 13, pp. 105–22.

DRIVER, R., GUESNE, E. and TIBERGHIEN, A. (Eds) (1985) *Children's Ideas in Science*, Milton Keynes, Open University Press.

EDWARDS, D. and MERCER, N. (1987) *Common Knowledge*, London, Methuen.

GENTNER, D. and STEVENS, A. (Eds) (1983) *Mental Models*. Hillsdale, N.J., Lawrence Erlbaum.

GUNSTONE, R. and WHITE, R. (1981) 'Understanding of gravity', *Science Education*, 65, 3, pp. 291–9.

JOHNSTON, K. (1989) *Learning and Teaching the Particulate Theory of Matter: A Report on a Teaching Scheme in Action*, Children's Learning in Science Project, Centre for Studies in Science and Mathematics Education, University of Leeds.

KUHN, K. and AGUIRRE, J. (1987) 'A case study — on the journal method — a method designed to enable the implementation of constructivist teaching in the classroom', in NOVAK J. (Ed.), *Proceedings of the Second International Seminar: Misconceptions and Educational Strategies in Science and Mathematics*, Vol. 2, Ithaca, N.Y., Cornell University, pp. 262–74.

NUSSBAUM, J. (1985) 'The particulate nature of matter in the gaseous phase', in DRIVER, R. GUESNE, E. and TIBERGHIEN A. (Eds), *Children's Ideas in Science*, Milton Keynes, Open University Press.

OLDHAM, V. (1989) *A Constructivist Approach to the Teaching of Plant Nutrition: A Report on a Scheme in Action*, Children's Learning in Science Project, Centre for Studies in Science and Mathematics Education, University of Leeds.

OSBORNE, R. and FREYBERG, P. (Eds) (1985) *Learning in Science: the Implications of Children's Science*, London, Heinemann.

ROGOFF, B. and LAVE, J. (Eds) (1984) *Everyday Cognition: Its Development in Social Context*, Cambridge, Mass., Harvard University Press.

ROWLAND, S. (1984) *The Enquiring Classroom*, Lewes, Falmer Press.

SCOTT, P. (1987) 'The process of conceptual change in science: A case study of the development of a secondary pupil's ideas relating to matter', in Novak J. (Ed.), *Proceedings of the Second International Seminar: Misconceptions and Educational Strategies in Science and Mathematics*, Vol. 2, Ithaca, N.Y., Cornell University, pp. 404–19.

SOLOMON, J. (1987) 'Social influences on the construction of pupils' understanding of science', *Studies in Science Education*, 14, pp. 63–82.

STRAUSS, S. and STAVY, R. (Eds) (1982) *U-shaped Behavioural Growth*, New York, Academic Press.

SUTTON, C. R. (1980) 'The learner's prior knowledge: A critical review of techniques for probing its organisation', *European Journal of Science Education*, 2, 2, pp. 107–20.

WIGHTMAN, T. (1986) *The Construction of Meaning and Conceptual Change in Classroom Settings: Case Studies in the Particulate Theory of Matter*, Children's Learning in Science Project, Centre for Studies in Science and Mathematics Education, University of Leeds.

Chapter 5

Science as a Discipline, Science as Seen by Students and Teachers' Professional Knowledge

Tom Russell and Hugh Munby

Scrupulous attention to data, fair consideration to alternative interpretations and theories, and an implicit understanding of the principles that warrant moves from data to constructs are among the features that set disciplined knowledge apart from opinion, folklore and mere whimsy. Yet these features are not the exclusive property of the scientific disciplines. Instead, and this is fundamental to the case we wish to advance, these features can be found in any enterprise in which rigorous thought is appropriate. So these features accompany thinking about science, about educational research and about one's own teaching.

To develop these ideas, we will consider two aspects of teaching and the possible relationship between them. The first aspect is the 'pictures of science' presented to children by the language of science teaching. The second aspect concerns the character and development of teachers' professional or practical knowledge — the (frequently) non-propositional or tacit knowledge called upon by teachers when they teach. The common element in these aspects is knowledge. In the first we are interested in how the nature of science and the nature of its knowledge are communicated in classroom discourse. In the second we extend our epistemological interests to the character and development of teachers' professional knowledge. We will begin with a consideration of language in science teaching. This section serves to introduce distinctions about the nature of knowledge that are employed later. Next we provide an account of the approach we are currently taking to the study of the nature and development of teachers' professional knowledge. Then we draw on two recent case studies to explore the possible relationship between the view of science held by two teachers and the ways in which their professional knowledge develops and is considered by them.

Language and Argument in Teaching Discourse

Because this section is about classroom discourse and the messages it sends about the nature of science and scientific knowledge, it is appropriate to begin by looking at an instance of science teaching. Lesson 1 is an excerpt from a lesson with a class of 9-year-olds in which the teacher is introducing biological classification. The distinction between living and non-living things has just been established, and the next distinction is just ahead:

> Lesson 1
>
> *Teacher*: Now we are going to leave the nonliving things for later and study just the living things. [writes 'living' on the board] Now, let's divide all the living things into two divisions. Into what two divisions can we divide every living thing? Every living thing is either a _____ or a _____ [signalling a blank with her hands]? Lucy, give me one division.
>
> *Lucy*: People?
>
> *Teacher*: People are just part of one of the two divisions.
>
> *Peter*: Plants and animals.
>
> *Teacher*: Good for you, Peter. That's right. Everything in this world is either plant or animal. People, Lucy, are animals, so they fit in this division.
>
> *Lucy*: People aren't animals, they're humans.
>
> *Teacher*: People are animals, the same as cats and dogs and so on. [Much laughter and several loud objections by a large number of pupils speaking simultaneously. It appears that they disagree with this last statement.] People *are animals*. What's wrong with that? They're not plants, are they?
>
> *Jimmy*: But people talk, and have two legs and arms, and move and can think. Animals aren't like that. [laughter]
>
> *Teacher*: People do think, and this makes them one of the highest forms of animals, but they are still animals. And other animals communicate with one another [Several children are noisy and visibly disturbed.] That's enough. People are animals. Now maybe it would help if we looked at the diffferences between plants and animals. What are the differences? There are at least three that you could name.

Something clearly 'goes wrong' in this lesson when Lucy and the teacher clash. We find that focus on the language allows us to account for the difference in view that has emerged. By attending to the language we can also draw attention to what is being said about science itself (Munby, 1982: 21–2). The language of science is different from ordinary language, and this can lead to similar terms from the two areas of discourse having very different meanings. Here scientific classification is up against the classification familiar to Lucy and her classmates, and science wins. Notably, however, nothing is said in the lesson to show why there is a difference. Instead, the lesson's language implies that Lucy's perspective is simply wrong, and that science is right. Science, the language seems to say, provides the correct way to organize our perceptions of the world. Because the teaching omits any discussion of how classification systems work, of how their conceptual bits fit with phenomena, and of how the systems themselves are created to perform specific tasks, it does not allow the children access to the intellectual processes underlying the lesson. So, left with working at the surface meanings, the children are not surprisingly upset. But there is more: bereft of a discussion about classification systems, the language conveys the picture that science simply does not deal with constructions of the world. Instead, the language suggests that science offers an unfailingly accurate and thoroughly acceptable description of it.

A very different image of science is presented by the teacher's language in the following excerpts from Lesson 2, a lesson that introduces static electricity to a class of 15-year-olds. At the beginning of this lesson the teacher rubbed an ebonite rod with wool and showed how small, light objects jumped around when the rod was brought close to them. During this time the teacher spoke (and had pupils speak) only about what could be seen.

Lesson 2

Teacher: And it was kind of an interesting curiosity for a long time, that when you cleaned and polished this piece of amber it had this magical property of being able to cause light little things to jump about.

[The teacher has asserted that this 'magical property' was first observed for amber. Next, the teacher gives the origin of some contemporary terms:]

Teacher: And the Greek word for amber was that [writing 'electron' on the board]. So he called materials like this — like the ebonite rod and so forth, the amber — he called them 'electrics' [writing it on the board], or 'amber like materials'. That's where we got the name. From this word that's in here.

[Once the phenomena are presented, the teacher invites explanations:]

Teacher: Now there are our observations. We've organized them. What conclusions can we come to? Can we come to any definite conclusions? How will you explain it? What, what theory can we advance to explain what we see here? Scotty.

Scotty: [an indistinct response]

Teacher: It's somewhat mystifying, isn't it?

Scotty: Yeah. [laughter]

Teacher: Certainly, we've probably never observed any behaviour like this before. [pause] Richard, have you got any theories to explain this?

Richard: Well maybe, um, just when you rubbed that rod with the cloth . . . .

Teacher: Uhuh.

Richard: . . . it attracts and then repels the thing. Um, it's . . . .[indistinct]

Teacher: Well, that's our . . . that's our observation, yeah.

Richard: Oh.

Teacher: That's what we observed. But what theory can we advance to explain it? Is it because the thing is clean?

Richard: No.

Teacher: Or is it because it's now highly polished? These are the only two things we can observe from this experiment. John.

John: Er, the friction makes it into a temporary magnet.

Teacher: The friction makes it into a . . . ?

John: Temporary magnet.

Teacher: A magnet? Then it should attract metals, should it not? Do you think if we tried that with metals . . . ?
[At this point the teacher finds some small metal pieces and brings the rubbed rod up to them several times. A few lines later, Richard introduces 'charge'.]

Richard: They've got an electric charge on it, like.

Teacher: Well, what are you talking about? I don't know what you're talking about. Dave.

Dave: When you rub the thing it builds up a static electricity — the ebonite rod. Then it attracts the . . . um.

Teacher: Well, what do you mean 'static electricity'? I've never heard of that. [some laughter] I'm just performing this experiment.
[This is followed by other attempts at explanation; for instance, Richard tries 'force'. Later, we hear:]

Teacher: There are other things people began to notice about the effect. It went away after a while. Although the object might still be clean and shiny, it did go away after a while. It sort of tended to destroy our theory that because it was clean and shiny that these effects occurred. [pause] People began to think of it as having some property all its own because of the fact that we had done this to it. [repeating the demonstration] Performing this operation on the rod that gives it some new property that it didn't have before that it could lose. That it somehow needed to be revitalized after a time or recharged. The use of the word 'charging' for 'filling something up' is not uncommon. So we came to think of these things as having some kind of property which needed to be recharged, or refilled, or redone periodically. And we came logically after a while to think of it having initially a charge. Whatever this property was we called it a charge. And since it was an electrical material, it seemed logical to call it some kind of electrical charge. So it's odd sometimes how these terms arise. Very odd indeed. These have come more through the language than anything else. There's no, er, logical reason for that to, er . . . no reason to lead us to the fact 'Well, obviously. . . .' Someone was trying to tell us earlier, 'Obviously, there are electrical charges or electrostatic charges' or something. These are terms that we didn't have before, and types of thinking that we didn't have before either.

Where explicit talk about language and its function is excluded from Lesson 1, it forms the focus of Lesson 2. Here the teacher takes pains to establish how language is incorporated into an explanatory construction of the phenomena in question. This working through of the link between language and phenomena offers the students a glimpse of what goes on 'behind the scenes' of science. The students are not left to work with the surface of scientific content; instead, they witness and can participate in some of the intellectual work that gives rise to this particular scientific construction. Lesson 2 clearly carries the message that science offers a construction of reality, a message that is not conveyed in Lesson 1.

Just as we can look at the language of teaching for messages conveyed about the nature of science,[1] so we can look at the argument presented by the discourse for messages about the nature of scientific arguments (Russell, 1983). Deriving an analytical framework from Toulmin's (1958) work on patterns of rational arguments, Russell analyzes arguments in several science lessons and identifies several ways in which arguments contained within teaching may not accord with our understandings of what disciplinary arguments should be. Warrants are central to his analysis: they are the devices that authorize moving from data to conclusions. In the transcript from Lesson 1 no warrant is provided to the children to permit them to understand how a category system is built and then legitimated by its usefulness as a conceptual tool. Instead, the children are presented with an assertion about classifying human as animals. Jimmy responds to this by identifying characteristics, yet his resorting to 'evidence' is met by the teacher's assertion, and again no argument is offered. Here the discourse is presenting a picture of how argument and authority are used in science, and the picture bears little resemblance to the features of science noted in our introduction. In contrast Lesson 2 provides important clues about the warrants used in formulating a construction of reality, because attention is paid to the relationship between constructs and data, and to the origin of constructs in language rather than in data. Because the final authority is evidence, Lesson 2 characterizes science very much as we have done in our opening paragraph.

The above excerpts and their analyses show that the language of teaching can be analyzed to reveal the implicit messages it sends about the nature of science — messages beyond the so-called scientific facts or factual content of the lesson. The excerpts invite relatively straightforward analyses that reveal how one can begin to deduce the consequences to children's understanding: *the intellectual provisions of the discourse can readily be made demonstrable.* In some respects our above analyses are similar to analyses of textbooks for their transmission of ethnic bias (Pratt, 1972) and sex-role stereotypes (Spender, 1982). Work of this nature flows directly from the view that language not only describes our world but substantially creates it. A sunset is the setting of the sun, not because it really is, but because we say it is so.

The idea that we construct our worlds is central to our current research on the nature and development of teachers' professional or practical knowledge. The analyses we have just presented are particularly germane to this research, because our concern for understanding teachers' professional knowledge can be enhanced when we consider the understanding science teachers have of science — their view of science. Particularly fascinating is the potential relationship of teachers' views of science *to the development and character of their professional knowledge and their views of their own knowledge.*

Metaphor, Reflection-in-action and the Nature of Professional Knowledge

Since 1984 we have been using Schön's (1983) work to highlight the significance of 'knowing-in-action' in describing, and eventually accounting for, that component of professional knowledge that is expressed in professional activity. Our particular interest in Schön's work begins with a fresh look at the generally accepted notion that one learns to teach by teaching. This apparently self-evident view is also a superficial one, because it fails to suggest how this learning occurs: it says nothing about the particularities of action that give rise to development of knowing-in-action, nor does it speak to the capabilities of the teacher that prompt this development.

Schön's account is helpful for its introduction of 'reflection-in-action'. Where knowing-in-action captures the idea that the essence of professional knowledge resides in action, 'reflection-in-action' suggests a process by which this knowledge develops. In an essay review (Munby and Russell, 1989) of Schön's (1983, 1987) two books, we differentiate this special sense of reflection from that used by Shulman (1987) and by Zeichner and Liston (1987). Their use of 'reflection' refers to a deliberate consideration of one's action, whereas Schön's concept refers to a non-logical process in which action reflects back on thought dialectically. The reflection that Schön calls attention to is *in the action* and contemporaneous with it; it is not in subsequent thinking about the action.

For Schön the central process by which reflection-in-action leads to the development of knowing-in-action is *reframing*, which refers to naming, describing or 'seeing differently' phenomena that are puzzling, with the result that they are cast in a fashion that admits of solution. 'The change, rather like a gestalt shift, does not necessarily come from a deliberate consideration of alternatives, because one has no control over the shift. Instead, *the shift is prompted by the events of action and by one's coming to see them differently*' (Munby and Russell, 1989: 78). The success of using the theoretical concept of reframing as a means of studying teachers' knowledge has been demonstrated in earlier work (Russell, 1986, 1988). Our research has capitalized upon the implicit relationship between reframing and language (if phenomena are 'seen differently', then they will be described differently), drawing upon earlier work (Munby, 1986) on metaphors and professional knowledge. This, in turn, is built on the assumption that a significant part of teachers' professional knowledge is not in the form of propositions but is to be understood in terms of how teachers construct their realities. The concept of metaphor emerges as a powerful tool for investigating teachers' thinking. This link between the development of teachers' professional knowledge and their language is consistent with Schön's view of metaphors as 'central to the task of accounting for our perspectives on the world' (1979: 254). Others (Reddy, 1979; Lakoff and Johnson, 1980) have pursued this perspective to show how metaphors reflect the ways in which we construct the world.

The case studies emerging from our 1989–90 work provide a wealth of information about the development of professional knowledge. Fifteen teachers have participated; of these, two are the focus of the present discussion. We invited teachers known to us who were considered likely to be interested in learning more about their teaching. Participation was voluntary, with a written understanding that anyone could withdraw at any time without explanation. Interviews were held at intervals of four to six weeks, and in most instances were preceded immediately by observation of a lesson by the interviewer. The line of questioning in the interview was informed by the observation just shared with the teacher, and built on themes apparent in previous interviews. Transcripts of the interviews were returned to participants for information and further comment. No teacher withdrew from the project, and all seemed to welcome the interviewer's visits and the associated opportunity to talk about their teaching.

For the purposes of this chapter we have selected two science teachers, here referred to as Wendy and Roger. Both were students in classes with one of us (Russell) during their BEd programme of pre-service teacher education. Roger has subsequently enrolled in an MEd programme. These two teachers have shown us two quite different approaches to science and to professional knowledge; our data suggest that the differences in reframing and thus in the development of knowing-in-action might lie in their different orientations to, and understanding of, science. Here we are not concerned with possible differences in the body of propositions that constitutes the discipline's content knowledge, nor are we interested in skills like 'problem-solving' and 'scientific thinking'. Instead, we are interested in the sorts of features about the nature of science that we discussed in analyzing the extracts from Lesson 1 and Lesson 2 above. In particular, we are sensitive to how the theoretical content of the discipline is 'fluid' (Schwab, 1978), and is characterized by attempts to capture the essence of phenomena with available language, much as the teacher in Lesson 2 was portraying the development of early concepts of 'electrics' and 'charge'. This view of the nature of science implies that the success of a theory depends in part upon linguistic inventiveness: as seen in Lesson 2, concepts that usefully capture the intricacies of phenomena are derived from sometimes imaginative and sensitive uses of language.

We are particularly intrigued with how this view of science is consistent with Schön's idea of reframing: a process that embodies naming an event differently, or 'seeing' it as something else. Quite clearly, inventive use of language plays a part here, just as it does in using 'electrics' to refer to materials just because they are observed to behave in certain ways. So it is reasonable to think that a science teacher who holds something similar to a constructivist view of science (Driver, 1983) might be accustomed to moulding novel language in framing puzzling classroom phenomena. This orientation informs our analysis of the cases of Wendy and Roger.

Wendy

Wendy has completed two years of science teaching at the secondary level. As we have watched her teach and listened to her discussions of her initial experiences of teaching, we have concluded that her learning from the experience of teaching seems constrained by her images of teaching and of the knowledge she teaches. Viewing teaching as the transmission of knowledge seems to prevent Wendy from relying on her own experiences and treating them as a valid source of professional knowledge. It has been her experience to obtain knowledge from external sources and so she does not seem to expect teaching experiences to inform or teach her. As a result, Wendy appears to be refining her teaching strategies, but not developing new perspectives on practice from her involvement with students and subject matter.

Wendy seems to regard knowledge as information that comes in packaged 'chunks'. The ways in which she is accustomed to learning seem to be reenacted in her actions with students. Transmission of information is directly from teacher to student, with evaluation in the form of tests as the only method used to see if the information has been received.

> I know that I feel I don't seem to be teaching if I'm not up there telling them what to do, or teaching them. And somebody said, 'Be easy on yourself; let the kids do the work.' I never thought about that before! I thought that was my job — to give them everything, to feed them information! But that's not really learning! If they learned it on their own, that seems to be learning.

Wendy describes teaching in images such as 'covering the curriculum' and 'getting it across'. In recent comments about her second-year experience, she discusses changes in her teaching in terms of different techniques that enable her to 'get it across' more effectively. She sees herself making more connections between topics, interrelating material for students and encouraging them to make their own connections. Up to this point in her professional development, learning from the experience of teaching seems to involve 'fine tuning' rather than reframing of experience through significant new teaching actions. Her metaphors for teaching appear stable.

> I know everything that I wasn't sure of last year with the subject matter. I'm more confident of that. That makes everything so much easier. I'm cutting out things I know didn't work right away, and I'm trying a few new techniques, especially in how I approach the subject in terms of, 'Do you do the lab first or do you do the lesson first?' I'm trying to get them to do more work than me, so I get them to do more learning themselves.

Wendy's ideal images for teaching appear to be held separate from her practice, but this is not because she wishes it so. She speaks of wanting to make science fun for her students and relevant to their lives, but she recognizes that achieving that goal would mean a lot of work on her part. She is uncertain where and how to begin. She says that she feels that students should learn to work independently, that school should involve 'learning how to learn', and that the learning process is more important than its product. Yet she lacks examples of how this might be done, and she teaches as she was taught. Wendy frequently relates her teaching to that done by other science teachers, in terms of rate of progress through the curriculum. It appears that she is willing and eager to bring her practices in line with those of colleagues in her department. Her situation seems similar to that of most beginning teachers.

> Right now as first year teachers, we're teaching the subject matter; we're not teaching them how to learn. The thought of me teaching them how to learn seems so strange! In the backs of our minds, that's what we're working for, but somebody tell me how to do it! I'm not sure how to do it, so I'm going to leave it out 'here' for now until I'm capable of understanding what I have to do in order to do it.
>
> Instead of learning science or learning English or French, learning how to interpret . . . how to form opinion . . . believing in something and sticking by it — making sure you can support what you believe in. As long as they learn those values they can apply them to any subject . . . it's an ideal thing that I would like, and it's the sort of thing that you think about and it seems really nice, and then you go on, and life is so hectic as it is, that it gets left out.

In contrast to this discussion of ideals we observe little evidence that Wendy's teaching is developing in ways that involve 'learning how to learn'. Rather, we see a teacher whose view of teaching remains relatively stable during her two years of teaching. We do not see a reframing of her perspectives on teaching, but we do see how her experience contributes to modifications in strategies that enable her to teach more effectively within her existing frame of teaching, in which covering the curriculum as effectively as possible is the core of her professional responsibility. Her experience in the classroom leads to refinement of her presentation strategies so that she is more confident that students are covering the curriculum productively.

Wendy espouses a view of practice that she says she would like to incorporate into her teaching, but she seems to find it very difficult to connect her actions and experiences in the classroom with the process of achieving that goal of modifying her teaching. When Wendy expresses her desire to change various aspects of her practice, she also acknowledges that thinking about her teaching is difficult and requires time that she has not yet found.

> The idea that I have is that if I thought more about how I wanted to approach my style of teaching, and how I could change it — if I thought about how kids learned, then I could change my style of teaching so they could learn better.
>
> Something I haven't done which I'd like to change: I still find I make myself the centre of attention. I'm up at the blackboard — I'm the one teaching them instead of having them teach themselves. I would like for them to do more self-learning instead of guided learning. Even I don't do guided learning — I'm more of a lecturer instead of guided learning or self-learning. I think I would

like them to do more of that, but for me to do that takes a lot of work — I've got a lot of thinking to do and I haven't got around to that yet! I have a lot of ideas but I haven't sat down to do something about them. And I'm sure that will come with time — even after a year it gets better.

When you 'want' to change things, you have to be — physically and actively thinking about it all the time. And I don't think about it enough to actually be thinking about changing it, and thinking about ways to change it. It's not something that I've done a lot with.

It seems clear to us that in her second year as a science teacher Wendy's professional knowledge developed in ways that did not enable her to reduce the gap between goals or values, on the one hand, and teaching practices, on the other. This stable state of affairs is corroborated by the images or metaphors apparent in her talk about her professional knowledge. Repetition of words and phrases such as 'too academic', 'stuff too much into one lecture', 'get it across', 'stick in a few more concepts', and 'get the content to the kids', leads us to believe that Wendy's central perspective relates to 'covering the curriculum'. She seems to view teaching through a 'conduit' metaphor (Reddy, 1979) in which knowledge previously taken in by the teacher is passed on to the students. Within this perspective Wendy's attention during her first year appears to be on herself and her presentation. Her repeated use of 'structure', 'organized', 'frustrating', 'doing all the work', 'can't seem to change it', and 'change means work' gives the impression that Wendy feels she could cover the curriculum better if only she were more organized and more structured in her presentation. In her second year Wendy continued to speak about structure and organization, but in ways that suggest she felt more comfortable with her organization of knowledge: 'getting all the key points in', 'cutting out things that I know didn't work', 'trying to interrelate', 'better in connecting ideas' and 'giving them a lot of work'.

In her second year Wendy's language contains other images that suggest a conduit metaphor. She wants to try different presentation techniques, but feels that she is not sufficiently knowledgeable about alternative strategies. She wants someone to 'give it to me, so I can give it to them'. Notice the view of knowledge suggested by these words; 'haven't come across any really neat ideas', 'getting bored', 'looking for something new', 'always have to provide them with new ideas', 'should have more detailed knowledge', 'running out of ideas' and 'if they are willing to give, you take'. These phrases suggest that Wendy feels that the professional knowledge she seeks must come from sources outside her present teaching, rather than from attention to the evidence of classroom events.

The process of change seems much easier to outsiders than to those who actually do it, or think about doing it. We value and respect Wendy's personal integrity, and are intrigued by the process by which she develops and refines her practices while declaring values not reflected in those practices. Wendy's openness has enabled us to see the very real tensions faced by the beginning teacher. As Wendy gains confidence and experience, it appears that the environment in which she finds herself does not encourage and support the reflection-in-action that would enable her to explore her ideals at the level of practice. However, we believe that more than the environment is at work here.

Wendy rarely speaks directly about her images of science itself; the two main images have already been noted, and they appear to be mutually exclusive. On one other hand, she stresses her responsibility to her students to cover the content; she wants them to understand the concepts of science, and she wants them to pass their tests. On the other hand, the idea of learning how to learn rarely appears in her teaching actions. From Wendy's various comments, which emphasize her responsibility to cover the curriculum, we infer a picture of science as unchanging content, content that is not subject to the vagaries of human inventiveness that accompany presentations of puzzling or anomalous phenomena. One relevant passage in Wendy's data shows her comparing her use of laboratory activities in her first year with that in her second year. She has made changes based on her initial experiences; the changes seem intended to improve students' understanding of a concept rather than to improve their understanding of how a specific concept is developed from observation and experimentation.

> I tried a few labs differently. I demonstrated a few labs that we did last year which were confusing for the kids. I spent more time explaining. I demonstrated it [rather than have them do it themselves]. Last year we had done it as a class experiment. Every kid had a set of equipment . . . And I didn't really get the concept over of what they were supposed to be getting out of these labs. And [so] this year . . . we had one set of equipment out, and everyone stood around and watched, and I asked questions, so I was asking them to interpret what was going on while we were doing it. So I asked more questions, and I think their understanding was better because of that.

Our inferences about Wendy's image of science are to some extent based on what she does not say. If she held unusual views of science, we assume that they would emerge in the context of discussion of laboratory work. Wendy appears to hold familiar and stable images of science, consistent with the practical priority of covering the curriculum in a responsible way that maximizes the understanding achieved by the greatest number of students.

Similarly Wendy's knowing-in-action about the curriculum also shows stability. The language she uses to speak about her curriculum concerns is dominated by a 'cover the curriculum' metaphor. In Schön's terms this metaphor is 'stale' because it appears to hinder the reframing of experience one might expect given the unresolved tension between Wendy's ideals and her teaching practices. Productive resolution of this tension, and hence growth in knowing-in-action, depends on Wendy's finding language that reframes the puzzle for her. Generative metaphors of this sort have not appeared in our interviews during her first two years of science teaching.

Roger

Data provided by Roger offer insights into the process of reflection-in-action that Schön argues is prompted by events of practice and generates new sequences of actions that involve seeing those events in new ways. Now in his fifth year of teaching, Roger teaches science in grades 7 and 8 (12–13-year-olds) in a special programme for gifted students. His own accounts of his development of professional knowledge articulate how listening to the 'backtalk' of events in his classroom changes his view of learning and his approach to teaching.

Through many years of schooling Roger experienced the frustration of not understanding what he was 'learning', yet doing well enough in school to gain entrance to university. After two years at university he withdrew for one year. When he resumed his studies, he found he received much higher grades. In particular, he recalls an enquiry-based research course that finally provided opportunities to *understand* the concepts he was studying. Roger also indicates that several years of experience as a Boy Scout leader provided him with what he now regards as 'a large knowledge base of how kids learn' prior to entering pre-service teacher education. His pre-service programme, which included a special emphasis on outdoor and experiential education, helped to confirm the personal value he associates with experiential learning. Once he began to teach in a classroom of his own, his students' responses showed him that enquiry-based learning has to be associated with content. If it is not, he explains, students learn that science is fun but they learn little about the concepts of science. At the same time that Roger's teaching experiences were generating puzzles about how students learn, he was exploring these questions in the work of Driver (1983) and Barnes (1976). This written corroboration of the importance of his puzzles led Roger to experiment with a new approach in which he combines content with an enquiry model of learning. The following data are taken from Roger's own accounts of the experience of working out these puzzles of professional knowledge.

> When I came here [to the Faculty of Education], I was very much experiential, very discovery-, enquiry-, process-orientated. And that was great because that was very much the kind of approach and philosophies that were being used here, particularly in

science. And when I went to try it, it worked very well. The kids love it and they really enjoy it, but what I noticed was that they were having a lot of fun and they loved science, but they weren't learning anything! And so I began to develop strategies that would deal with that as a side issue. 'Yes we'll have some fun, but now we've had some fun, we sort of have to learn some things!' I thought, 'This is really stupid. You can't have sort of two parallel approaches to teaching.' Anyway, the more I started to read about teaching, and think about it, I really began to look at trying to sort out that dilemma of how is it that people learn so much by *doing* things and yet, when you give kids things to do in science, they don't really learn anything about science other than 'science is fun', and 'science is enjoyable', and that kind of thing, which is very worthwhile, too.

Here we see quite clearly that Roger has reframed his understanding of teaching as a result of bringing written analyses of teaching to bear on his teaching practices in the science classroom. His understanding of science and his understanding of teaching parallel each other and interact, and his professional knowledge develops accordingly. Roger describes a crucial aspect of reframing as he continues his account of how his professional knowledge has developed.

And I guess the thing that really struck me was I read Ros Driver's book, *The Pupil as Scientist?* At first, I was really annoyed with the book because basically what it says is that enquiry is screwed up — I mean, kids can't do anything if they don't know anything, and they can't discover anything or plan their own experiments or whatever if they have no background. It was so obvious that it annoyed me; basically, she's saying that enquiry doesn't work. But I didn't want to know it. It was almost as if I believed in it so strongly that there must be a way to make it work. Anyway, the outcome of that book, really, was to lead into the whole 'cognitive science' approach to teaching, and looking at how people learn. And I basically got involved in that sort of thing . . . . And that has led to all kinds of reading on top of that, and discovering, actually, now, there are a lot of people who feel that way. Not that the sort of philosophy or the spirit of enquiry is wrong, but just that there has to be some associated content to go with it, and that this can happen in specific ways so that people have some things, some tools to work with when they go to do this experiential kind of thing. So that's what I played with last year, with my kids, and it was dynamite.

One major theme in Roger's accounts of his teaching involves *helping students make sense of science.* In the following excerpts we see how Roger's perspective on teaching influences the events he attends to in his classroom. He is very concerned that students be able to make sense of science. This concern, combined with his view of teaching as content *plus* enquiry and his view of science as searching for answers, influences the events of practice that interest him most. He actively seeks information about how his students are seeing science.

> Now, the other thing that I've spent quite a bit of time doing is trying to identify how kids see those ideas as well. I present what *I'm* thinking of, get them to present what *they're* thinking of, and then we have a place to start negotiating what this is really about. I'll have the kids work on activities and ask them to use some of their ideas to explain things and then, when *their* explanations don't work so well, I have them go back and say, 'Well, maybe there's something not so good about that explanation', and offer them alternative explanations. I have them look at it and, once those alternative explanations are accepted as being reasonably plausible, I then provide more activities and give them opportunity to use that explanation to explain other things.
>
> I spend a lot of time, often, as things are happening, saying 'Gee, I wonder what the difference is between what I did this time, or what happened last time and this time that caused the difference?'
>
> I end up learning so much, working this way, about how the *kids* learn, and it helps me enormously. I end up going back and changing all my things immediately, and saying, 'Well, I'll have to change that around!' because something that I thought was fairly obvious clearly wasn't!
>
> But there were some very nice things that came out of those discussions and you can't ignore that. I love the way they think out loud, which is great, and I guess because of all the dialogue I encourage in the class they do that, and so in this little discussion group they will think out loud. And that's a very profound kind of insight because, you know, we had to deal with that right then and say, 'Well, in fact, there *are* two things.' And then we got into quite the discussion about it, and it was great. But that was never on the lesson plan . . . for this group, actually, it was important right then.

A second major theme in Roger's accounts of his teaching involves *stepping back to look at his practice*. The ability to step back from the immediacy of classroom activities to see what is happening to his students seems to play an important part in his learning from classroom experiences. He speaks of taking time to step back and see what is happening and being continually fascinated by student responses.

Because things are fairly well laid out now, I can stand back from things a bit and concentrate on the kids who aren't getting into it as much and to look at some aspects of why they don't. And how you can move them from this very structured position to one where they're quite willing to suspend things. One girl, when she started out in grade 7, was quite lost without any kind of structure and now she really enjoys being confused. And it provides a challenge for her. But that took a long time, about three-quarters of a year. But it took a lot of work to get her to that stage, and a lot of that comes in the feedback that I give in the reports and things that they write. Once the kids are allowed to *believe* that they have some ability to solve these kinds of problems, then everything opens up.

It's much easier now to step back and look at what's happening as opposed to 'Where do we go next?' And I'm also able to predict fairly well the kinds of things that will come up and to get a sense of the kinds of things that kids will understand, the kinds of interesting conceptions that they'll have of things.

In Roger we see a teacher who does construct a personal interpretation of teaching from his classroom experiences and from theoretical positions about how children learn. His experiences prior to entering the profession helped him to develop his educational ideals and gave him an opportunity to explore and sort out the 'how' of teaching. Once in his own classroom, he quickly began to listen to the 'backtalk' of events, and at the same time to explore his ideals through experimentation with his practice. Through his experiences of teaching he continues to construct his professional knowledge.

An analysis of images in Roger's discussion of his professional knowledge parallels closely the significant reframing already described. Roger's dominant metaphor of practice involves creating conditions that foster students' development of knowledge. One of his key phrases is 'making sense'. He searches for explanations that make sense, he ties ideas together and he makes connections that are real for his students. These language patterns reflect a perspective on teaching that is similar to a constructivist view of knowledge (Driver, 1983). Roger talks about 'playing', 'exploring', 'investigating', 'fiddling around', 'experimenting' and 'beginning to wonder' both in relationship to his own learning and in relationship to his students' activities in the classroom. For Roger both science and teaching science are 'fascinating, exciting, and fun'. He 'relates', 'coalesces', 'integrates' and 'pulls together ideas' in his teaching. Two features of these figures demand attention. First, one does not have to look far to see that they could characterize an intellectual orientation to science just as easily as they characterize Roger's approach to having his students learn about science *and* his approach to attending to the evidence of his own teaching. Second, and in contrast to the stability of Wendy's talk about her teaching, Roger's language seems bounded only by the need to give precise expression to his thinking.

Intellectual Orientations and Reframing

We find it particularly productive to frame the obvious contrasts between these two teachers in terms of views of knowledge — both scientific knowledge and professional knowledge. Wendy and Roger both teach science, but their understandings of what this means result in very different teaching. For Wendy teaching science is a matter of transmitting the subject matter, in a fashion that is defensible when the task is to present science as normal science (Kuhn, 1970). Wendy's teaching conveys to students a picture of science that has propositional content front and centre. Roger's orientation to science is markedly different, as is his approach to teaching it. Nor is the contrast adequately captured by the difference between 'content' and 'process' approaches. We have seen from the interviews that Roger has moved away from the latter position, prompted by his reading and by his thinking about his teaching. Roger's teaching has many elements of the 'constructivist' position, and in Kuhn's (1970) terms we could say that he wants students to understand the revolutionary features of paradigm shifts in science.

Also striking in these cases is the contrast we read in their discussions of their teaching (and by inference the nature of their professional knowledge). After the rush and uncertainty of the first year Wendy is focusing on her responsibility to cover the curriculum. Her accomplishments are impressive, for she is modifying her teaching to maximize understanding. Yet her ideals of teaching are still at a distance from her practice, and she has not developed a 'knowing-in-action' that satisfactorily meshes the two. In contrast, after several years of experience Roger has realized that a constructivist approach enables him to combine his ideals about science and science teaching with his desire to have students enjoy science. Their enjoyment, to him, appears inseparable from their intellectual involvement with constructs and experiences of phenomena. He takes a similar stand in terms of his own professional knowledge of teaching.

The varied backgrounds of Roger and Wendy defy any attempt to trace the movement of Roger toward a constructivist orientation to science or to explain why this movement occurred when it seems not to occur for many teachers. Yet the common theme of knowledge compels us to attempt to explain the differential development we see in the two teachers' professional knowledge, specifically in their knowing-in-action. Schön's account of the development of this little understood type of knowledge seems to be closely linked to the essence of science itself. Rather than the typical problem-solving of 'normal science' (Kuhn, 1970), the essence of conceptual invention lies in a fruitful dialectic between phenomena and language. Schön's concept of reframing, set within reflection-in-action, is reminiscent of Kuhnian paradigm shifts, in which familiar events are quite suddenly seen differently. Our data suggest that Wendy is not aware that her own professional knowledge could develop in this way, possibly because she is unaware that the development of science can be seen in this way. Roger, on the other hand, has come to terms with this aspect of the development of science, and he views the development of his own knowledge similarly. The apparent correspondence between one's intellectual orientation to science and one's ability to reflect-in-action is intriguing.

Our continuing work with case studies of teachers and their teaching constantly reminds us that understanding how people learn to teach is very complex. The cases of Wendy and Roger have provided us with a promising direction for this research, and have shown the power of Schön's basic theoretical work. We are increasingly aware of the importance of careful and ongoing attention to similarities and differences among a teacher's intellectual orientation to science, images of science presented to students and understanding of how professional knowledge of teaching develops.

Acknowledgments

The case studies reported here are from the research project 'Metaphor, Reflection, and Teachers' Professional Knowledge', funded by the Social Sciences and Humanities Research Council of Canada. Phyllis Johnston has given invaluable assistance to the research.

Note

1 In a much earlier study Munby (1973a) developed an analytical scheme based on philosophy of science, and showed that it could be applied to science teaching in a way that allowed one to determine the view of science presented to children by the discourse. Texts can also be examined from similar perspectives (Munby, 1973b; Kilbourn, 1974, 1984).

References

BARNES, D. (1976) *From Communication to Curriculum*, Harmondsworth, Penguin.
DRIVER, R. (1983) *The Pupil as Scientist?* Milton Keynes, Open University Press.
KILBOURN, B. (1974) *Identifying World Views Projected by Science Teaching Materials: A Case Study Using Pepper's World Hypotheses to Analyze a Biology Textbook*, Unpublished doctoral dissertation, University of Toronto.
KILBOURN, B. (1984) 'World views and science teaching', in MUNBY, H., ORPWOOD, G. and RUSSELL, T. (Eds), *Seeing Curriculum in a New Light: Essays from Science Education*, Lanham, Md, University Press of America, pp. 34–43.

KUHN, T. S. (1970) *The Structure of Scientific Revolutions*, Chicago, 2nd Edn., University of Chicago Press.
LAKOFF, G. and JOHNSON, M. (1980) *Metaphors We Live By*, Chicago, University of Chicago Press.
MUNBY, H. (1973a) *The Provision Made for Selected Intellectual Consequences by Science Teaching: Derivation and Application of an Analytical Scheme*, Unpublished doctoral dissertation, University of Toronto.
MUNBY, H. (1973b) 'Some implications of language in science education', *Science Education*, 60, pp. 115–24.
MUNBY, H. (1982) *What Is Scientific Thinking? A Discussion Paper*, Ottawa, Science Council of Canada.
MUNBY, H. (1986) 'Metaphor in the thinking of teachers: An exploratory study', *Journal of Curriculum Studies*, 18, pp. 197–209.
MUNBY, H. and RUSSELL, T. (1989) 'Educating the reflective teacher: An essay review of two books by Donald Schön', *Journal of Curriculum Studies*, 21, pp. 71–80.
PRATT, D. (1972) *How to Find and Measure Bias in Textbooks*, Englewood Cliffs, N.J., Educational Technology Publications.
REDDY, M. (1979) 'The conduit metaphor', in ORTONY, A. (Ed.), *Metaphor and thought*, Cambridge, Cambridge University Press, pp. 284–324.
RUSSELL, T. (1983) 'Analyzing arguments in science classroom discourse: Can teachers' questions distort scientific authority?' *Journal of Research in Science Teaching*, 20, pp. 27–45.
RUSSELL, T. (1986) 'Beginning teachers' development of knowledge-in-action', Paper presented at the annual meeting of the American Educational Research Association, San Francisco (ERIC Document Reproduction Service No. ED 270 414).
RUSSELL, T. (1988) 'From pre-service teacher education to first year of teaching: A study of theory and practice', in CALDERHEAD, J. (Ed.), *Teachers' Professional Learning*, Lewes, Falmer Press, pp. 13–34.
SCHÖN, D. (1979) 'Generative metaphor and social policy', in ORTONY, A. (Ed.), *Metaphor and Thought*, Cambridge, Cambridge University Press, pp. 254–83.
SCHÖN, D. (1983) *The Reflective Practitioner*, London, Temple Smith.
SCHÖN, D. (1987) *Educating the Reflective Practitioner*, San Francisco, Jossey-Bass.
SCHWAB, J. J. (1978) 'What do scientists do?' in WESTBURY, I. and WILKOF, N. (Eds), *Science, Curriculum, and Liberal Education: Selected Essays by Joseph J. Schwab*, Chicago, University of Chicago Press, pp. 184–228.
SHULMAN, L. (1987) 'Knowledge and teaching: Foundations of the new reform', *Harvard Educational Review*, 57, 1, pp. 1–22.
SPENDER, D. (1982) *Invisible Women*, London, Routledge and Kegan Paul.
TOULMIN, S. (1958) *The Uses of Argument*, Cambridge, Cambridge University Press.
ZEICHNER, K. and LISTON, D. (1987) 'Teaching student teachers to reflect', *Harvard Educational Review*, 57, 1, pp. 23–48.

Chapter 6

The Social Construction of School Science

Joan Solomon

There are many reasons for expecting that secondary school science lessons will have a strong social character. The age of silent pupils working at separate desks under threat of immediate punishment for any unsolicited word to a neighbour is over. Some may mourn its passing, but gone it is. In the UK the 1989 National Curriculum for science gives its official recognition to the value of working in groups (DES, 1989). In the laboratory there are simply not the resources for each pupil to have a set of experimental equipment, so group activity has become the norm to such an extent that few can now recall whether it was expediency or design that first promoted collaborative practical work. Groups of pupils are bound to interact together, and so it has come about that silence has been vanquished by various kinds of pupil talk some of which are positively encouraged by teachers.

But peer groups of talking teenagers, once permitted and established, cannot so easily be engineered to work according to adult expectations for learning. Adolescence is a period when approval from friends becomes more important than parental or teacher influence, as developmental psychology, the slavish following of teenage fashion and the existence of street gangs bear ample witness. In the school laboratory we find substantial consequences from this new learning mode. 'Doing science lessons' is a social activity which is governed every bit as much by the rules and rituals of group activity as by the exposition and questions posed by the teacher. Such factors will affect every aspect of learning science, from entry into the laboratory to the understanding of concepts encountered during experimental work.

However pervasive is this social influence — and years of teaching and classroom research have left me in no doubt whatever of its importance and reality — trying to describe its influence is seriously hampered by a paucity of research results. Many of the data in this chapter are from small-scale studies with which I have been personally involved in either an active or advisory capacity. Far more research needs to be done; nevertheless, this is an interesting moment to reflect upon what has been achieved so far. Not only is this social constructivist approach still novel enough to be little known to many science educationalists, but I have been forced to choose some data for its illustration which are culled from sources where they were mere unremarked details in a more traditionally personal view of learning science. However, the approach should not be uncomfortably eccentric. Even if the social perspective has been largely ignored in the field of education, in the study of laboratory action (for example, Latour and Woolgar, 1979) it has already proved its worth. In this chapter I will take advantage of what research data are beginning to show, and of what social theory suggests, to focus on just three aspects of social action in the science classroom: on pupil behaviour vis-à-vis the teacher, on doing practical work, and on discussion among pupils about the concepts and implications of the science that they are learning.

Of Groups, Spaces and Behaviour

It is many years now since the work of Goffman (1959) and Harré (1979) demonstrated the value of analyzing the social scene in terms of actions designed to be read by the other actors present. Not only has little use been made of this for explicating normal school behaviour in the special setting of the school laboratory, but no account at all seems to have been taken of the pressures of group values, of task-related acts or of pupil and teacher spaces on the smooth progress of learning. There may be recurrent outcry from the Inspectorate and in the press about disruption in the schools, yet the normal run of group activity, how it is influenced by teacher action and how it influences pupil learning has been left unexplored. The intellectual tools for its examination are ready to hand, but ignored. Knowledge about how such activity usually operates exists only precariously, as anecdotes rather than more general rules, within the tacit understanding of practising teachers.

In that situation it was clear to some of us that the starting point should be an ethnomethodological study of laboratory behaviour by the science teachers themselves. The STIR (Science Teachers In Research) group set out in 1985 to begin this study, and it proved to be most challenging in terms of method, interpretation and validation. After two years of trial, error and retrial, the preliminary results are now in press (Solomon *et al.*, 1989). Of the method used we wrote, '. . . a common theoretical perspective is the only tool which can bind together the observations of different teachers and, if successful, make their practitioner knowledge explicit and accessible'.

This filter for observation and guide to reflection about 'doing science lessons' was provided by four general points which were borrowed from the field of social psychology.

All pupil actions are to be considered for the meaning they have for the pupil in the context of all the others present, and for the social honour to be derived from them.

These social acts build up performances from which the 'moral career' of a pupil develops.

Groups have their own conceptions of the reputation they wish to achieve, which varies with age and with gender.

All space within the laboratory has social and behavioural significance and the boundaries between spaces are not crossed without consequences.

Case study records were drawn from the teachers' own dairies of four classes learning science. Two of these were mixed ability second year classes and two were post-adolescent fifth year groups — one of middle ability and the other both less able and less socially settled. The teachers considered their own actions and reactions not only as relevant from the point of view of their teaching intentions, but also as an integral part of the social context of learning science. Thus their informal chat with the pupils, their movement from one group to another and the space that they normally occupied in front of the blackboard all became valuable items of data for the research.

This work indicated that all four general points listed above were important for interpreting many of the vagaries of classroom behaviour and learning success. In particular the research suggested that the older, post-adolescent pupils had a far more developed sense of group identity and reputation than those in the younger classes. Pupils whose personal values were different from those of their group, or who had poor social skills (see also Gray, 1986), upset the classroom rituals of activity and learning. Paying attention to the teacher's explanation, as well as moving to watch a demonstration or a video excerpt, became explicable in terms of social space. The teachers also claimed that their results made new sense of some of the problems associated with use of supply teachers, with differences between groups of girls and boys and with the effects of approaching external examinations.

Talking during practical Work

In the previous research the content of talk was only recorded if it was a part of the behaviour between teacher and pupils. To determine what is said as pupils carry out experimental work within their groups a quite different research perspective is required. It calls for non-participant observation. There are also different expectations of such task-related talk, including a new and influential wave of interest in 'working in groups' which is encouraged as far afield as industrial management courses.

The commonest claim made for group talk is that it helps in the planning and designing stages of practical work. The APU studies of investigation (Assessment of Performance Unit, 1988), to which we owe so much, were too individual and research-based to suggest how group work in the ordinary school laboratory might affect the mode of operation or the learning outcome. Some educationalists already had a strong predisposition to argue for its value (for example, Baxter, 1988). In the run up to GCSE some of these ideas became enshrined in recommendations for preparing students for assessment.

The only empirical study of pupils talking together during practical work of which I am aware comes from a very patient listening and observing study of a second year science class by June Wallace (1986). The pupils worked in pairs or trios which continued unchanged from one lesson to the next, as they so often do in science classrooms. Wallace reported snippets of discussion from five different groups and, although these short extracts could often seem banal in themselves, her analysis showed clearly the different types of talk, their function for different purposes and the different periods of the lesson which they characterized.

1   Negotiating doing (e.g., arranging collection of apparatus and turn-taking in the experiment);
2   Removing tension (e.g., when disappointments or near quarrels have occurred);
3   Giving help and tutoring;
4   Non-task talk (e.g., for greeting and 'stroking' as they settle into their pairs);
5   Negotiating knowledge (e.g., agreeing or disagreeing about what colours, measurements or tastes they perceive);
6   Constructing meaning (see the next section of this chapter).

The point that Wallace makes many times in her commentary, and substantiates from the literature of social psychology, is that all this talk is essential for smooth social operations. If teachers choose, for whatever reason, to encourage group practical work, then all these kinds of pupil talk will be bound to occur. Without (1) the pupils would continually bump into each other, without (2) they might fight and without (4) it is almost impossible for any two humans, adults or children, to enter into such close and active proximity.

It seems likely that children need to do a number of things outside the formal organisation of a lesson. They need to chat and play. Children within a small group seem to form a relationship with each other, and the degree to which that is successful influences the success of the work they do. They need each other for practical help and for confidence about what they have noticed. Developing the relationship seems, as in adults, to arise from informal chat. It looks as if children need to chat about anything as well as

129

Joan Solomon

their work. Similarly play, another informal activity, seems to give
opportunity for developing understanding. (Wallace, 1986: 72)

Group Discussion of Science Concepts

The group construction of meaning is probably much nearer to the science
teacher's intentions than the 'chat' and 'messing about' that has just been described. Indeed class–teacher interaction through brainstorming or question
and answer has long been advocated to help pupils understand new pieces of
theory, or for eliciting their own meanings for everyday happenings. Un-
fortunately the style and location of the talk bring other messages to the
pupils, like 'getting it right' or 'winning teacher's approval'. The power
balance is far too much weighted towards the knowledge of the teacher for
an easy and equal flow of contributions to come about. As Edwards and
Mercer (1987) and others before them have shown, teacher-led classroom
discussion can all too readily degenerate into a kind of verbal 'follow my
leader'. 'The teacher seems able, despite what appears to be a relatively
open pupil-orientated and conversational style of teaching, to maintain a
close control over the selection, expression and direction of ideas and activities' (Edwards and Mercer, 1987: 112).

Group constructions of meaning do take place, but more often when
the teacher is absent from the discussion. In a small-scale piece of research
by Kennedy (1984) an unexpected happening during elementary learning
about electricity illustrated this very clearly. She had tested all the pupils'
conceptions of current flow in an electrical circuit by means of the diagrams
that Osborne (1981) developed following his own research on young
children's ideas about electricity. After this test, these first year pupils learnt
about electricity from a set of simple experiments with circuit-boards performed in groups from identical worksheets. Then they were tested again,
individually, by means of the same circuit diagrams. To the chagrin of
teacher and researcher alike, very little progress towards the 'correct' view
of electric current seemed to have been made. Only when the data were re-
explored, with reference to the groups in which the practical course work
had been carried out, was any pattern discernible. It seemed that a consensus within each practical group had emerged which even forced some
pupils who originally held the 'correct' view to be converted by the majority
to another 'incorrect' view. The most probable explanation for this seemed
to be that the pupils had been speaking together about the experiments in
terms of their preferred meaning for current, and this had produced distinct
clusters of meaning in the post-test results.

This sort of effect can be the result of overt argument, or of minority or
majority influence (for example, the experiments on groups discussing the
comparative length of two rods (Ashe, 1955)). However, this consensus can
just as easily be the result of talk in which the meaning of current flow is only

130

suggested by ways of connecting the wires while talking about the current or the brightness of bulbs. In the commonsense mode of learning implied meanings in general conversation are more common vehicles of persuasion and even conversion than is deliberate argument. Indeed the single comment, 'D'you know what I mean?', is all that is usually necessary to effect a change of meaning within the flexible logic of life-world knowing (Schutz and Luckmann, 1973).

Perspectives from the sociology of knowledge (for example, Berger and Luckmann, 1967) indicate that all of us, adult and child alike, need the corroboration and participation of others if we are to be comfortable with our own tentative construction of the world's happenings. The modern emphasis on 'learning by discovery' without any authoritative model supplied in advance of experiment by the teacher (Solomon, 1980) places the pupils in a singularly insecure position. What is it that they are supposed to be seeing? What should they be thinking? In such circumstances even half-formed suggestions are at a premium and may be seized upon by the group to fill a conceptual vacuum. Then, as they speak about it together, the picture implicit in the suggested meaning grows steadily clearer and brighter.

Even without any experimental work pupils may be encouraged to speak together to 'clarify' their ideas about a particular concept. To judge from the following extract of classroom conversation, the same urge to reach group consensus may have anything but a clarifying effect on pupils' ideas from the point of view of the teacher's objectives!

P1: You get energy from exercise.
P2: By doing exercise.
P3: You lose it by doing exercise.
P1: . . . You may lose energy.
P4: It makes your body fit.
P1: Yes . . . I think both (Solomon, 1984: 4).

Despite the logical contradiction between the two views about energy and exercise, pupil P1 participates so readily in the meaning of what the others say that s/he manages to agree with both views at the same time.

At other times, by listening to the sequence of pupil talk in a classroom, it is possible to detect a different manifestation of the consensus effect. Instead of trying to accommodate the conflicting meanings, pupils may pick up the ideas of other pupils and build upon them either immediately or after a pause. Figure 6.1 shows 'topic trails' of slightly shortened responses to the teacher's original question, 'What is energy?', repeated three times. The trails show this input by an arrow; the substance of the following comments suggests both the social chaining effect and some slightly delayed references back to the sun.

Undoubtedly there are also occasions during group talk when the drive to reach consensus is exploited by an influential character and gives rather

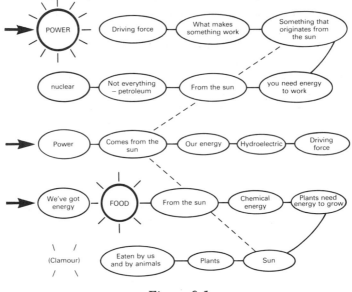

Figure 6.1
Flow Diagram of Energy Ideas

Source: Solomon (1985: 158)

less happy results from the point of view of learning 'correct' science. The classic work of Ashe (1955) on minority influence in the adult group decision-making process has already been mentioned. In the context of learning science this effect can be seen in some of the vivid accounts of the work of the Children's Learning In Science (CLIS) Project. The following extract comes from the diary of 'Robert' who reports on a lesson in which he and 'Pete' had different ideas about why two blocks could be the same size but have different weights. The outcome of what appears to have been a civilized discussion was decided, it seems, more by force of character than by the logic of a well chosen model.

> I thought it was something to do with atoms being compressed densely in (block) A and not so packed in B. Pete said something about air trapped in B and so it made the weight lighter.
>
> After this we got into fours....I decided to try to convince Pete about my idea by saying if you get two bins and put boxes in A and compacting it and then putting more in. Then you just put non-compacted boxes in B. I think he agreed but still pressed on with his idea.
>
> After we had to make a poster. I settled to go along with Pete's idea (Children's Learning in Science Project, 1987: 44).

This extract, written after the lesson was over, raises many questions about the long-term effect of forced social constructions. One interpretation is to see Robert's acquiescence to Pete as no more than a social ritual demanded by greater authority or prestige. Some of the research on football gang behaviour (for example, Marsh, Rosser and Harré, 1978) would appear to support such a view. Moscovici (1976: 106) writes that 'in social influence, relations with others takes precedence over relations with objects.' This is especially important in the field of education, where the purpose of group discussion may be thought of as collective information-processing in which each contributes to make the total the sum of the parts. In social processes, where agreement has to be achieved in the face of both conflict and disagreement, no such additive result is possible: '. . . judgment is the establishment of agreement in the context of disagreement. Judgment is a type of negotiation' (Churchman, 1961: 293).

However, it is better to see the tension between social and personal constructions of knowledge, including the changes of opinion which seem to be forced by subservience to a stronger character, as a continuous and organically changing process. All kinds of situational cues affect our picture of reality; so long as no external orthodoxy obtrudes, each external signal or pressure can be considered simply as a part of the continuous learning and constructing process.

> Thus, throughout a conversation, speaker–hearers do not only 'speak' and 'hear', but they also construct a cumulative and idiosyncratic account of what has been going on. This construction . . . does not necessarily end when the talking stops and the conversers separate: it continues when participants reflect on what was said . . . But even this is not fixed: the reflective meaning is always open to change because of new information available, or new insights achieved by the speaker–hearer as he reflects on events that are past, or talks about them to others (Barnes and Todd, 1977: 100).

Discussion of Science-based Social Issues

During the last ten years or so a new field has emerged for the operation of social constructivism within the learning of science. In science, technology and society (STS) courses, or even in the odd lesson of this kind, there may be group discussions of science-based social issues. The requirements for this kind of discussion are probably more complex than either of the two we have explored so far. Almost all the categories Wallace identified, with the possible exception of (1), may be important. If the peer group discussion follows the viewing of a video excerpt, as in the present research of the Discussion of Issues in School Science (DISS) Project (Solomon, 1988), even category (5) may occur. Pupils often feel they have to describe to each other what they saw on the screen and how they reacted to it before they are ready to comment on its societal implications.

Topics such as providing kidneys for transplant operations or deciding on a national energy policy involve feelings, attitudes and evaluation as well as a sifting out of appropriate knowledge. All of these will be both facilitated and influenced by the social context of the small friendship group in which discussion takes place. It may even be that strategies will be suggested, at the culmination of the discussion, based on these values and knowledge. For many of us this progression — from elicitation of *personal values*, through consideration of *relevant knowledge* inputs to agreeing upon a *solution strategy* — is the expected outcome of any successful discussion of an STS issue.

Experience suggests that this may be an ambitious programme for informal discussion, especially if the topic is new to the participants. In such situations we would all need help in picturing how it might affect us or those near us before we could begin to feel our way into an evaluative response. In group discussion there will be both support from friends and the kind of minority influence from a strong character which was noted in the previous section. But there will also be a different and more tentative character to the talk if the participants are intent on putting into words their own value positions in a situation where they have not done this before.

David Bridges, in *Education, Democracy and Discussion* (1979), argues that there are four functions that discussion can provide in this evaluation process. All begin with a sharing of perspectives on the topic. With slight adjustments to his categories and the addition of a fifth and final stage we can arrive at the following list of possible and valuable outcomes in any discussion about values.

a   There are personal statements of differing value positions.
b   These lead to an understanding of alternative responses to a situation.
c   Some preferences between different views are expressed.
d   A cogent choice between alternatives leads to a sense of resolution.
e   From this consensus the group feels ready to suggest some action strategies.

Knowledge of various sorts is used in the presentation of different perspectives. Some of these may contribute in a significant way to the formation of a consensus. But it is the last stage, when the group begins to consider possible strategies for social action, that most clearly shows the need for new knowledge inputs. Now the pupils will need to reveal their picture of a social world of power and civic rights, and this is an area which reveals attitudes towards political forces in society at large. Lack of knowledge can induce a sense of powerlessness or disenfranchisement, which is followed by inaction. In group discussions this may be evinced by a comment like, 'We cannot know, we can never be sure.'

In this, the last of our tentative categories for the social influences on the construction of a scientific picture of the world, school pupils begin to move towards a citizen science. This might well be the paramount goal of all school learning, practical or theoretical, personal or social, but it is rarely presented as such. Group experimental work is unlikely to turn up in everyday life, and only university students and the attentive few who follow science seriously in the media will go on acquiring conceptual knowledge. But issues thrown up by new technologies are becoming a commonplace. When they touch us personally, possibly through the construction of a nearby motorway or some invasive medical treatment, discussion may become a vital mode of social learning. Once again, as at school, we shall explore our knowledge and our values through interchanges with friends and neighbours who have goals which are similar to our own.

References

ASHE, S. (1955) 'Opinions and social pressure', *Scientific American*, 193, pp. 31–5.

ASSESSMENT OF PERFORMANCE UNIT (APU) (1988) *Science at Age 15: A Review of APU Survey Findings 1980–84*, London, HMSO, Chs. 10–11.

BARNES, D. and TODD, F. (1977) *Communication and Learning in Small Groups*, London, Routledge and Kegan Paul.

BAXTER, M. (1988) 'Working in groups', in Open University Course PSEH545, *Physics for Science Teachers*, Block A: Issues in Science Teaching, Milton Keynes, The Open University, pp. 68–77.

BERGER, P. and LUCKMANN, T. (1967) *The Social Construction of Reality*, Harmondsworth, Penguin.

BRIDGES, D. (1979) *Education, Democracy and Discussion*, Windsor, NFER.

CHILDREN'S LEARNING IN SCIENCE PROJECT (1987) *Approaches to Teaching the Particulate Theory of Matter*, Centre for Studies in Science and Mathematics Education, University of Leeds.

CHURCHMAN, C. W. (1961) *Prediction and Optimal Decisions*, New York, Prentice Hall.

DEPARTMENT OF EDUCATION AND SCIENCE, (1989) *Science in the National Curriculum*, London, HMSO.

EDWARDS, D. and MERCER, N. (1987) *Common Knowledge*, London, Methuen.

GOFFMAN, E. (1959) *The Presentation of Self in Everyday Life*, Harmondsworth, Penguin.

GRAY, J. (1986) *Classroom Disruption and Social Skills*, Unpublished DPhil thesis, University of Oxford.

HARRÉ, R. (1979) *Social Being*, Oxford, Blackwell.

KENNEDY, J. (1984) *Some Aspects of Children's Ideas in Basic Circuit Electricity*, Unpublished MSc thesis, University of Oxford.

LATOUR, B. and WOOLGAR, S. (1979) *Laboratory Life: The Social Construction of Scientific Facts*, London, Sage Publications.

MARSH, P., ROSSER, E. and HARRÉ, R. (1978) *Rules of Disorder*, London, Routledge and Kegan Paul.

MOSCOVICI, S. (1976) *Social Influence and Social Change*, European Monographs in Social Psychology, London, Academic Press.

OSBORNE, R. (1981) 'Children's ideas about electric current', *New Zealand Science Teacher*, 29, pp. 12–19. (This work is also discussed in OSBORNE, R. and FREYBERG, P. (Eds) (1985) *Learning in Science: The Implications of Children's Science*, London, Heinemann, pp. 21–6.

SCHUTZ, A. and LUCKMANN, T. (1973) *Structures of the Life-World*, London, Heinemann.

SOLOMON, J. (1980) *Teaching Children in the Laboratory*, London, Croom Helm.

SOLOMON, J. (1984) 'Alternative frameworks and the epistemology of Jean Piaget', Paper presented at the British Educational Research Association Conference, University of Lancaster.

SOLOMON, J. (1985) 'Classroom discussion: A method of research for teachers?' *British Educational Research Journal*, 11, 2, pp. 153–62.

SOLOMON, J. (1987) 'Social influences on the construction of pupils' understanding of science', *Studies in Science Education*, 14, pp. 63–82.

SOLOMON, J. (1988) 'DISS — Discussion of Issues in School Science', *Education in Science*, 129, p. 18.

SOLOMON, J. and the STIR group (1989) 'A study of behaviour in the teaching laboratory', *International Journal of Science Education*, in press.

WALLACE, J. (1986) *Social Interaction within Second Year Groups Doing Practical Science*, Unpublished MSc thesis, University of Oxford.

Chapter 7

Writing and Reading in Science: The Hidden Messages

Clive Sutton

It seems to me that pupils in school quickly develop expectations about what a normal piece of writing in science is like. They sense intangible rules about what can be said, and what is allowable in the way you say it. Since such rules or conventions have been imbibed by generations of learners, they also affect us as teachers. For instance, the phrase, 'It seems to me that . . .', is rather rare in the books and papers found around a school laboratory. Some internal censor screens it out. I almost feel that I should apologize for using it, but I am going to break other rules as well, and I hope that the contrast created by doing so will sharpen our awareness of what these rules are. Then we can discuss their functions, their value and their limitations.

If this chapter were a scientific report, I would probably start by listing forty or so of the textbooks and pupils' notebooks which I have surveyed, explain how they were selected and then describe some features they exhibit. That would lead to conclusions about them, and I would take great care to show that those conclusions are firmly based upon empirical evidence. Anyone who is going to be a scientist must learn that style, but since this chapter is mainly about possible unintended effects of its routine use in schools, I will write in a different way, exploring possibilities, trying out a point of view, arguing a case. This way is much less certain, *pre*-scientific perhaps. It is less formal, more personal than would be accepted in many academic contexts. Please bear with me if it seems too 'familiar'. I shall also set out tentative conclusions near the beginning, and then try to support them — the opposite of the system encouraged in school science. Overall, the case I wish to make is that some of our major traditions in writing and reading support images of science that differ markedly from those which teachers claim or hope to convey.

Science as 'Describing What Happens'

Let me begin by deliberately overstating the case, in a generalization to which there are bound to be exceptions. I believe that there was a *de facto* consensus about how pupils should write in science, which was dominant for nearly a century, up to about 1960. It was linked with widely held views about the nature of science and with a partial agreement about the major purposes of science education, and it was entirely to do with writing about practical work. Other writing seemed to be unproblematic, a matter of notes, or stocks of information, and not something that required a policy, but for writing about practical work teachers did have policies.

The consensus recognized at least four components in a report of laboratory work:

(AIM) METHOD RESULTS (CONCLUSIONS)
(or PROCEDURE)
with DIAGRAM

The middle two of these loomed largest in the experience of many pupils. 'Aim' was often reduced to a title, and decided directly or indirectly by the teacher, and therefore quickly passed over. 'Conclusions' were a source of worry, even to the point where some teachers felt they had to resort to a dictated conclusion. 'Method', however, appeared to be much safer ground, a manageable task for everyone. It was sometimes outlined on the board or a worksheet, but of all the four components this was the one most likely to be the pupil's own composition, and to consume his or her time. Some pupils probably found security in writing it carefully, and getting the teacher's commendation for doing so. Similarly for 'Results' the task seemed clear, and pupils were encouraged by such phrases as 'Just write down what you see', 'Say what happened', 'Put the figures in the table' and 'Make sure you get some readings down — borrow your neighbour's if necessary'.

If I am right, some may have been left with an impression that science is essentially doing things and 'describing what happens'. You have to describe what you are told to do, and then you have a section called 'Results' where you describe what happened (or what should have happened). Of course, the most sophisticated pupils would see more in each lesson, especially after a sequence of linked lessons. Here I am just trying to evoke the image remaining for those who experienced the lessons but took away only the loudest message.

This impression of science elevates *doing* above *thinking*, especially above *thinking beforehand*. It also implies that results emerge automatically as long as you are not clumsy, and that somewhere there exists a set of *the* results, known to your neighbour who is 'good at science' and to the teacher.

The downgrading of thinking was not intended; teachers have generally regarded the aim or purpose of any laboratory work as the starting point for it. To a pupil, however, the reason for doing anything is easily read as 'Teacher says' or 'It's on the syllabus', and so there is little need to enter into preliminary reasoning. If the teacher lets you get on with the procedures, you do so, and you may not see those procedures as a test of previous thoughts.

Looking into the origins of this pattern of writing, I searched out some examples of advice about it given by teachers in earlier decades, and it is very interesting to see the variation in the flexibility allowed, and in how much emphasis is placed on the preliminary statement of ideas. One extreme may be represented by C. B. Owen of Stowe School in his *Methods for Science Masters* (1956). He offered the mnemonic: High Powered Motors Often Crash, to trigger recall of the need for Heading, Picture, Method, Observations and Conclusion. As a reminder of what makes an acceptable diagram he offered A L C O H O L — Accurate, Large, Clear, Own work, Hair line, One plane and Labelled. He also recommended that 'I' and 'We' should be avoided in accounts, but 'initials such as C.B.O. or V.L.G. are good' — because you can attribute the observation to someone (yourself seen as a third person perhaps?).

Many other patterns of headings have been tried. For example, MacNair (1904) suggested: 'The Object Aimed at', 'What Was Done', 'What Was Seen' and 'What the Result Proved'. The word 'prove' appeared in the titles of many practical experiences in physics up to the 1960s. Kerr's survey of school practical work in 1963 indicated that over 60 per cent of such lessons were concerned with 'verification' of facts or principles. Later there were changes in spirit (or in fashion?) over titles, and 'To investigate how . . .' replaced 'To prove that . . .'. There may also have been an influence from falsificationist philosophy of science which made the word 'verify' unacceptable. Nevertheless, the emotional tone of these older words, 'prove' and 'verify', is important. It communicated the solidity and reliability of scientific knowledge. You could feel that you were describing real facts.

F. W. Westaway (1929) favoured the past tense for describing, but he did not like the passive voice, whereas Newbury (1934) recommended the passive voice 'because it is used in the chemical literature'. He seems to have had a clear idea that the major objective of chemistry teaching was apprenticeship to future chemical laboratories.

A. G. Hughes (1933) advocated the headings, 'Purpose', 'Apparatus', 'Observation', 'Inference', but described a system of three columns on the page as too rigid, even with more child-centred headings such as 'What I Did', 'What I Saw' and 'What I Learned'. He stressed the importance of discussion before practical work to clarify its purpose, and his book gives many ideas about how writing can aid thinking, and how a notebook can become a prized personal possession.

For an outstandingly distinct set of opinions we can go back to H. E. Armstrong before the turn of the century. Writing in 1898, he was characteristically uncompromising in his views about writing. Pupils must write as they go along, and not 'pretty up' the work later, and the writing should be personal to them. In comparison with the others that I have quoted he demanded more from the young investigators at the beginnings and the ends of each episode of inquiry. They should begin with a statement of 'Motive' for what they planned to do, and then 'Justify' the form of the investigation. Only after that would they come to making an exact account of observations made and results obtained, and they should end with a discussion of 'How These Results Bear on the Original Question', and what could be done in 'The Next Stage of the Investigation'.

Armstrong's advice was intended to raise the importance of *ideas* in the learner's experience of investigation. In his scheme practical work is intimately linked with thought, before, during and after the bench activity. The image of science is investigational and cyclical. It involves having ideas, planning and carrying out tests of them, and so developing successive refinements of the ideas. His description of practical enquiry re-emerged in the teachers' guides of the Nuffield O level chemistry course in the 1960s, and soon most science teachers of that period claimed to be teaching an investigational kind of science. Pupils would be engaged in cycles of enquiry, even if strongly 'guided' by the teacher. Leaders of the curriculum teams were themselves skilled in engaging youngsters in a process of collaborative enquiry, but in other classrooms the dominance of doing over thinking was consolidated because there was a lot more laboratory work to get through. In a crowded timetable discussion beforehand might be sacrificed, and one suspects that the essence of the session became 'do what the teacher says, and come to the expected conclusions'.

I believe that the tension between wanting learners to think, to plan and to write about their ideas on the one hand, and yet making them follow instructions on the other, has not yet been resolved, and I shall return to this in a later section about the most recent teaching schemes.

Science as 'Data First and Theory Later'

If we examine the history of science rather than just that of science teaching, we can see that scientists themselves often appear to downgrade the importance of ideas. There is a long tradition of trying to separate one kind of statement from another: 'observations' from 'interpretations', evidence from conclusions, facts from speculations and mere opinions. Newer epistemologies reveal problems in maintaining such strict distinctions, especially between observation and interpretation, yet much effort in science and science teaching has been motivated by an unquestioning belief in the possibility and value of doing so. How did that come about?

In this section I want to survey the rise of an idea which may reinforce the picture of science as 'describing what happens' rather than 'testing ideas'. I am calling it 'data first and theory later', using the word 'first' in two senses, of priority and timing. It includes the notion that data are more important, and much more trustworthy, than theorizing, and that they properly come earlier in time.

We find this idea as an active influence in the seventeenth century, when many of the leaders in what was then called natural philosophy had strong convictions about observing the real world — a desire to reject mere argumentation as a source of new knowledge, and a belief that you could refer to nature instead. Would there have been any science without such a simple faith? Descriptive, factual, 'this is what happens' accounts excited the early experimentalists (and continue to excite us). They took (and we still take) a pride in basing ideas on what you can find in nature. By joining the ranks of science you can feel that you are a practical person, basing your knowledge on empirical experience. Your statements about nature will be statements about real things, and not just flights of fancy. I am not at this point concerned with the correctness or otherwise of such views; I just want to evoke the feeling that goes with them.

By the mid-1600s that attitude to firm knowledge was also associated with a style of language oriented towards things and their description rather than to theoretical disputation.[1] The notebook that you would keep yourself and the paper that you might send to a learned society gradually became objects of pride for anyone with aspirations in science. Both would need to exhibit standards of accuracy, reliability and repeatability, and their importance probably helped to focus attention on the *recording of data* as what scientists do (rather than, say, *musing in a study*).

The importance of recording defensible data led eventually to systems for training people how to write them down. A particularly interesting one dates from the nineteenth century, and that is the notebook format for a record of qualitative chemical analysis (see Brock, 1967). It had three columns, headed 'Test(s)', 'Observation(s)' and 'Inference(s)'. What ideas about science do we get from this system? Data are carefully recorded, theorizing is held back in a disciplined way until the data has been put down. But that is not really how it is done. No thinking analyst would work in that way only, and there should at least be another column at the left headed 'Possibilities', 'Ideas' or 'Hunches', and then the choice of a 'test' would make sense. If I have a dry white powder and think 'Hmm — might be a carbonate, and not of a transition metal', then it makes sense to carry out tests with dilute hydochloric acid, and to miss various other tests. Otherwise I do not investigate, I just follow the tables mechanically, doing every test regardless of its likely relevance, relying on the algorithm of the system to tell me what ions are present. Possibly the fact that analysis can be rendered in this algorithmic manner may have encouraged the view that scientific enquiry in general consists in following a set of rules to elicit discoveries.

'Test, Observation, Inference' offers a view of science which is long out-of-date amongst philosophers, sociologists and historians of science, and it should be amongst teachers. It suggests that preliminary thoughts are not needed, which is particularly wrong when trying to identify a substance. A hypothetico–deductive view of science would require the addition of a first column, or an opening section headed 'First Ideas and Reasons for Them'. But then, the system was not intended to give a view of science at all. It was simply a training or apprenticeship in one small part of science.

The Value of 'Data First' When Training Young Scientists

The columns do not tell the whole story of how an intelligent analyst solved a particular problem, but they do provide *defensible evidence for conclusions*. If you are learning to be a scientist, the presentation of evidence to a critical public is an important part of your craft, and so the system is appropriate where the purpose of science education is apprenticeship. By using it, *one part* of what is good practice in science can be learned.[2]

When science education is primarily a training for future scientists, then learning to present evidence in the style of a scientific paper also has a prima facie validity. In the early 1960s Sir Peter Medawar (1963) made an amusing analysis of the standardized structure of these papers, and posed the question: 'Is the scientific paper a fraud?'; that is, does it misrepresent the thought that led to what the author is describing? He argued that it does. It parades the experimental procedures and the presentation of data before discussion of their significance in a way that hides the preliminary thoughts, conjectures and hopes that the experimenter probably had. One reason is that the authors of a scientific paper are not trying to tell the whole story of their thought. They are preoccupied with 'the context of justification', rather than the 'context of discovery'. They are trying to set out an unassailable case that centres on the data. In Medawar's own terms they describe the 'checkwork' rather than giving the wider picture of 'guesswork and checkwork'. Defenders of the existing format argue that the rather peculiar conventions of a modern scientific paper are well adapted to these limited purposes.

This raises problems in wider education, where there is a need for a fuller story, both about the thoughts that scientists had, and about the thoughts that the learner has. It may not matter in the research world if the whole story is not told in a journal report, but *in school* the suppression of first thoughts, conjectures, preliminary beliefs, hopes or reasons for doing an experiment could be both a misrepresentation of science and an interruption in the development of the learner's own thought.

Problems Caused by Suppressing the Observer

Trying to separate facts from ideas is linked with efforts to separate the fallible observer as well, and with a gradual suppression of 'I' in the reporting. If the data will 'speak for themselves', then the writer can hold back from personal involvements such as 'It seems to me that...'or 'I think...'or 'I wonder if...'. Although scientific accounts in earlier centuries were not markedly depersonalized, the ambition to make them factual reports independent of the observer has always been powerful, and is probably responsible for the growth of the third person style which implies detachment. The relegation of the discussion of ideas to the *end* is a further way of holding back the person.

All this fits some very early ideas of the nature of science: observe the world, collect observations, think about them, see the patterns in them, build more general laws and theories. The thinking comes mainly after the looking and doing. This view is no longer accepted in science studies, but it still has a powerful emotional appeal for scientists and teachers.[3]

The most extreme examples of this view are found in certain curriculum schemes which make a great fuss of separating observation statements from inferential statements. For example, the two schemes *Warwick Process Science* (Screen, 1986) and *Science in Process* (Wray *et al.*, 1987) both ask pupils to practice 'observation' separately from 'inferring'. To see some of the effects of trying to maintain that distinction I have selected a detailed account from an older source, but a version of this same activity with a candle was published in the Warwick scheme in 1986 (see Figure 7.1).

The passage in Figure 7.1 is taken from a prestigious American chemistry course of the 1960s. Learners were asked to observe and describe the candle, and then to compare their own accounts with this one by an experienced scientist. The superscript numbers in the text are intended to indicate the separate and distinct points remarked upon, and the editor's commentary on certain features of the account is given in the bottom right-hand corner. Point 4 of that list is particularly important to the present discussion, indicating the attempt to separate 'observations' from any kind of inferential statement, interpretation, theory, opinion or judgment of significance.[4]

We all want our students to be accurate and reliable reporters of what they notice, and I have myself used the extract many times to teach about the use of different senses and the opportunities for semi-quantitative estimates. Once one gets into the spirit of it, writing a description like this can be fun — especially for the articulate (usually male) leaders in the game of 'I can show you an even better list'. But in terms of teaching strategy I no longer accept the example. The images of science it projects, both in an emotional sense and in terms of philosophy of science, are far from those which I now hold.

Let's take the emotional images first. Some of my pupils, and also adult

A drawing of a burning candle is shown[1] in Figure A1-1. The candle is cylindrical in shape[2] and has a diameter[3] of about ¾ inch. The length of the candle was initially about eight inches[4] and it changed slowly[5] during observation, decreasing about half an inch in one hour[6]. The candle is made of a translucent[7], white[8] solid[9] which has a slight odor[10] and no taste[11]. It is soft enough to be scratched with the fingernail[12]. There is a wick[13] which extends from top to bottom[14] of the candle along its central axis[15] and protrudes about half an inch above the top of the candle[16]. The wick is made of three strands of string braided together[17].

A candle is lit by holding a source of flame close to the wick for a few seconds. Thereafter the source of flame can be removed and the flame sustains itself at the wick[18]. The burning candle makes no sound[19]. While burning, the body of the candle remains cool to the touch[20] except near the top. Within about half an inch from the top the candle is warm[21] (but not hot) and sufficiently soft to mold easily[22]. The flame flickers in response to air currents[23] and tends to become quite smoky while flickering[24]. In the absence of air currents, the flame is of the form shown in Figure A1-1, though it retains some movement at all times[25]. The flame begins about ⅛ inch above the top of the candle[26] and at its base the flame has a blue tint[27]. Immediately around the wick in a region about ¼ inch wide and extending about ½ inch above the top of the wick[28] the flame is dark[29]. This dark region is roughly conical in shape[30]. Around this zone and extending about half an inch above the dark zone is a region which emits yellow light[31], bright but not blinding[32]. The flame has rather sharply defined sides[33], but a ragged top[34]. The wick is white where it emerges from the candle[35], but from the base of the flame to the end of the wick[36] it is black, appearing burnt, except for the last 1/16 inch where it glows red[37]. The wick curls over about ¼ inch from its end[38]. As the candle becomes shorter, the wick shortens too, so as to extend roughly a constant length above the top of the candle[39]. Heat is emitted by the flame[40], enough so that it becomes uncomfortable in ten or twenty seconds if one holds his finger ¼ inch to the side of the quiet flame[41] or three or four inches above the flame[42].

The top of a quietly burning candle becomes wet with a colorless liquid[43] and becomes bowl shaped[44]. If the flame is blown, one side of this bowl-shaped top may become liquid, and the liquid trapped in the bowl may drain down the candle's side[45]. As it courses down, the colorless liquid cools[46], becomes translucent[47], and gradually solidifies from the outside[48], attaching itself to the side of the candle[49]. In the absence of a draft, the candle can burn for hours without such dripping[50]. Under these conditions, a stable pool of clear liquid remains in the bowl-shaped top of the candle[51]. The liquid rises slightly around the wick[52], wetting the base of the wick as high as the base of the flame[53].

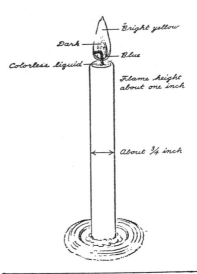

Several aspects of this description deserve specific mention. Compare your own description in each of the following characteristics.

(1) The description is comprehensive in *qualitative* terms. Did *you* include mention of appearance? smell? taste? feel? sound? (Note: A chemist quickly becomes reluctant to taste or smell an unknown chemical. A chemical should be considered to be poisonous unless it is *known* not to be!)

(2) Wherever possible, the description is stated *quantitatively*. This means the question "How much?" is answered (the quantity is specified). The remark that the flame emits yellow light is made more meaningful by the "how much" expression, "bright but not blinding." The statement that heat is emitted might lead a cautious investigator who is lighting a candle for the first time to stand in a concrete blockhouse one hundred yards away. The few words telling him "how much" heat would save him this overprecaution.

(3) The description does not presume the importance of an observation. Thus the observation that a burning candle does not emit sound deserves to be mentioned just as much as the observation that it does emit light.

(4) The description does not confuse observations with interpretations. It is an observation that the top of the burning candle is wet with a colorless liquid. It would be an interpretation to state the presumed composition of this liquid.

Figure 7.1
A scientist describes . . .

Description of a burning candle, presented as a model of how to describe, with editor's commentary on certain features. From George C. Pimentel (Ed.) (1963) *Chemistry, an Experimental Science.*

students, have been markedly inhibited by the scientist's account. Younger children can generate long lists of things they notice, in a quite unself-conscious manner, but for those beyond the age of 12 an encounter with the model description signals inadequacy to some of them. They feel that they have missed too much, or they are repelled by its coldness, or they sense a set of rules that are too tight for them. 'If that's what you've got to do, then I'm not going to be much good at it, am I?' The rules *are* very tight, and distinctly unaccepting of any personal foibles, or of the humour of adolescent learners, or indeed of any personal aspect of knowing or thinking. Was it written by a person, or a Nuspeak Robot: 'The kandel . . . is . . . cylin . . dri . . cal . . . in shape'?

As well as the features which the authors point out, the following further rules might be felt to apply:

1   Do not use I, we or you, but write in the third person, and when you start a sentence, refer to things rather than to yourself.
2   Use the passive voice; 'a drawing is shown' will avoid the embarrassment of having to say 'I have shown a drawing'; 'a candle is lit . . .' will save you from saying 'I can light the candle . . .'; and 'heat is emitted by the flame' will be better than 'the flame gives out heat'.
3   Do not express your thoughts about all this; observing does not need thoughts, but just a keen eye; thoughts come later.

As a model to place before beginners, the whole account is pedantic and too clever by half. It leaves an image of science quite lacking in person-appeal. Of course, there *was* a human author behind it, but he (am I correct in thinking it was a he?) has held himself so far out of sight that it is almost as if a machine had written. I believe that he hid himself for highly laudable reasons, in the name of detachment and objectivity, and to demonstrate the care that a scientist might take in attending to detail, and trying to make an unbiased record. I do not quarrel with those purposes, but it seems a mistake to equate 'objective' with 'non-personal'. A valuable message is swamped by other unintended messages.

In relation to the epistemological aspects of the account, it is a pretence that 'all' things are noticed, and that theoretical ideas can then be derived from these jottings. The writer did not really notice a set of disconnected facts: the solid wax, the shape, the colour of the wick, etc. Being a good chemist, he already had clear theoretical ideas about its mechanism. He 'saw' it working and so was able to select many important points. Notice how his eye scanned the pool of liquid which 'rises slightly around the wick, wetting the base of the wick as high as the base of the flame'. Once you have seen or guessed that the wick is a fuel pipe you can more easily see the flow of liquid towards and then up the wick, a constant current of further fuel to feed the flame.

Personally I could give many different accounts of a candle, all strongly influenced by scientific theories that I have. The modern theoretical 'spectacles' through which the candle can be seen were formed by chemists from Lavoisier onwards, and were brilliantly used by Michael Faraday in his *Chemical History of a Candle* in 1860–61. All modern accounts would draw, directly or indirectly, on Faraday's, but I want to put some parts of them in my own words to make a strong contrast with the allegedly 'pure' description quoted.

I might choose to focus upon the flame as a reaction zone — hot wax vapour on the inside, air on the outside, churning together at the junction. In my mind's eye I visualize molecules of oxygen and molecules of hydrocarbon colliding, breaking, reassembling as carbon dioxide and water with quite a bit of carbon left over. Even without looking up Faraday's demonstrations, I know how I could collect wax vapour from the interior of the flame, and carbon dioxide or water from above it. The yellowness at the top of the flame I see as a glow from thousands of hot particles, and again I could collect them. My theoretical knowledge and what I notice in the ragged top of the flame are closely interrelated.

At a simpler level I see a candle is an ingenious device, an 'engine' if you like, that not only generates light, but is so constructed that it can turn solid fuel into liquid continuously, pipe it upwards in a wick and vaporize it ready for burning. The hot flame is hot enough to melt some of the wax below it, but not so hot as to reduce the stock of wax to an unmanageable puddle.

I see many lamps and stoves as basically flames sitting on top of a fuel supply. If the fuel is gaseous, as in my propane camping light, you just turn the tap and gas emerges at the top ready to burn. In a Primus stove the fuel is a liquid in the tank below, and it has to be pre-heated before you can ignite it — a procedure which has defeated many of us in getting such a stove going, but which is self-sustaining once you establish the system. A solid fuel might well cause bigger problems, and you certainly cannot ignite a lump of wax directly. In a candle the problem is solved using waste heat from the flame to 'ready' the fuel. A cleverly designed wick allows it to flow up at a suitable rate, and someone has also found a way to make the wick curl over at the top and slowly self-destruct in the hottest part of the flame. That stops us being left with a dirty and drippy piece of string to collapse into the mechanism and muck it up. Altogether the candle is a technological masterpiece, no doubt socially and economically well adapted to the times of its invention, and still quite serviceable and important to us today.

In all these accounts I have mixed together quite highly 'theoretical' statements, such as those about molecules, with rather less theoretical ones, and with 'technological' statements about problems human beings have faced. Do I have to apologize for doing so? Each kind of idea informs and enriches the others, and at the level of learning about and appreciating any new topic I want to retain the mixture.

From a teaching point of view the candle offers access to important *ideas*, to *ways of seeing*, not just 'seeing'. These ideas include appreciation of changes of state and perhaps of the kinetic theory as an interpretation of them, i.e., there are two levels of concepts in what we might call pure science. There is also a close link with applications and uses and human problems, so to me the candle is also an inexpensive piece of kit that introduces the connections of science with technology. I visualize a study unit in which pupils might be asked to design a lamp for some other fuel such as animal fat or sunflower oil, so that they may come to *feel* how scientific concepts have been needed in the improvement of even the most basic devices of our civilization. If the appreciation of these points is to strike home, they will have to be taught some theory. It will not be enough to give them a challenge to 'observe' something. We shall need to educate their eyes. Observations are theory-laden. To notice key points about the candle, you have to link them and to see, not a set of unconnected observations, but the possibility of a whole mechanism.[5]

Failure of the Traditions

I have dwelt at some length on this example of observing and the observer because it links past traditions with present problems, and the observing game has emerged again in the 1980s, in the UK at least, as part of some people's hopes for getting children to 'be scientific'.

In the 1960s and early 1970s British science teachers encountered many changes associated with the formation of comprehensive schools and the extension of secondary education to the whole population. In retrospect we can see that the long-established traditions would be unlikely to match the whole of this new task, not only because some of the new clientele might not cope with sophisticated writing, but also because of the heavy dependence on forms designed for future scientists. Adaptation was only gradual, and it included many attempts to carry over to the new school population the experiences that had been developed for the smaller, academically select, group. When teachers encountered mixed ability groups, one change was a move away from whole class teaching and an increase in the use of prepared worksheets so that subgroups could get on at their own pace. Many worksheets of that period were essentially guides for what to do, supplemented with questions. They reinforced the image of science already mentioned, about doing what you are told and describing what happens. Few of them required the pupils to engage in discussion *before* practical work, or to commit themselves to any extended statement of purposes.

More recently, however, some curriculum projects have explored a wider range of writing activities in the classroom, some which *do* involve learners to clarify ideas, and also some which cater more effectively for pupils at different levels of attainment. In a case study entitled 'How We See Things' Crookes *et al*. (1985) described a series of lessons based on their 'idea-testing' view of science. Pupils were required to commit themselves to paper about their existing understanding of illumination and vision, and then the ideas of the class were pooled and used as the basis for discussing what experimental evidence would distinguish between these ideas. In the teaching approaches outlined by the Children's Learning in Science project (Needham and Hill, 1987) provision is made for structured discussion about ideas in pupil committees and presentation to the rest of the class using posters. The Teachers' Resource Pack of *Science in Process* (Wray *et al.*, 1987) gives ideas for more varied writing tasks, and draws a distinction between 'presenting' ideas to various audiences and 'recording' in something like the traditional manner. Possibly the variety of different forms of 'presenting' might ultimately give an idea of science as an activity that involves clarifying and communicating thoughts.

However, old assumptions do not die easily. Teachers may not be drilling pupils in the use of headings, crossing out 'I' and 'We', or *forbidding* 11-year-olds to venture an opinion about what they do. But it seems that we do guide pupils gradually in that direction, so that certain kinds of statement are quickly eliminated from written accounts. Humour, pleasure, concern about the value or importance of the ideas they encounter, personal feeling of any kind and speculative musing are soon excluded from repertoire of permissible expression in the science book. Dobson (1986) suggests a simple enquiry on this point which any teacher could carry out in their own school.

There are many conflicting influences on teachers in the early years of secondary schooling, even assuming that the basic problems of organizing activities in a mixed ability class have been solved. One is the ideal of scientific detachment to which I have already referred. Is there any science teacher who is not influenced by the feeling that school science should include a training in how to write a dispassionate, accurate account of things? Some image of a reliable account guides the way we influence our pupils, and it is an image containing less opinion and conjecture and more factual, reproducible description. Running partly counter to that influence is the desire to engage pupils in active thinking for themselves: say what you see; write down your ideas and thoughts. Encouragement of 'we did' and 'I thought' probably comes more from that pressure than from a view of science. It is largely a matter of tactics, a signal that the teacher concerned is at least moderately child-centred with youngsters. 'What We Did', 'What We Found Out', 'What We Thought' are headings that try to combine the personal involvement and the detachment, but the notion that the impersonal report is nearer the ideal in science has seldom been fundamentally questioned.

Reading Material to Support Alternative Images

The main missing ingredients in the popular image of science picked up from classroom experience are those outlined in the section on 'seeing' the candle: science is about *ideas* and *theories*, as well as *actions*; and these ideas are made by people. If these features could be more adequately felt by school pupils, their own personal involvement in starting to possess and rework the ideas would probably follow easily. The alienation of learner from knowledge that can develop when that knowledge is treated just as 'information' would diminish, and the personal, social and technological relevance would be accepted into the learning process where it belongs, and not relegated to a sort of luxury or frill quite outside the understanding of the concepts themselves.

It is unlikely that classroom techniques such as a greater use of discussion in committees will be sufficient by themselves to provide a feeling for the personal nature of scientific knowledge, when it is absent from so much of what pupils read. Models or exemplars are needed that show the personalization in action — writings by scientists and perhaps by other learners. To explore this idea I present a couple of historical examples in Figures 7.2 and 7.3.

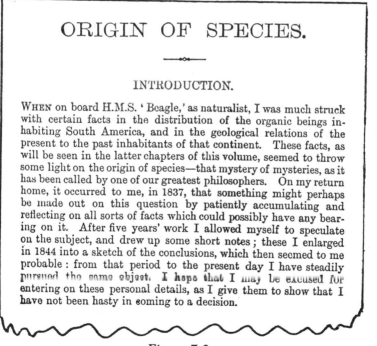

Figure 7.2
Darwin (1859) 'hopes he may be excused . . .

. . . for entering on these personal details', but demonstrates the full interaction of himself, his ideas and the evidence he presents — the opening sentences from the preface to the *The Origin of Species*.

Figure 7.2 shows the introductory paragraph from *The Origin of Species*. Darwin's writing in this book never suffers from that separation of person and ideas to which I have referred, and we see this from his very first sentences. At every stage it is clear that the writer is a real person, putting forward certain propositions or ideas, inviting consideration of the evidence and weighing the evidence himself. Throughout the book, and not just in the Preface, the discussion is personal in a much fuller sense than the mechanics of using 'I' and 'We'. He never tries to hide himself or his own thoughts, but stays very close to his own knowledge-claims. There is something very dignified, but a little sad, in his plea to be 'excused for entering on these personal details', responding perhaps to the popular belief that such things are not relevant.

Darwin was, nevertheless, a stickler for knowing when he was dealing with evidence and when with speculations, and certainly he was never 'hasty in coming to a decision'. He marshals an immense amount of evidence, and always signals its difference from what he knows to be speculative. The ability to do this is an important part of the system for defending ideas in science, and the thing that mostly marks *The Origin of Species* as a book of science rather than of general literature is that it is a *defence* of ideas by means of factual evidence. Ideas and evidence are clearly distinguished, but they are also held together in an active dialogue.

Using the accepted language of the day for a post hoc explanation of this disciplined distinction, he pretends that one activity preceded the other — patient accumulation of facts until 'after five years I allowed myself to speculate'. That is not quite true, because his notebooks show an active speculation from a much earlier stage, but it was important to him as a way of saying that his claims would not be mere speculations, but grounded in knowledge of the real world. Overall, the image in this work is of one particular scientist: humane, personal, cautious, with the constant habit of working on ideas that concern him greatly and with a strong sense of discipline about evidence and the danger of leaping to conclusions too soon.

Figure 7.3 is from Lavoisier's major work in which he began to systematize chemistry as we know it (1789). In this passage he sets out to explain how he believes all substances can change their state from solid to liquid to gas ('elastic aeriform vapour' is the term he uses; the word 'gas' had not then come into general use).

He debates with himself and with the reader what might be happening to separate the particles of something as it gets warmer. What exactly is heat, and how shall we talk about different degrees of hotness? Shall we admit the idea of heat as a sort of subtle lubricant between the particles of things, overcoming their attractions one to another, and perhaps actually repelling them from each other? Shall we call it 'hotness-stuff' or 'matter of heat' or 'igneous fluid' or something like that? No, let's give it a new name: 'caloric', then we shall not confuse it with real substances (weighable substances) if it turns out to be hypothetical and not actually there at all. The

The fame may be affirmed of all bodies in nature: They are either folid or liquid, or in the ftate of elaftic aëriform vapour, according to the proportion which takes place between the attractive force inherent in their particles, and the repulfive power of the heat acting upon thefe; or, what amounts to the fame thing, in proportion to the degree of heat to which they are expofed.

It is difficult to comprehend thefe phenomena, without admitting them as the effects of a real and material fubftance, or very fubtile fluid, which, infinuating itfelf between the particles of bodies, feparates them from each other; and, even allowing the exiftence of this fluid to be hypothetical, we fhall fee in the fequel, that it explains the phenomena of nature in a very fatisfactory manner.

This fubftance, whatever it is, being the caufe of heat, or, in other words, the fenfation which we call *warmth* being caufed by the accumulation of this fubftance, we cannot, in ftrict language, diftinguifh it by the term *heat;* becaufe the fame name would then very improperly exprefs both caufe and effect. For this reafon, in the memoir which I publifhed in 1777 *, I gave it the names of *igneous fluid* and *matter of heat:* And, fince that time, in the work † publifhed by Mr de Morveau, Mr Berthollet, Mr de Fourcroy, and myfelf, upon the reformation of chemical nomenclature, we thought it neceffary to banifh all periphraftic expreffions, which both lengthen phyfical language, and render it more tedious and lefs diftinct, and which even frequently does not convey fufficiently juft ideas of the fubject intended. Wherefore, we have diftinguifhed the caufe of heat, or that exquifitely elaftic fluid which produces it, by the term of *caloric.* Befides, that this expreffion fulfils our object in the fyftem which we have adopted, it poffeffes this farther advantage, that it accords with every fpecies of opinion, fince, ftrictly fpeaking, we are not obliged to fuppofe this to be a real fubftance

Figure 7.3
Lavoisier Debates With Himfelf

. . . how to explain the nature of heat and its effects in causing changes of state. From the *Traité Elementaire de Chimie* (1789), English translation by Robert Kerr.

151

debate is all the more poignant in that the theory he is developing proved dominant for a time, and is still usable today in calculations of 'heat transfer', but it was ultimately rejected when changes of state were adequately explained within a general kinetic theory of matter. I am arguing here not just for the caloric theory to be taught as an example of a provisional, transitional and temporarily useful theory, but for *the mental struggle to formulate it* to be seen as a human effort.

Extracts such as those in Figures 7.2 and 7.3 are not intended as 'illustrations from history' of the kind found in some textbooks. In selecting them I was looking for passages to help a reader to enter imaginatively into the world of the author and to *feel the problem*, not just to find out the answers as understood today. If we want the popular image of science to include that kind of appreciation, then materials capable of generating it will have to gain a much more prominent place in school. They will need to be a main focus of attention and to occupy time in classrooms, so that 'doing science' is felt to include working on the interpretation of an author's words and thoughts.[6] For the most part, when people have tried to include such material in textbooks, it always appears as an adjunct to the main task. We need another kind of book: something like *Scientists and Learners Thinking Aloud*.

Strengths and Limitations of the Traditional Textbook

To clarify this point, let me now consider what textbooks are, what they are good at and the features that prevent them from accommodating uncertainty. Textbooks concentrate on presenting answers and solutions, not problems. They set out the main theories as held now, the meanings of technical terms as we understand them now and the information that can be taken as fact to confirm this way of looking at things. They are not well-suited to exciting in their readers a sympathetic appreciation of the mental struggles that were involved in formulating ideas; indeed, part of the purpose of a textbook is to help a new generation to avoid those struggles, and to come quickly to a position of taking the established ideas for granted.

Especially when there have been great theoretical advances in a subject, the main purpose of a textbook is to define the fields anew, and to determine what shall count as part of it. It maps the area of knowledge, and shows how the various concepts interconnect. Kuhn (1970, 1977) has argued that textbook writers are so intent on presenting the current map of the field that they frequently ignore or misrepresent the meanings of their predecessors' statements, or quote selectively so that it seems as if the route to our present ways of thinking was an accumulation of happy discoveries overcoming earlier errors. Textbooks as he describes them re-write history; they bypass some of the preoccupations of earlier generations, and portray the growth of scientific knowledge as a success story of progress on progress.[7]

They make invisible the revolutions in thought that led to our present ways of seeing things, largely because they change the meanings of key terms. That in turn makes it appear that scientific knowledge is simply a set of 'discoveries' ('un-coverings'), rather than the product of mental effort. To change the metaphor from mapping to building, textbook writers set up a structure of thought; they build afresh, somewhat regardless of what previously occupied the site. Like some real builders, they may use bits of the previous structures that fit conveniently into the new edifice and claim that this shows that they have maintained continuity with the past.

From their nature, we can see what textbooks are good at. They are good when you want to get to grips with the current structure quickly. In a sense anyone picking up a textbook is offering himself or herself for indoctrination into the existing theoretical structure. Textbooks are at their best for learners who have already acquiesced in the current paradigm; they have some idea of its form, and wish to gain a fuller command of it. Because the organization of a textbook is related to the logic of the subject, it is invaluable for a reader who is seeking those linkages; it is much more than a list of information, more of an expression of the language that he or she is trying to learn.

But what proportion of school pupils does that represent? It obviously includes those who aspire to become scientists, once they have arrived at a particular state of readiness, which might be within days of entry to secondary school, or after years! It surely also includes a section of the wider public too, again at the points of needing and wanting to know. To other readers textbooks seem to be just stores of facts, and their dominance in people's experience at school leaves an image of science as just a lot of information. If that impression is to be overcome, books that inform will need to be supplemented by other books whose function is to inspire, provoke, amuse or persuade in relation to scientific topics.

The history of didactic books about science is interesting. 'Catechisms' of science and then 'conversations' on science from the very early part of the nineteenth century show some of the didactic features mentioned above. Later that century textbooks as we know them triumphed over other types of book, at least in the school and college context. These books achieved a fully dominant position in the period when school science essentially meant grammar school science. Lynch and Strube (1983, 1985) argue that their general form has changed little in this century, and that when publishers use sophisticated illustrations and page layouts, or more 'modern' titles, the changes are essentially cosmetic.

If a textbook is to do the job of expounding the structure of a subject, then it has to retain a corresponding structure itself, so there is nothing strange about the persistence of form. Titles may change to reflect particular trends, such as the hope in the 1960s that the content would be 'investigative' and in the 1970s that it would be 'relevant'. Some topics drop out and new ones appear, e.g., vibrations and waves in physics, or the structure of solids in chemistry. Nevertheless, the books retain their form as a survey of the principal themes in the modernized plan of each science. Some school science books that try to break away from that mould face other problems, and may actually be losing their coherence as texts.[8]

There will always be a place for textbooks in science education. The problem seems to be how to get them into a useful relationship with other reading material that a teacher might need in order to engage the minds and feelings of learners, especially of learners who are not initially seeking to understand the grammar of a subject. I suspect that the most effective relationship would be divorce. Separate the textbook with all its implied certainty and deliberate avoidance of ambiguity, and have another kind of book that really does offer uncertainties for the learner to resolve.

In other sectors of education engaging people's minds nearly always involves exposing them to doubt or ambiguity so that they *have* to engage in the activities of interpretation. In a poetry class it is taken for granted that you have to spend some time considering, say, what Shakespeare might have meant when he wrote, 'All the world's a stage . . . .' In a physics class people do not expect to devote a corresponding effort to what Boyle meant by 'the spring of the air'. This is unfortunate because it takes away much of the capacity of the written word to tease the mind into action.

Future Policies for Science in General Education

If science for general education is ever established successfully in schools, the images of science that pupils take from their experience will be rather different from those they carry away now. The routine experiences they encounter are likely to include some that *counteract* the currently dominant images. The models of good writing that they see and the range of reading material they use will change. So too will the learner's sense of how writing and reading help your understanding.

Writing. The main purpose of writing will not be to report experiments, but to help the learners to reformulate their own understanding — reflecting on what they are learning, coming to terms with new ideas, building up fluency in using these ideas to interpret aspects of the everyday world. Where writing is associated with practical work, there will be more emphasis on first thoughts, but generally writing will be less closely tied to experiments than at present. A more important kind of writing might be 'Our understanding of what the book is arguing'. Certainly the stylized laboratory report is not how a learner would write to get to grips with ideas. An educated citizen should know about such reports, see some and perhaps practice trying to write that way once or twice. He or she will not engage in poor mimicry of the scientists' ways week in week out for years.

Reading. Textbooks may be reserved for 'second-rank' use after other reading which draws the reader into an engagement with ideas. Perhaps this 'first-rank' reading should be published separately, and not bound into the covers of the textbook. Some lessons should be entirely interpretive work with such material, and science courses might have to be redescribed as a two-stage or two-level activity:

1 interpretation of ideas and their significance; and then
2 mastery of maps of the subject matter.

The two components have always been present in good teaching, but the first has become an endangered species, and is now in need of special protection and cultivation.

One of the most hopeful developments towards a separation of interpretive activities from information is found in lessons supported by materials from the SATIS collection (Holman, 1986). These contain reading material accessible to pupils of a wide range of ability — everything from a food label to a health leaflet, from directions in a foreign language to evidence concerning a possible crime. The diversity is especially refreshing because people who make the sort of case I have attempted in this chapter commonly end up by recommending extended historical case studies, or J. D. Watson's *The Double Helix* (1970), or passages like Figure 7.3, all of which seem suitable for older and abler learners. Historical material does offer important aspects of an alternative image of science, when learners can emphatize with the historical characters, but there are many other kinds of problematic source material that could influence their feelings about scientific knowledge, and their understanding of the idea-generating and idea-criticizing aspects of science.

Science for general education might also make greater use of extended narratives, fiction as well as biography, and evocative non-fiction (see, for example, Arabella Buckley's *Fairy-Land of Science*, 1878 — still usable today despite the quaintness of its title). Extended reading for pleasure could come higher on the agenda for science education in schools, and television productions such as *The Germ Theory of Disease* and *The Voyage of the Beagle* could make a major contribution to that part of the work.

In teacher education there is also a need for more explicit use of books that provoke or inspire in addition to those that inform. That includes books of scientific thoughts stated with passion (for example, Richard Dawkins' (1986) *The Blind Watchmaker*) or books that use scientific understanding in autobiographical settings (for example, Primo Levi's (1984) *The Periodic Table*). When these are part of the currency of learning to be a teacher, people's confidence may be raised over how to use ideas in the classroom in an atmosphere of greater uncertainty.

Teachers in Search of a New Paradigm

Much of the problem is one of paradigms, so let me start with the original sense of that word that led Kuhn to use it — a paradigm as an outstanding example which one can try to imitate or emulate. (That was before he and others started to use it in an enlarged sense of the associated sets of assumptions, world views, taken-for-granted procedures, etc.).

The professional practice of science, Kuhn argued, is guided by what are felt to be good examples of how to do it. I suggest that the predominant ways of teaching science have been similarly guided. For writing, the paradigmatic examples were reports of experimental work. Other writing which scientists do, some of which could have acted as exemplars to learners for the organization of their own thoughts, has not influenced classroom practice nearly so much. For the printed word the great exemplars have been the textbooks which established chemistry, physics, etc. Both of these were sustained for decades because of their value in a science education that was mainly for future scientists; and both of them too readily give an impression of science as depersonalized information, rather than as ideas open to debate. Although they began as paradigms in Kuhn's first sense, they also created a paradigm in his enlarged sense, so that it came to be seen as if science scripts and science books *must* be like that.

These felt guides to what constitutes proper science in school are now proving inadequate to the task of developing scientific awareness for all youngsters, and also to the job of projecting an adequate image of scientific thought. There is, however, unlikely to be a shift in the dominant ways of working until outstanding success with the alternatives has been demonstrated. We may all cling to the existing patterns by default, until new practices can be inspired and guided by a compelling and appealing example of a different approach.

Notes

1   Sprat (1667), in his history of the Royal Society of London, comments on the style of reports written by Fellows. 'Their purpose is . . . to make faithful Records of all the works of Nature . . . . And to accomplish this they have indeavour'd to separate the knowledge of Nature from the colours of Rhetorick, the devices of Fancy, or the delightful deceit of Fables' (pp. 61–2). An interesting discussion of early scientific writing style is provided by Dear (1985).

2   Other traditional systems can also be understood in terms of the vocational objectives which they may have served before becoming cultural fossils. For example, consider the double-page spreads prepared by those who experienced what Layton (1975) has called 'a starvation course on the precise measurement of physical quantities'. Their practical books were works of great craftsmanship, containing accounts with titles like 'To find the specific gravity of paraffin oil using a relative density bottle'. For those going into laboratories where the craft of exact measurement would be required, the experience of making such a report at least offered a clear example to

follow, and the actual techniques themselves were probably useful at the time they first appeared in syllabuses. Some of these accounts were accompanied by background theory, the headings on the lined page being: 'Theory', 'Apparatus', 'Procedure', and the measurements appearing on the facing page, with the conclusion in the form of a calculation. You could certainly learn an important part of the craft from this disciplined system.

3   Department of Education and Science (1985) *Science 5–16: A Statement of Policy*, para. 11, gives priority to introducing pupils to 'the methods of science', and places 'making observations' first amongst these. Both *Warwick Process Science* (Screen, 1986, 1987) and *Science in Process* (Wray *et al.*, 1987) provide activities which are supposed to offer practice in the skills of observation, independently of concepts that might steer the selection of relevant things to observe. To that extent they both subscribe to the idea of naive, virgin or unbiassed observation. Some pages of the Teachers' Resource Pack for *Science in Process* mention that there is more to observation, suggesting a divergence of understanding amongst the contributing teachers. *Nuffield 11–13 Science* (Lyth and Head, 1986) is markedly different in stressing the influence of expectations on observation.

4   The editors of *Chemistry an Experimental Science (Chem Study)* (Pimentel, 1963) were quite explicit about their philosophy. Science is 'done', they said, by inductive reasoning. They surveyed the 'activities of science', beginning with observation and description, in order to accumulate information. Organizing your observations will lead to general laws which can form the basis for the more speculative theory-building activities of science. Their first chapter included 'The Fable of the Lost Child', to illustrate how they believed an inductive generalization might be formed, used, rejected and replaced by another. In this charming story, the Child, hoping to collect fuel for a fire, made a generalization that was reasonable on the basis of his early experience with broom handles and tree trunks. He thought: 'Perhaps cylindrical objects burn'. Pieces of pipe that he collected in consequence forced a reassessment, and eventually 'Wooden objects burn' turned out to be a better guide.

In fairness I should mention that other parts of the same course materials express a rather different philosophy of science (e.g., stressing the need for 'pre-lab discussion'), but in Chapter 1 the authors claimed an inductive approach, and they were not deterred by two centuries of debate over its logical impossibility. The idea of naive and unbiassed observation had for them the strong appeal to which I have already referred. How sweet to think that we are all unbiassed recorders of nature as she truly is.

5   Many enquiries into human perception, the sociology of knowledge and the history of ideas indicate that observations are theory-laden. Preliminary thoughts and commitments steer and motivate the observer's quest, and the sense that he or she makes of the candle, or whatever. For an introductory account of these ideas see Chalmers (1982). Commonly they are summed up in the statement that observation is 'theory-laden', and if that phrase sounds rather overformal to describe children noticing things, it might be better to say that seeing and noticing are 'expectation-stored'. Expectations guide what you attend to and what you neglect; although they *can* cause you to notice the unexpected, more often the absence of clear expectations makes certain things 'invisible' to the newcomer. Hacking (1983) argues against a hasty acceptance of the term 'theory-laden observation', and believes that 'noticing' can be distinguished from observing, but in my view these are both encompassed in the idea of human perception as an active mental process.

6   The proposals for a UK National Curriculum in science (DES, 1988) incorporate suggestions on this point from the Science Working Group. They are quite specific (p. 133) on the need to have certain *occasions that are just* for the study and discussion of other people's theories, relating them to one's own emerging understandings and to the available evidence.

7 See also the accounts by Factor and Kooser (1981, 1982) of some features of American texts, including the projection of an image of 'truth and progress'.

8 Some current books for school science are in danger of losing their clarity as texts in a welter of glossy illustration and other material such as cartoon strips (some excellent, some trivial). What exactly are these books: part worksheet, part inspiration, part wallpaper, trying to cater for several ability levels, but not really meeting any one level in a sustained way? They resemble a magazine in format rather than a vehicle for an extended argument, yet the implication remains that there is a body of knowledge somewhere in them. Their heterogeneity seems to make them increasingly ephemeral. They invite scanning, and engagement on the particular section, but not engagement on the totality of the book. Within such a book a boxed panel about Madame Curie might well leave a very superficial impression of a heroine of science. These newer 'composite' books also exist in a culture where colour magazines are constantly seen briefly and discarded, and where documentary television programmes can suffer a similar fate from switch of channel, or from premature overlay by another experience before the first has been fully reflected upon.

References

ARMSTRONG, H. E. (1898) 'The heuristic method of teaching, or the art of making children discover things for themselves', reprinted in VAN PRAAGH G. (1973), *H. E. Armstrong and the Teaching of Science*, London, John Murray.

BROCK, W. H. (1967) 'An attempt to establish the first principles of the history of chemistry', *History of Science*, 6, pp. 156–69.

BUCKLEY, A. (1878) *The Fairy-Land of Science*, London, Edward Stanford.

CHALMERS, A. F. (1982) *What Is This Thing Called Science?* 2nd ed., Milton Keynes, Open University Press.

CROOKES, J. *et al.* (1985) *Leicestershire Secondary Science Curriculum Review: Science as a Process*, Leicester, Leicestershire County Council.

DARWIN, C. (1859) The *Origin of Species*, London, John Murray.

DAWKINS, R. (1986) *The Blind Watchmaker*, London, Longmans.

DEAR, P. (1985) 'Totius in verba: Rhetoric and Authority in the Early Royal Society', *ISIS*, 76, pp. 145–61.

DEPARTMENT OF EDUCATION AND SCIENCE (1985) *Science 5–16: A Statement of Policy*, London, HMSO.

DEPARTMENT OF EDUCATION AND SCIENCE (1988) *National Curriculum: Science for Ages 5 to 16*, London, DES and Welsh Office.

DOBSON, K. (1986) 'How is science taught and learnt', in NELLIST, J. and NICHOLL, B. (Eds), *ASE Science Teachers' Handbook*, London, Hutchinson.

FACTOR, R. L. and KOOSER, R. G. (1981) *Value Presuppositions in Science Textbooks: A Critical Bibliography*, Galesburg, Ill., Knox College.

FACTOR, R. L. and KOOSER, R. G. (1982) 'Does Chemistry really work that way?' *Journal of Chemical Education*, 59, p. 1010.

FARADAY, M. (1860–61 lectures) *The Chemical History of a Candle*. (I have used the London Unit Library edition, 1904).

HACKING, I. (1983) *Representing and Intervening*, Cambridge, Cambridge University Press, Ch. 10.

HOLMAN, J. (Ed.) (1986) *SATIS: Science and Technology in Society*, Teaching Units and Teachers' Guide, Hatfield, Association for Science Education.

HUGHES, A. G. (1933) *Elementary General Science: A Book for Teachers*, London, Blackie and Son.

KERR, J. F. (1963) *Practical Work in School Science*, Leicester, Leicester University Press.

KUHN, T. S. (1962, 1970) *The Structure of Scientific Revolutions*, Chicago, University of Chicago Press, Ch. 11. 'The Invisibility of Revolutions', pp. 136–43.

KUHN, T. S. (1977) *The Essential Tension*, Chicago, University of Chicago Press.

LAYTON, D. (1975) 'Science or Education?' *The University of Leeds Review*, 18, p. 100.

LAVOISIER, A. (1789) *Traité Elémentaire de Chemie*. (The English translation by Robert Kerr (1965) is available as a modern reprint: New York, Dover Publications.)

LEVI, P. (1984) *The Periodic Table*, English translation from Italian, London, Sphere.

LYNCH, P. P. and STRUBE, P. (1983) 'Tracing the origins and development of the modern science text: Are new text books really new?' *Research in Science Education*, 13, pp. 233–43.

LYNCH, P. P. and STRUBE, P. (1985) 'What is the purpose of a science text book? A study of authors' prefaces since the mid-nineteenth century', *European Journal of Science Education*, 7, pp. 121–30.

LYTH, M. and HEAD, J. (Eds) (1986) *Nuffield 11–13 Science: How Scientists Work* and *Teachers' Guide I*, London, Longman.

MacNAIR, D. S. (1904) *Chemical Laboratories for Schools*, London, George Bell and Sons.

MEDAWAR, P. (1963) 'Is the scientific paper a fraud?' *The Listener*, 12 September, pp. 377–8; reprinted in JENKINS, E. W. and WHITFIELD, R. C. (Eds) (1974), *Readings in Science Education*, London, McGraw-Hill.

NEEDHAM, R. and HILL, P. (1987) *Teaching Strategies for Developing Understanding in Science*, University of Leeds, Children's Learning in Science Project. (For teaching schemes which embody these strategies, see Childrens' Learning in Science Project (1987) *Approaches to the Teaching of Energy, Approaches to the Teaching of Plant Nutrition, Approaches to Teaching the Particulate Theory of Matter*, Centre for Studies in Science and Mathematics Education, University of Leeds.)

NEWBURY, N. F. (1934) *The Teaching of Chemistry*, London, Heinemann.

OWEN, C. B. (1956) *Methods for Science Masters*, London, Macmillan.

PIMENTEL, G. C. (Ed.) (1963) *Chemical Education Material Study. Chemistry an Experimental Science*, San Francisco, W. H. Freeman.

SCREEN, P. (Ed.) (1986, 1987) *Warwick Process Science*, Southampton, Ashford Press.

SPRAT, T. (1667) *The History of the Royal Society of London for the Improving of Natural Knowledge*, available in reprint (1959), London, Routledge and Kegan Paul.

WATSON, J. D. (1970) *The Double Helix*, Harmondsworth, Penguin.

WESTAWAY, F. W. (1929) *Science Teaching*, London, Blackie and Son.

WRAY, J. *et al.* (Eds) (1987) *Science in Process*, Pupil texts and Teachers' Resource Pack, London, Heinemann.

Chapter 8

Waves or Particles?
The Cathode Ray Debate in the
Classroom

Ton van der Valk

Do we really give our senior high school physics students an accurate impression of what physics is about? Most teachers would want to answer in the affirmative: we consciously try to teach good physics. But do we, along with physics knowledge, communicate a valid image of science? The image which many students perceive may be that physics simply reveals the truth about nature. It may suggest that the great physicists have revealed (and continue to reveal) this structure. The whole community of physicists then quickly accepts the newly revealed truth. Students may get the impression that almost all physics researchers fail to contribute to physics and only the cleverest, or possibly the most fortunate, ones succeed. Is there an alternative image of science which we could present? Modern philosophy of science portrays physics knowledge as provisional (Kuhn, 1962). It is continually subject to adaptation and sometimes to radical change. But can we present this view in the classroom; and what would be the impact on learning and on student motivation if we were to teach physics from such a point of view? Many students say: physics must tell us what nature is *really* like. They do not want uncertainty and qualified answers. Many physics students may choose the subject precisely *because* of the certainty they feel it offers (Head, 1980). This is something with which any attempt to broaden the image of science will have to contend.

This chapter deals with an evaluation study of a teaching unit, *Around 1900*, which the Physics Curriculum Development Project (initials PLON, in Dutch) (Hooymayers, 1982; Eijkelhof and Kortland, 1988; Lijnse and Hooymayers, 1988) has developed for use with 17-year-old pre-university students (Dekker and van der Valk, 1986). The unit tries to incorporate some elements of current perspectives in the philosophy of science. As one of its main aims, the authors wanted to give students some insight into theory development and theory change in science using a historical case study. The cathode ray controversy between adherents of atomic theories and wave (or continuum) theories between 1880 and 1900 was chosen as the case study. Other authors have also noted the potential of this topic for raising questions about the nature of science and of theory (Arons, 1982). The unit was also written to cover an essential part of the pre-university physics curriculum, introducing concepts of physical optics, particles in fields and the wave-particle duality of light and electrons. The unit has been extensively evaluated with particular attention being paid to its core activity: the cathode ray debate.

It is this aspect of the evaluation study which is reported in detail here, dealing with the experiences of teachers and students, and looking at the quality of the discussion between students in the classroom during the debate activity. The results have forced us to reflect on the aims of the unit and have led to guidelines for a radical revision of the unit as a whole.

The feature of *Around 1900* which, perhaps, differentiates it from some other attempts to include historical and philosophical perspectives within the school science curriculum is that it aims to teach some science *at the same time.* By looking in detail at the evolution of one teaching package through several stages of evaluation and revision, we may gain some more general insights into the issues which are raised when knowledge about the nature of science becomes an objective within science courses, and into strategies for tackling these ideas in the classroom.

The Unit *Around 1900*

Are the 'new rays' which were discovered towards the end of the nineteenth century wave-like or particle-like? This is the central question which underlies the unit *Around 1900* (PLON, 1985a, 1985b, 1985c). The first of these 'new rays' were cathode rays; intensive research into these lèd to the discovery of X rays and of the radiation from radioactive materials. The period of very fruitful research on cathode rays which led to the discovery of the electron and of X rays was attended by controversy between a 'particle' and a 'wave'-school about the nature of these rays. The controversy dealt with ideas and concepts which are covered by school physics syllabuses. The resolution of the controversy itself can be seen as a classic example of a paradigm shift (Kuhn, 1962). So it seemed a good case study to choose to introduce within pre-university physics education both the physics of free electrons in fields and historical/philosophical issues. The result of this attempt was the unit *Around 1900.*

A Short Historical Background of the Cathode Ray Controversy

As early as 1838 Faraday observed a pink glow when he passed an electric current through a partially evacuated glass tube. In 1856 Geissler succeeded in producing a better vacuum, and Plücker was able to observe many new phenomena caused, apparently, by rays coming from the cathode (the electrode connected to the negative terminal of the high voltage supply). Between this initial observation and 1880 ten properties of these so called *cathode rays* were found (see Table 8.1).

Table 8.1
The Ten Properties of Cathode Rays Known in 1880, as Stated in the Unit, Around 1900

1 The rays originate from the cathode.
2 The rays are always emitted perpendicular to the cathode.
3 The properties of the rays are always independent of the cathode material.
4 The rays propagate in straight lines.
5 The rays are deflected by a magnetic field, as though they are negatively charged particles.
6 The rays are not deflected in an electric field.
7 The rays cause fluorescence of the glass behind the cathode and of the gas in the tube. The fluorescence of the gas is, in appearance and intensity, strongly dependent on the pressure in the tube.
8 The rays can turn a little paddle-wheel in the tube.
9 The rays can heat the anode enormously.
10 The rays are able to blacken photographic emulsions.

Cathode rays became a major focus of research for many groups from 1880 onwards, as the techniques of evacuation and of producing high electrical potentials quickly developed, offering the opportunity for many new experiments. The results of these experiments were often disturbing and open to various interpretations, giving rise to many theories. These theories can be divided into *particle theories*, originating from the kinetic theory of gases which was then being developed mathematically, and *wave theories*, which viewed cathode rays as a candidate for inclusion in the 'family' of electromagnetic rays, predicted theoretically by Maxwell. In this view the cathode rays might 'fill the gap' in the spectrum between the radio waves recently discovered by Hertz and light itself. As atoms themselves were still hypothetical with no direct evidence available, there was a strong anti-atomic tendency in some sections of the physics community, especially in Germany. The great successes of thermodynamics and electromagnetism, neither of which required atomic ideas, gave encouragement to the anti-atomic factions.

Particle theories, which claimed that the rays were negatively charged atoms, could not explain why no deviation in electric fields was observed. On the other hand, wave theories had problems in explaining deviation in magnetic fields and emission perpendicular to the cathode. Experimental results were interpreted by both sides as supporting their predictions, with the result that from 1885 onwards the positions were immovable and almost all progress ceased. Cathode ray research became an obscure field in the eyes of fellow researchers, until von Lenard in 1894 succeeded in bringing the rays outside the glass tube, under normal air pressure. This seemed to be a decisive experiment in favour of the wave position, as no particle theory could explain the transparency of air and the newly discovered element aluminium which formed the window. The von Lenard tube enabled Röntgen to make his discovery of X rays. For the cathode ray researchers X rays opened up the possibility of interpreting all kinds of puzzling phenomena. At last, however, improved evacuation techniques led Thompson to his decisive experiments which showed that cathode rays do deflect in electric fields and that they carry negative charge. So evidence was found of the existence of the hypothetical 'electron', the subject of Lorentz's theories. The discovery of the Zeeman effect and its theoretical interpretation by Lorentz in terms of electrons was the final piece of the jigsaw. The physics community rapidly adopted the particle theory.

In the process cathode ray research had given rise to an avalanche of new discoveries in the years 1895 to 1897, including the X rays of Röntgen, radioactivity by Becquerel and the controversial N rays of Blondlot (Klotz, 1980).

Structure and Aims of Around 1900

As explained above, the aim of the unit *Around 1900* is to give students some insight into the way science progresses in the period leading up to and including a paradigm shift. *At the same time* it aims to teach the physics of electrons in fields and the behaviour of electron beams. Koningsveld (1978) lists five rules to describe scientific progress and paradigm change. The authors of the unit *Around 1900* made use of these five rules, stated in simpler language, to frame the philosophical goals of the unit (see Table 8.2).

In the 'Orientation' to the unit students are given the task of decoding a fictitious medieval document. As they perform this task, the students are supposed to reflect on their experience in the light of these five rules.

The remainder of the unit is divided into three parts. The first part, 'Settled Theories', consists of two chapters. The first deals with particle theory: forces and deflection in magnetic and electric fields, acceleration in an electric field and mean free path. The second chapter deals with wave-theory in the historical context of the particle/wave debate about light. The

Table 8.2
The Five 'Rules' Describing Scientific Progress, as Stated in the Unit,
Around 1900

1 Many phenomena can be interpreted in different ways.
2 Observation without theory is meaningless.
3 We try to understand new phenomena using old theories and concepts.
4 As you make theories to try to understand a new phenomenon, you are inclined to ignore counterexamples.
5 In science, old settled theories are replaced by new theories only if:
   a counterexamples to the old theory accumulate;
   b there is a new theory that can explain those counterexamples;
   c a new generation of physicists comes along to elaborate the new theory.

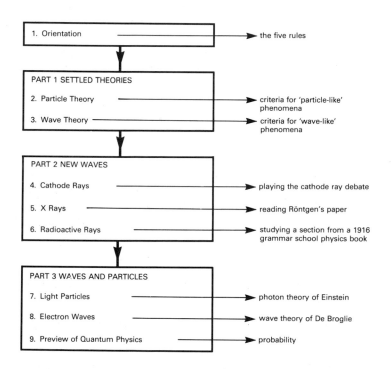

Figure 8.1
Flow Diagram of the Unit Around 1900

aim of this chapter is to introduce the students to all those aspects of wave theory which are needed for discussing the cathode ray debate. In this chapter the 'criteria' for regarding a phenomenon as 'wave-like' are identified: interference, diffraction, refraction, Doppler effect and polarization.

The second part of the unit is called 'New Waves'. It consists of three chapters: 'Cathode Rays', 'X Rays' and 'Radioactive Rays'. It starts with the discovery of cathode rays by Plücker, the technical equipment needed for demonstrating cathode rays and the ten properties of the rays (see Table 8.1). The particle model of Crookes and the wave model of Goldstein are presented. These form the starting point for re-enacting the cathode ray debate in the classroom. The cathode ray chapter ends with the Thomson model of the atom. In the X ray chapter the students read a translation of Röntgen's original paper about X rays and answer questions. These set the paper in the context of the cathode ray controversy, which was at its height at that time. Some attention is also given to the rapid application of X rays in medicine. In the 'Radioactive Rays' chapter (we now prefer the expression 'radioactivity or ionizing rays' (Eijkelhof *et al.*, 1987)), a section from a 1916 grammar school physics book is reprinted.

The third part of the unit, 'Waves and Particles', focuses on developments in the early part of the twentieth century: the photon theory of Einstein and the Compton effect, the de Broglie wavelength of the electron and the Davisson and Germer experiment, ending with a 'preview of the quantum theory'. This third part aims only to give a general overview of this material (see Figure 8.1).

The Intended Approach

The unit was designed to be taught in twenty-four lessons of fifty minutes each, though, having completed the unit, the authors estimated it would require twenty-eight to thirty lessons, in spite of their efforts to reduce this number by minimizing the subject matter. The authors intended the unit to be varied and interesting for the students, and so included many types of student activity:

playing observation games in the 'Orientation';

doing experiments as well as reasoning and calculation tasks in the 'Settled Theory' part;

observing demonstrations of historical experiments in the classroom;

debating the cathode ray issue, looking at experimental evidence from both the wave and particle points of view;

evaluating the debate in the classroom from the point of view of the five philosophical 'rules';

reading historical texts;

consolidating parts of a new theory by calculations and reasoning tasks.

Many of these activities are designed to take place in groups of three or four students. We shall now examine how far the unit's aims were realized by teachers and students.

The Development of the Cathode Ray Debate

Finding a suitable vehicle for the cathode ray debate in the classroom turned out to be complicated. Between 1984 (when the first edition of the unit was trialled) and 1986 two revisions were made. The authors tried to incorporate feedback from teachers who had used the unit into these revisions. On the one hand, this was positive, showing that students and teachers are interested in historical/philosophical issues; but on the other hand, it appeared that the attempt to attain the unit's goals made demands on teachers and students which could not be met.

In this section we shall describe the debate and the changes in its presentation through the various revisions of the unit. This description will focus on the question of how the historical/philosophical goals were elaborated in successive editions and will look at the nature of the feedback and the discussions it generated, which led to the particular revisions made.

The Trial Edition

The main objectives of the first edition of the debate were historical/philosophical. During the debate students were involved in discussions about the interpretation of new phenomena related to cathode rays. Then the main experimental outcomes had to be evaluated using the five rules of scientific progress (see Table 8.2).

As the debate was designed, it was assumed that the students already understood the physics which they needed to understand the controversy. The philosophical objectives were reflected in the tasks students had to perform during the debate, re-enacting aspects of the original discussion, in which arguments both internal and external to physics are of importance. One of the external arguments concerns the rivalry between two nations, Germany and England. To stress this, the section in the first edition was called 'The Debate between the Germans and the English'. The information the students needed during the debate was provided on colour-coded cards which were given to the groups at various stages during the debate. At the start of the debate the class was divided into two groups, the Germans and the English. The debate was held in four rounds, with the titles shown in

Table 8.3
Titles of the Cathode Ray Debate Cards (First Trial Edition)

Green/particles (for the English group)	Blue/waves (for the German group)	White/information (for both groups)
First round		
1 Crookes' particle view	2 Goldstein's wave view 3 Goldstein's arguments against Crookes' view	4 Goldstein's experiment
Second round		
5 The Schuster model	6 The Hertz hypothesis	7 Hertz' pure cathode rays being shown
Third round		
	8 von Lenard's hypothesis	9 von Lenard's tube
Fourth round		
10 Do cathode rays have a charge?	11 Perrin's hypothesis	12 Cathode rays and charge

Table 8.3. By giving arguments both for and against the views of both groups, and ending with the decisive Thomson experiment, the authors wanted to give an illustration of all the five rules.

Experiences of the Teachers Leading to the First Revision

When the first edition of the debate was trialled in schools, only the historical/philosophical parts of the unit were complete. The chapters dealing with the core material of the unit, the wave theory and charged particles in fields, were still to be written.

Three teachers took part in the trials. A short evaluation study was carried out (Tenhaeff, 1984). The teachers were enthusiastic about the ideas behind the unit and so, according to them, were their students. Trying out the debate in the classroom, however, revealed some important imperfections. In the first place more time was needed than planned. Teachers had no time at the end to evaluate the discussions in the light of the five rules. In addition the tasks of the two groups turned out not to be balanced, with the Germans having to work through more cards than the English, as can be seen from Table 8.3. Not all students became fully involved in the discussions, as the groups were too big (half class groups) and students were not equally adept at debating. The quality of the arguments seemed often to be of less importance than scoring debating points. The *main* problem, however, appeared to be that not all the physics needed to understand the debate had yet been dealt with in class. So the teacher had to incorporate theory on centripetal force, electric and magnetic fields and so on, as the debate proceeded.

So in the revised and completed edition of the unit the design of the debate was changed in some respects. All students were now given the same information, so that the tasks for the groups were equivalent. Only one kind of card was supplied. These gave information about the two theories and about experiments done from the viewpoint of one or other theory, but the students were left to discover for themselves which theory each piece of evidence supported. Each card contained tasks for students which challenged or supported either one or both theories (see Table 8.4).

Table 8.4
The Titles of the Cards (First Revision)

Card number	Card title
1	Doppler Effect
2	Mean Free Path
3	Positive Rays
4	The Hertz Model
5	von Lenard's Tube
6	The Hertz Charge Experiment
7	The Perrin Charge Experiment
8	The Thomson Experiments

To reinforce the physics topics on the cards, questions and exercises were included. One example was the task of calculating the mean free path of the Crookes particles in the tube and comparing the result with the observed mean free path; another was calculating the speed of the Crookes particles and predicting the Doppler shift. As well as reinforcing the subject matter, the tasks were intended to stimulate the participation of all the students in the debate.

Experiences of the Teachers Leading to the Second Revision

The revised debate was tried out as part of the completed unit. The unit was found to be 'interesting', but to set unrealistically high goals. All the teachers involved in the trial reported problems when dealing with the debate in the classroom. All had difficulties dealing with all the cards. The addition of the exercises was appreciated, but doing these was very time-consuming. The division into tasks for and against each position was seen as too complex and led to confusion amongst the students about which tasks to do. Some teachers preferred to organize discussion in small groups rather than hold whole class discussions. Another important problem appeared to be the knowledge of the teachers themselves about historical/philosophical issues. They felt uncomfortable in not having enough background knowledge. One teacher reported having stopped the debate after the second card because he could not answer the questions put by the students.

As a result, the authors decided to make a further revision of the debate. The tasks were simplified and the idea of discussion between particle and wave adherents was dropped. This was replaced by the idea that the students themselves have to make up their minds which theory they choose, and are provided with information which tries to pull them to and fro between both points of view. So the goal of the debate had moved from illustrating the five rules to assimilating subject matter within a historical context; the philosophical aspects had become less prominent. The titles of the cards were not changed. One card was added about Schuster's calculation of the e/m-ratio from the deflection of cathode rays in a magnetic field. This was an interesting experiment but Schuster did not publish his results because the calculated ratio was so incredibly different from Faraday's e/m-ratios. The authors knew that they had not really tackled the time problem, but they hoped it would resolve itself through the improved efficiency of the new tasks and the increased experience of the teachers with the unit.

Evaluation Study on the Cathode Ray Debate

In the 1985/86 school year an evaluation study was carried out using the unit in eight schools. The study was in three parts:

1 an evaluation meeting with ten teachers using the unit;
2 a written test for the students on the development of the electron concept;
3 analysis of tape recorded and transcribed discussions during the debate, involving two groups of four students.

Feedback from Teachers

Ten teachers, five of whom had already taught the unit in the previous year, took part in the evaluation. All had attended an in-service course on the unit. They appreciated the aims of the unit and the way these were developed. One of them wrote: 'I enjoyed teaching the unit. I felt it was very satisfying that the electron didn't come out of the blue.' Teachers with prior experience of the unit reported that things had gone much better in the classroom than the year before. They had more support from the revised *Teachers' Guide* (PLON, 1985b) and the accompanying *Reader* (PLON, 1985c). They also felt that the tasks on the debate cards had been improved, though they regretted that no solution had been found for the shortage of time, and made a plea for fewer cards. This problem was felt even more acutely by those teachers who had come new to the unit. The debate in particular demanded a great deal of these teachers. As one teacher put it: 'the most difficult part to supervise was the cathode ray debate. Here my lack of experience and the class's came home to roost.' These new teachers said that they did not have enough time to read all the information available in the *Teachers' Guide* and the *Reader*. Several teachers reported that students simply assume that the cathode rays are electrons. This problem was greatest for those teachers who had already dealt with electrons in fields with their classes: their students already *knew* that cathode rays are electrons. For these students the debate ceased to be interesting. It was not enough for the teacher simply to state that electrons had not yet been discovered at that time; this was not satisfying to the students, or stimulating enough to promote discussion. Some teachers reported that their students tried to reconcile both views: 'Isn't it possible that waving particles exist?' In other parts of the study this view comes up again. Teachers note this as a misconception which often develops as students try to come to terms with wave-particle duality.

Results from the Written Tests

Written tests were completed by three classes (forty-eight students) before the unit, and one class (twenty students) after the unit. There are some striking differences between these groups, but as the pre- and post-tests were not given to the same students and as the post-test group is small, we can draw only tentative conclusions. We shall concentrate on those which relate directly to the debate or to student misconceptions.

In the pre- and post-tests students were asked to judge the correctness of thirty statements about electrons. Table 8.5 gives some examples of these statements. In the post-test some evaluation questions were asked about their change of views during and after the cathode ray debate.

The results showed clearly that after the unit the students knew more about electrons than before. The large number of 'don't knows' in the pre-test (20 per cent) decreased to 5 per cent. Both before and after the unit an electron was, for most students, a particle with mass and charge (95 per cent). Hearing about the dual wave-particle character of the electron did not affect this view. Both before (84 per cent) and after the unit (60 per

Table 8.5
Some Statements from the Written Test
(Students had to judge these as true or false)

---

3   An electron is as big as an atomic nucleus.
6   Under the influence of a magnetic field, the speed of an electron
     may increase.
8   Every molecule contains electrons.
15   Electrons do not experience gravity.
17   A beam of electrons can show diffraction.
23   All materials with electrons are conductors of electricity.

---

cent), most students held the misconception that the speed of an electron increases in a magnetic field. The percentage who answered (correctly) that
this is not so did, however, increase after the unit from 2 per cent to 40 per
cent. Nevertheless, this means that this misconception was quite persistent.
The students remained sure that electrons are not a sort of wave. Most
students, however, said in both the pre- (74 per cent) and post-test (85 per
cent) that a beam of electrons can show diffraction. This answer may be
explained by the similarity of the words for diffraction (Dutch: *buiging*) and
deflection (Dutch: *afbuiging*). It is probable, especially in the pre-test, that
students thought of deflection instead of diffraction. A remarkable number
of students (43 per cent) in the pre-test said that the wavelength of a beam of
electrons can be measured. This number increased to 65 per cent in the post-
test. This may be due to the misconception of 'undulating electrons' mentioned above. In the post-test five out of twenty students explicitly referred
to this kind of image in the evaluation questions. One student wrote:
'[cathode rays are] particles, that move in a wave movement.' Another
made a drawing of an undulating electron (see Figure 8.2).

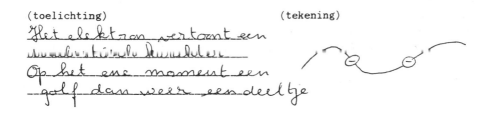

Figure 8.2
A Student's Drawing of an 'Undulating Electron'
(She gives the explanation: 'The electron shows a dual nature. At the one
moment a wave, the next a particle.')

From these data we can conclude that the students have learned a great deal about electrons. The students who reported that they had changed their mind about the nature of cathode rays were very positive about the debate and felt that they had learned many things. They gave the impression that the discussion in their groups was of a high quality. On the other hand, many students were rather critical of their learning outcomes. A major objection of the students was: 'one first has to learn things which are wrong.' This objection, and the uncertainty it produces about what to learn from the debate, seemed to be the main reason for much of the criticism. Teachers reported that it appeared to be very difficult to stimulate groups which had problems at the start of the debate. In those groups where the debate failed the students reported that they had learned nothing from it. This finding does not corroborate the impression, reported by the teachers, that students were generally interested in the unit. Perhaps this is due to some special characteristics of the classes observed, but it is more probable that the teachers' impressions were unduly optimistic.

Analysis of Students' Discussions during the Debate

The discussions of two groups of students during the debate were tape recorded and transcribed. One group consisted of four girls (age 17), the other of four boys (ages 17 and 18), one of whom was absent for the first lesson. Both groups had the same teacher, but were from different classes. The teacher took three lessons for the debate. The groups continued the discussion while the teacher had supervisory talks with each of the groups in turn. As he supplied each new card, he gave a short introduction to all the groups at once. There are striking differences between the two groups, but also some similarities. We shall describe the main lines which both discussions had in common, and then try to draw some conclusions.

The Girls' Group. In this group's discussions three stages can be discerned: an *orientation* stage, a stage of *model formation* and a stage of *conviction* to a view.

The *orientation* stage in the group is characterized by carrying out the set tasks very carefully. At this stage no particle or wave arguments are put forward by the students. They simply follow the tasks on the cards. As a result, they feel they are being manipulated, as this transcription makes clear:[1]

> *Mari:* All these things are about the wave model.
> *Anna:* On the next card they force the particle model on us.
> *Mari:* No.
> *Anna:* Yes they do.
> *Mari:* On card 3 we still have to reject the particle model.

Anna: Do we?
Mari: Yes, for the e/m ratio doesn't fit.

They do not have many problems in doing the calculations. One exception is when they need to use the idea of potential difference decreasing between two points, to discuss Schuster's hypothesis about dissociation. They assume a constant voltage instead and get into difficulties with the task. This leads them to make explicit their image of particles moving through the tube. So the *model formation stage* starts:

Mari: Behind the cathode there is light. So the negative particles are going that way. So the negative particles give out light.
Toos: Negative particles arrive pprrr ... takkkk ... at the glass surface ... eeeaaa ... eeeaaa ... light, light, light [she tries to illustrate the collision and the emitting of light with sounds]
Mari: Then the negative particles could cycle ... or scoot.

A less than completely serious discussion follows about 'cycling', 'scooting' and 'flying', but arguments about the fact that a surface is needed for cycling and about the pressure needed for flying in air are included. It ends with ideas about collisions of flying particles with one another, which makes them crack apart. However, even this discussion does not lead to a solution of the problem. So they begin another card, about positive rays. By this stage they have an image of cathode rays as particles with mass and charge, and the ability to emit light. So the arguments on the card about mean free path and Doppler effect can be evaluated. This results in a point of view (a conviction) about the character of the cathode rays, supported by arguments. The *conviction stage* has been reached:

Anna: They have to be waves, for particles cannot pass [through the aluminium window of the von Lenard tube].
Toos: They are waves. There's no doubt about that.
Anna: [to teacher] Why do we have to do two more cards?
Teacher: Maybe some of the others will bring up something new.
Toos: Particles that can run through the wall?
Mari: They might be different particles.
Anna: That send out waves.
Toos: Yes, so that it emits energy.
Mari: Electrons with no mass. Electrons are the only particles with no mass.
Teacher: Yes but they didn't yet exist at that time in physics.

Mari is now thinking of particles, even of electrons, Toos is sure it is a wave phenomenon and Anna seems to want it to be *both*! In spite of these different views the discussion remains animated, the girls continue listening to each other and new details are added to their models. For example, Anna suggests particles that emit waves or energy in collisions:

Mari: Let us imagine they are negative particles.
Anna: But how can they pass through the window?
Mari: If they collide, they will emit energy.
Anna: Yes, and at the end of the tube they collide against the window and then they send out energy.
Mari: And that carries on for another 10 cm after the window. That's right! [all laugh]

This is quite surprising, for it looks very like a description of X rays, which they have not yet met! This discussion does not mean that the other two girls have been converted to this view. They are still considering a wave explanation. With the same kind of inventiveness other topics like deflection in electric and magnetic fields and mean free path in the tube are also discussed.

In this group it is clear that an orientation period is very necessary before the students can really choose a point of view and make their models explicit in the model formation stage. After they reach the conviction stage the discussion continues to be fruitful because of their wish to understand each other and to come to an agreed solution. The discussion also shows that the students are able to discuss in an inventive and creative way. It seems possible that these students have experienced something like a paradigm shift. They have enjoyed the discussions, but the fact that they did not have enough time to discuss all the questions raised on the cards makes some of them feel uncomfortable. To them the purpose of having the debate is unclear and they have the feeling of not having learned what they should have learned. So they are critical of the debate.

The Boys' Group. With the boys' group the same three stages can be observed as with the girls' group. However, the *stage of conviction* is reached rather sooner. We shall argue that is the main reason why the debate is not a success in this group.

For the first lesson one of the four boys is absent. The other three boys begin the debate by discussing the ten properties of cathode rays (see Table 8.1) in order to make up their minds on the wave/particle question. This clearly is the *orientation stage*. During this discussion many good physics arguments are used. For example, as they try to interpret deflection in a magnetic field, Paul puts the argument: 'The only way light can be deflected is by diffraction or refraction. And neither of these is the case here.' When they get to the last property, they continue immediately to the *model formation stage* and Paul puts forward the idea: 'I see. They are radioactive particles. Proton, neutrons, etc.' The others accept this model and the group again goes down the list of properties to interpret them using this model: '[property] 9. They can heat the anode. Think of radioactivity. Yes that's right! Look at the neutron bomb.' They do not, however, make explicit the properties they are attributing to 'radioactive particles'. They propose a decisive experiment, which involves placing a Geiger-Müller counter near the anode. They ask the teacher whether the counter will record any counts.

The teacher encourages them to elaborate their theory, but asks them to do this in words which could have been used around 1900, and not to use words like 'neutron' and 'proton', as these particles have not yet been discovered. He refuses to answer their question about the Geiger-Müller counter: 'That apparatus didn't exist at that time.'. The students grumble a bit about this answer. At the end of this lesson all three are proud of their 'fluorescence theory', as they call it, and are convinced of its correctness.

For the next two lessons of the debate Martin is present. Unlike the others, he has met cathode rays in the previous year and has learned that they are electrons. So when the debate restarts, Martin begins by saying in an authoritative way: 'The cathode ray is an electron, so...'. But he is interrupted by the other three who say: 'That is not our theory.' He tries to explain his view to his fellow students, but they succeed in giving counter-arguments which he is not able to parry:

Marti-
n: No, they are electrons that are liberated from the cathode, from a piece of metal by the heat and they shoot out.

Paul: No, look at [property] 3: properties independent of the cathode material.

Jack: Yes [ironically] so let's forget about the cathode.

Here a misunderstanding is clearly developing. Martin's model is of electrons which are present in the metal being emitted. Later it appears that he thinks of cathode ray tubes as fluorescent tubes, about which he, unlike the others, was taught the year before in another PLON unit called *Light Sources* (PLON, 1984). Paul and Jack at this point seem to be thinking that it is the atoms of the metal which are being sent out. Again, their ideas about the properties of the particles are not made explicit.

Later Paul, Jack and Kees try again to interpret all the properties from the point of view they prefer. Martin now listens rather cynically; at one point he is on the verge of getting into discussion again, when the other three state that the particles are uncharged. Paul agrees with Martin's argument that there cannot be a magnetic force on an uncharged particle. So one observation has been explained using an accepted scientific property of a particle! The question of where the charge comes from is solved in this way: 'It comes close to the cathode and picks up a charge'. No explanation is given of what 'it' refers to here: a gas molecule, a radioactive particle or what? Martin is astonished by this argument: 'How can you turn it around?' That is to say, how is it possible for particles not to come from the cathode, but from within the tube?

After they have decided that charged particles are involved, the problem of the absence of deflection in an electric field arises. An ad hoc argument is produced: 'Well the neutrons get pushed to the plus pole and the protons get pushed to the minus pole and they compensate each other.' The students have clarified some aspects of their image of the property 'radio-active', but they appear to have forgotten charge conservation.

From this point on Martin begins to lose interest in the discussion, and appears to feel that his colleagues do not want to listen to him. When the teacher comes to speak to the group, Martin tries to get his support for the electron theory. The teacher is faced with a problem: to agree with Martin means to give the solution. He is interested by the 'fluorescence theory' of the three others and would like it to be developed further. So he decides to say the group should discuss Martin's model too; he then, however, only asks questions about the fluorescence theory, trying to point out some of its internal contradictions. By the time the teacher leaves the group Martin has completely lost interest and tries to distract the others, succeeding after some time. The teacher repeatedly tries to pull them back to the discussion, but with little success. The group answers only a few of the questions on the cards.

Somewhat later, after having dealt with the discovery of electrons by Thomson, the teacher comes back to the group to evaluate their 'theory'. Martin says proudly: 'I was right.' The others also feel *they* were right to a considerable extent: the rays *were* particles. Martin indicates that he feels he has not learned anything from the debate and did not enjoy the discussion. Paul, Kees and Jack have learned that molecules are split up by collisions, not by the electrical field. Paul and Jack say they liked the debate, but Kees, who participated less, reports that he did not.

After a successful start this group has fallen into a trap which the design of the debate has itself created: to reach a point of view about the character of cathode rays and to defend this. Once they have reached a view (a conviction), only the authority of the teacher is able to change it. The lack of discussion between the three boys and Martin is illuminating. So too is their resistance to looking at new information and considering the implications of the tasks on the cards provided. Their repeated interpretation of the ten properties also points in the same direction. From their discussion another flaw in the design becomes apparent: there is a lack of incentive to make explicit the mental models (for example, of various particles and of wave ideas) being used.

Conclusions

The unit appears to show that it *is* possible to teach physics ideas *and* historical/philosophical ones *at the same time*. Teachers who used the unit liked it, in spite of the problems it caused them. Major problems remain to be overcome, both for teachers and for students. Perhaps some of these problems are general and relate not only to this unit, but to any historical/philosophical unit which might be developed.

The experiences of the authors and of the teachers in the classroom show a tension between the need for basic knowledge to understand the main points of discussion, and the need to avoid giving the solution of the debate to the students. One of the aims of the unit is to show that knowledge is only temporary and may change a great deal in a short time (a paradigm shift). This however entails that students must learn ideas which later appear to be 'wrong'. We might conclude that a student has not grasped the idea of a paradigm shift if he or she regards all the initial measurements and interpretations as useless because these appeared to be 'wrong'. It is, of course, a very general finding that there are always some students who miss the main learning points which the developers have intended for their curriculum units! Particular attention must be paid to this issue in developing this kind of material.

Another question which arises concerns students who miss the point of the wave-particle duality idea with which the unit ends, by adopting the compromise image of a 'waving particle'. For a student who misses the idea of a paradigm shift there is a danger that they develop a misconception which may block further concept development. Perhaps, however, this kind of misconception is also likely to arise in more traditional instruction. The approach used in the unit *Around 1900* at least offers the opportunity to address this misconception by discussing it.

Our overall conclusion is that it *is* worthwhile to strive to give students some direct personal experience of a paradigm shift through a unit like this. But this paradigm shift has to be planned very carefully to ensure that the experience 'works' for most students.

From our experiences we have to conclude that the aims of the unit *Around 1900* should be less ambitious: fewer physics topics to be learned, fewer philosophical ideas to be introduced, a less complicated debate. We still feel that the cathode ray controversy offers the possibility of realizing the aims identified earlier. The *Around 1900* unit, however, may still need to be revised radically.

> The central question should be simplified to become: *is it possible to interpret the new rays using an atomic theory?* In this question the wave view is not present, and all the emphasis is on the question of the reality of atoms. This is, both historically and didactically, a valid emphasis. The particle-wave emphasis is interesting only in the light of the growth of quantum physics, and that may be better as the subject of another unit.
> The subject matter should be limited to particle physics, including the kinetic theory of gases.
> The central question of the cathode ray debate should become: *is the nature of cathode rays particle-like?*

The debate should be held in four rounds: the orientation, the model formation and the conviction stage as before, together with a fourth, the paradigm shift. The four rounds might be designed as follows:

1 interpretation of the ten properties using Crookes' particle model, including some questions which arise from the model and some experiments which challenge these (orientation stage);

2 more extensive treatment of one experiment and of the new problems which it raises, stimulating the formation of particle models by students (model formation stage);

3 the von Lenard tube: a decisive experiment? (conviction stage);

4 the Thomson experiments (paradigm shift).

More attention has to be given to the teacher support material, especially as regards techniques for encouraging the development of the students' skills of reflection. Reflective activities might also be provided which relate to the individual learning outcomes of the unit, as well as to the social process of knowledge construction in the classroom, asking students to consider how well the philosophical rules fit.

In this chapter the focus of discussion has been on the *problems* arising from the unit *Around 1900*, but readers may also have recognized *successful* aspects as well. I am indebted to my co-authors of the unit, all the teachers and students who cooperated in this research, especially those who agreed to be tape recorded. They made *Around 1900* a successful subject for development oriented research (which is continuing). We hope the directions for revision identified here may soon play a part in a further revision of the unit, and be evaluated in their turn!

Note

1 It is impossible to translate student utterances with complete accuracy from Dutch to English. In translating we often imply an interpretation. Even so, it seems worth presenting as accurate a translation as possible here, to give an impression of the students' discussions.

References

ARONS, A. B. (1982) 'Phenomenology and logical reasoning in introductory physics courses', *American Journal of Physics*, **50**, 1, pp. 13–20.

DEKKER, J. and VAN DER VALK, A. E. (1986) 'Pre-university physics presented in a thematic and systematic way: Experiences with a Dutch Physics Curriculum Development Project', *European Journal of Science Education*, 8, 2, pp. 145–53.

EIJKELHOF, H. M. C. and KORTLAND, K. (1988) 'Broadening the aims of physics education', in FENSHAM, P. L. (Ed.), *Development and Dilemmas in Science Education*, Lewes, Falmer.

EIJKELHOF, H. M. C., KLAASSEN, C. W. J. M., LIJNSE, P. L. and SCHOLTE, R. L. J. (1987) 'Public and pupils ideas about radiation: Some lessons from Chernobyl to science educators', in RIQUARTS, K. (Ed.), *Science and Technology Education and the Quality of Life*, Vol. 2, Kiel, FRG, IPN, pp. 688–93.

HEAD, J. (1980) 'A model to link personality characteristics to a preference for science', *European Journal of Science Education*, 2, 2, pp. 295–300.

HOOYMAYERS, H. P. (1982) 'Teacher training and curriculum development in the Physics Department of the University of Utrecht', *European Journal of Science Education*, 4, 4, pp. 463–70.

KONINGSVELD, H. (1978) *Het verschijnsel wetenschap*, Meppel, Netherlands, Boom.

KLOTZ, I. (1980) 'The N-ray affair', *Scientific American*, 242, 5, pp. 122–31.

KUHN, T. S. (1962) *The Structure of Scientific Revolutions*, Chicago, University of Chicago Press.

LIJNSE, P. and HOOYMAYERS, H. (1988) 'Past and present issues in Dutch secondary physics education', *Physics Education*, 23, 3, pp. 173–9.

PLON, (1984) *Lichtbronnen* (Light Sources), Zeist, Netherlands, NIB Publishers. (An English translation of this unit has been prepared by the Department of Curriculum Studies, University of Saskatchewan, Saskatoon, Canada.)

PLON (1985a) *Rond 1900* (Around 1900), Utrecht, Utrecht University.

PLON (1985b) *Lerarenhandleiding bij Rond 1900* (Teacher's Guide), Utrecht, Utrecht University.

PLON (1985c) *Leesteksten bij Rond 1900* (Reader), Utrecht, Utrecht University.

TENHAEFF, B. (1984) *Verwarring of verdieping? Verslag van het project Rond 1900*, internal publication, University of Amsterdam.

Chapter 9

Adventures with N Rays:
An Approach to Teaching about
Scientific Theory and
Theory Evaluation

Patricia Burdett

Science education in the UK in the 1980s is being shaped by demands for new structures of learning and assessment. The National Criteria for Science courses for the General Certificate of Secondary Education (GCSE) examination, taken by pupils at age 16, require that pupils, in addition to gaining some knowledge and understanding of scientific concepts and theories, should be able to 'draw conclusions from, and *evaluate critically*, experimental observations and other data' (my emphasis) and 'recognise and explain variability and unreliability in experimental measurements'. They should be able to 'make decisions based on the examination of evidence and arguments' and 'recognise that the study and practice of science are subject to various limitations and uncertainties' (DES, 1985: 3–4). These aims, if they are taken seriously, imply a move away from the following of practical 'recipes' to 'confirm' the results presented in textbooks and their writing up in transactional prose. At present the idea of a 'scientific theory' is rarely explicitly raised; the aims and purposes of science and the nature of its theories are rarely discussed.

The GCSE criteria, and their more recent articulation in the National Science Curriculum (DES, 1989: 36–7), direct teachers' attention towards these more philosophical aspects of science. They suggest and offer new possibilities for exploration, a chance to people science with episodes, anecdotes and case studies drawn from records of active science communities. Procedures of theory-making and validation in such case studies invariably raise issues of variability, unreliability and uncertainty which may, in turn, be used to reflect on pupils' own experience of practical science.

The use of historical cases must, however, be more than mere storytelling if it is to hold the attention of most students in mixed classes, and to engage them actively in thinking about science and scientific theory. For this reason these new aims for science education pose a challenge and perhaps a threat to many teachers. Didactic methods will not always suffice and a more participatory style of classroom management is needed to facilitate learning. This chapter reports on the development and evaluation of one possible approach, based on simulation of a historical controversy in science through role-play. Participants are given background information but are then left to create and develop their roles as the simulation proceeds. Drama is only infrequently used as a method in science classes. It may, however, provide a means of making the often implicit theory-making aspects of science more explicit, and form a useful addition to the science teacher's range of strategies for encouraging active learning about the nature of science.

Sociologists of science have commented on the particular value of case studies of *controversial* episodes (Pinch, 1986). In these, aspects of science which are normally hidden are laid bare, as protagonists argue over the significance of their results, ideas and theories. The simulation described in this chapter is based on the N-ray affair of the early 1900s. It is one of three simulations of controversial incidents in science which have been developed for use with secondary school pupils (Burdett, 1982). The chapter begins by giving a brief account of the N-ray affair itself. This is followed by a description of the simulation materials and its enactment in school. Then some prominent ideas from the literature on theory change in science are outlined briefly. This leads on to a consideration of the learning outcomes which might be promoted by the use of this particular simulation.

The N-Ray Affair

The N-ray affair is a well known example of deviant science. It is particularly interesting because it shows how an established researcher can misunderstand the significance of his observations to such an extent that a whole research field is set on a deviant course. Useful accounts of the affair can be found in articles by Klotz (1980) and Nye (1980), the Klotz account being particularly accessible. Original sources of information are the journal of the French Academy of Sciences, *Comptes Rendus*, and correspondence in *Nature* during 1903 and 1904.

The central figure is René Blondlot, an established and respected scientist, a member of the French Academy of Sciences and a Professor at the University of Nancy. His reputation was based on experimental work on electromagnetic radiation. Following Röntgen's discovery of X rays, he became interested in experiments to determine the nature of these rays — were they waves or particles? Part of his investigation involved setting up an experiment to discover whether a beam of X rays could be polarized. His detection technique was routine, involving estimating changes in the brightness of an electric spark. The beam of X rays would fall on a spark gap at varying angles. If X rays were polarized electromagnetic waves, they might make the spark brighter in certain orientations. To Blondlot's delight, this experiment yielded positive results (see Figure 9.1). But he then discovered that the radiation affecting the spark appeared to be bent (refracted) by passing through a quartz prism. It was known at this time that X rays are not refracted by quartz. Therefore, reasoned Blondlot, the radiation under investigation could not be X rays, but must be a new form of radiation (which he called N rays, after his home university). This was a disastrous conceptual leap, since he had not made any serious investigation into possible sources of error or carried out any reappraisal of his basic techniques of detection. A little further work convinced Blondlot that N rays could pass through many materials, wood, paper and thin sheets of metal. Water, however, could block them out and so Blondlot used wet cardboard as a screening material in many of his experiments.

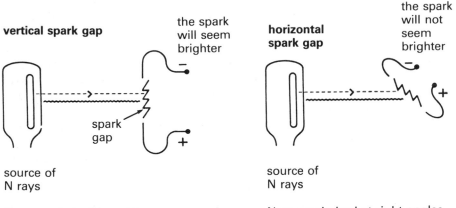

Figure 9.1
Blondlot's Original Method for Detecting N Rays

That Blondlot should have believed he had found a new form of radiation appears more reasonable when the research context of the time is considered. Blondlot's working paradigm was well defined and he had no particular reason to be alert to anomaly. Knowledge of atomic structure was still very sketchy. Techniques for detecting and measuring radiation were difficult to use and subject to considerable unreliability. New discoveries of radiations, notably Röntgen's X rays and Becquerel's radioactivity, were fresh in their minds, and auxiliary research fields were developing fast. Physicists were disposed to believe that new kinds of radiation with new properties and hence new applications might be announced at any time.

So the scientific community and, to a lesser extent, the public were receptive to the idea of N-rays. Blondlot even suffered claims to primacy from lesser workers, a sure sign of success! Meanwhile, new developments in the technology of radiant sources offered opportunities for more exact work. The Nernst lamp, in which a metal oxide rod is heated electrically to become incandescent and emit light, was reported by Blondlot to be a particularly rich N-ray source and was used by him in much subsequent work.

Blondlot and his colleagues at Nancy rapidly developed a research programme around N rays. He published copiously in *Comptes Rendus*, beginning with four papers between January and June 1903, and increasing to fifty-four in the same period in 1904. Many of his colleagues began researching N rays in relation to their own interests. Jean Becquerel (son of the discoverer of radioactivity, Henri Becquerel), Charpentier and d'Arsonval all contributed to the fund of N-ray 'knowledge'. In 1904 Charpentier published a series of papers dealing with physiological phenomena and N rays. This led quickly to the hope that N rays might give three-dimensional images of living tissue once a good photographic technique had been developed. The basis for this was Charpentier's reports that tissue emits N rays at varying intensities. His papers refer particularly to active muscle and nerve tissue. Another paper suggested that N rays, as energizing radiation, could be focused on to sense organs to improve their efficiency. There were further claims that certain metals, such as heated pieces of silver and sheet iron, emitted N rays. If this seems fanciful, it needs to be remembered that there was still no account available to explain the emission of radiations from uranium, a process which appeared to continue indefinitely with no obvious energy source.

Eventually the physiological claims, and a rather bizarre report by Becquerel that, when anaesthetized with chloroform, metals cease to emit N rays, galvanized other researchers into action. R. W. Wood, professor of physics at Johns Hopkins University, went to Nancy to investigate the N rays work. Wood was an internationally known figure in optics and spectroscopy; he was also something of a showman, given to hoaxing and practical jokes, and with a reputation for attempts to unmask fraudulent spiritualist mediums. At Nancy he was taken through a series of experiments designed to show that N rays could influence the brightness of a spark. These used photographic techniques, with a technician in charge of exposures. Wood pointed out that error could easily creep into such experimentation, specifically noting the possible variations in exposure times for photographs. He also noted peculiarities in the set-up used for the prism experiment. Here a slit 3 mm wide was used to produce a narrow beam of N rays. Blondlot claimed that an aluminium prism dispersed these into a spectrum. His detector was a fluorescent strip, only 0.5 mm wide, which was supposed to glow more brightly when N rays fell on it. Blondlot claimed that movements of as little as 0.1 mm made the strip go from bright to dim and back again. Wood was highly sceptical that a 3 mm wide incident beam could be resolved into spectrum components less than 0.1 mm wide. He also questioned the reliability of using subjectively perceived brightness of a fluorescent strip as a detection method (see Figure 9.2). Wood decided to take action and surreptitiously removed the aluminium prism during a demonstration in a darkened laboratory. The technician continued to read results without noting any change!

Perhaps in response to previous criticisms of the rather subjective nature of the N-ray detection system — involving direct assessment of the brightness of a fluorescent strip — the N-ray researchers had begun to claim that physiological, rather than merely physical, effects were involved. They suggested that the rays acted to enhance the senses, particularly vision. Klotz describes Wood's reaction to one demonstration of these 'effects':

> In a dimly lighted room a large steel file — an N-ray source — was held near an observer's eyes. On the wall of the room was a clock. The subject of the experiment assured Wood that the hands of the clock, which were not normally visible to him, became brighter

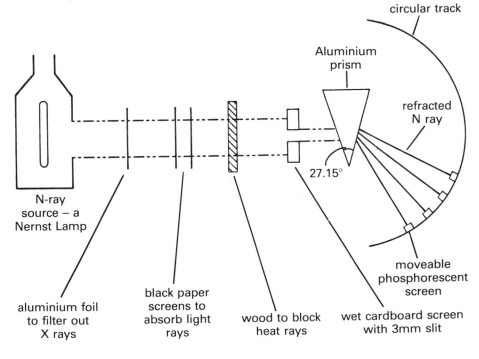

Figure 9.2
Refraction of N Rays

and much more distinct when the file was nearby, a phenomenon credited to the peculiar effect of N-rays on the retina. Again Wood was 'unable to see the slightest change.' Since the room was not completely dark, Wood could not perform quite the same kind of control experiment he had performed by removing the aluminium prism. He was nonetheless equal to the challenge. As he wrote, 'the substitution of a piece of wood of the same size and shape as the file in no way interfered with the experiment.' The substitution was of course made without the knowledge of the observer (Klotz, 1980: 129).

Despite Wood's report on his visit to Nancy, the N-ray affair was far from closed. Conflicting results continued to be published. A close analysis of Blondlot's calculations was carried out by Schenck at McGill University in Montreal. Schenck checked Blondlot's values for refractive index and argued that their accuracy was far beyond that possible for the experimental techniques employed. His view was that it was not possible to calculate reliable refractive indices for readings only fractions of a degree apart. He spoke too of the limitations of size and also of Blondlot's own admission that N rays are weak and difficult to detect.

Alternative explanations of N-ray effects were also emerging. Two Edinburgh physiologists, McKendrick and Colquhoun, investigating muscle contraction, attributed changed luminescence in detectors to warmth and not to N rays. They also ascribed the widely reported variations in observations of brightness to wavering ciliary muscles as the eye adjusted to objects at middle distance. Lummer, a respected German researcher, also offered alternative explanations of the reported phenomena. He wrote a detailed and closely argued paper analyzing Blondlot's experimental procedures and pointing out problems of perception associated with recent discoveries about the physiology of the eye. He noted that the eye takes time to adjust to changed lighting conditions, so darkening of a screen would be difficult to detect; and that semi-darkness provides conditions where there is 'shadowy vision', with only the rods in the retina functioning. His interpretations were supported by another German professor, Rubens.

Although Blondlot and his colleagues tried to respond to these criticisms, their cumulative effect was to put an end to support for N-ray research outside France. The N-ray workers in France, however, pressed on with their work for a few more years before French science also decided to regard N rays as a mistake — a piece of deviant science.

Simulating the N-Ray Affair

A simulation of a historical episode is a kind of playlet, where each character is given a separate role. All the players are given some background reading and information about the historical episode. Role cards contain additional specific information and clues about each character and are given only to the person playing this role. There is no script, the dialogue being made up as the simulation goes along. For this to work each player must try to 'be' the character described on the role card. The more they succeed in 'getting inside the skin' of the person described, the better the simulation will proceed — the better also, of course, will they experience something of the emotions and feelings involved in the original incident and in doing science generally. The result is something like a play, but is never the same on two occasions.

In the case of the N rays simulation, role cards are provided for ten of the main actors: Blondlot, Charpentier, Becquerel and Le Brun (Blondlot's technician) from the Nancy group, Wood, Schenck, Lummer, Rubens, Colquhoun and McKendrick representing various degrees and varieties of critique, reinterpretation and opposition. The setting for the action is contrived. It purports to be in Blondlot's laboratory at Nancy, where there is an informal gathering of all those interested in, or sceptical about, N rays. Blondlot and his co-workers are going to demonstrate and defend their work against queries and criticisms from the visitors.

The simulation is designed to run for one lesson of approximately seventy minutes, though the ensuing discussion may take at least as long again. It has been enacted several times by school pupils of age 16–17, and on two occasions these enactments have been recorded to allow some analysis and evaluation of the discourse produced. Excerpts from these transcripts are discussed later in this chapter.

It is essential to brief the players fully beforehand about the N-ray affair and its major actors. Care is taken at this stage to present only an outline of the controversy and to avoid directing the participants (as far as this is possible) towards a foregone conclusion. Following this, players need time, perhaps a few days, to consider and construct their roles. The simulation also benefits if players confer in advance and agree strategy. The 'technician' has some specific preparations to make. If the class has more than ten members, then doubling up allows each pair to discuss their role in advance. They may choose to share the role during the enactment, or (though this has not been tried) two parallel enactments could go on together, leading to a common debriefing. The debriefing is planned around a series of checkpoints for discussion which may be issued to participants at the original briefing session or kept until after the simulation.

As the main aim of the simulation is to provide an opportunity for students to improve their awareness and understanding of issues about the nature of scientific knowledge and theory change in particular, let us now turn to consider some theoretical perspectives on theory change and to identify realistic learning outcomes for this simulation.

Interpreting Theory Change

The N-ray affair raises issues about the reception of novel ideas and about theory change, in this case theory about the nature and even the existence of N rays. Amongst scientists and science teachers a widely received view of theory change is that of Popper. Popper's view is that theories stand until they are deemed inadequate by falsification. Mulkay comments on this view:

> This argument seems initially plausible because, in principle, although an immense number of positive observations is insufficient to prove a generalisation, one negative observation seems enough to disprove it. However, this thesis would only hold in relation to isolated theoretical propositions which could be compared with absolutely unproblematic observations. As soon as we take into account that any theoretical proposition is linked to and depends upon others, that observation is itself an interpretative act and that some theoretical assumptions must be made in order to establish the meaning of an observation, the appealing simplicity of the criterion of 'resistance to falsification' is lost. We are never in a position where we can measure an isolated and simple theoretical statement against an unmediated natural world (Mulkay, 1979: 54).

So the situation in reality is more complex. In elaborating his view on the development of knowledge and ideas, Popper (1972) postulates three worlds: an objective world of material things (World 1), a subjective world of minds (World 2) and a third world of objective structures which are the products of minds but, once produced, exist independently of them. Scientific theories belong in World 3. Sensory inputs from the first world of physical states can reach World 3 of abstraction and theory only by interaction with World 2 of subjective or personal experience. According to Popper, researchers may allow World 2 to intrude too far between Worlds 1 and 3; those who succeed do so only by constant monitoring to keep the influence of World 2 at bay.

Others, however, have not been so certain that the elimination of Popper's World 2 is either possible or desirable. Polanyi's work emphasizes the *personal* involvement of a researcher as ideas crystallize. He writes of a sense of 'otherness' as nuances of meaning come to seem to stand apart from their origins. This view of objectivity pays attention to deeper personal feelings and thoughts associated with formulation of new knowledge. Polanyi does not advocate cold detachment, but speaks of using the experience of our senses as clues until it 'transcends this experience by embracing the vision of reality which speaks for itself in guiding us to an even deeper understanding' (Polanyi, 1962: 5). Polanyi provides valuable insights into the feelings of researchers such as those involved in the N rays affair. The main actors had strong commitment to their work, which may have led them to make mistakes of interpretation, followed by misconceived theory. Their mistakes may be shown to have arisen because contextual factors were allowed to influence their interpretation of observations and experimental results, leading to deviations from accepted norms. These could only have been ignored by a kind of self-deception, by the attitude of mind described by Gould (1981) as 'unconscious finagling'.

Gould describes 'unconscious finagling' as a process whereby a researcher is so guided by his or her preconceptions that inconsistencies in results, omissions and miscalculations bring about the desired conclusions. It is perhaps worth noting in passing that if such selection results in findings and interpretations which are subsequently accepted and pass into accepted science, the scientist's actions are interpreted positively, as indicative of a good 'intuitive feel' for his apparatus and for the phenomenon (see, for example, Holton's (1978) account of Millikan's work on oil-drops). Gould is arguing that contextual factors such as beliefs extant in society at the time and held by the investigator can, quite independently of the researcher's conscious intentions, affect the conclusions of a 'scientific' investigation. In terms of Popper's schema of the three worlds this amounts to allowing the second world of subjective experience to influence theory-making activities. Gould is careful to distinguish 'unconscious finagling' from deliberate fraud.

Gould's ideas are supported by studies on perception, where we are becoming increasingly aware that, in Hanson's celebrated phrase, 'there is more to seeing than meets the eyeball.' Hanson (1969) distinguishes between visual experience as sense-datum experience and interpretation of that experience as perception. This distinction is also noted and elaborated by Bruner (1957) in a paper 'On Perceptual Readiness'. For Bruner perception involves the selection of sense-data by 'gating' and the interpretation of sense-data in the light of experience. Both are open to influence from existing knowledge. Bruner emphasizes that these are for the most part rapid and unconscious processes.

Applying this to the context of scientific research, it may be that repeated observations tend to build expectations. These then serve to direct thought about consequent observations, i.e., we tend to select certain aspects of natural phenomena as we carry out scientific observations, expecting to see certain regularities in the pattern of results. So perception is influenced by a biassed selection of only some aspects of what is observed — we see what we expect to see due to interaction of existing knowledge with the process of observation.

The contextual factors which influence scientific work may be 'internal' to science and relate to ideas, frameworks of understanding and theoretical perspectives which the researcher accepts almost without conscious reflection. They may also include 'external' factors such as questions of status, both gaining and maintaining it, desire for primacy, desire for eponymy (having an effect, unit or law named after you), financial pressures such as returns on previous funding and desire for future funding, and an altruistic desire to contribute to the good of mankind. All of these may lead to moral dilemmas when research is not progressing as rapidly or as well as expected. Several examples of scientific fraud resulting from such pressures are described by Broad and Wade (1985). More commonly, these external influences stop short of what we would normally term 'fraud'. Rather, they challenge conventional understandings of what is meant by 'objectivity' in scientific investigations.

Ziman defines objective knowledge in science as 'knowledge without a knower' or 'knowledge without a knowing subject' (1978: 107). This echoes Popper's conception of World 3. Ziman (1968), however, draws particular attention to the role of the scientific *community* as the means by which objectivity is achieved, through the imperative to convince one's peers of the validity of findings. Others too have noted that observations become scientific 'facts' only when the scientific community accepts them as such. This shifts the emphasis somewhat from the 'discovery' (or 'invention') of new knowledge to its *reception* by the scientific community. Here too social factors can play a significant role.

Mulkay (1972), in a study of social pressures surrounding innovation and knowledge-claims in science, argues that it is possible to elucidate social and cognitive norms for acceptance of new knowledge. In a case study of Pasteur, pursuing 'normal science' within established procedural and cognitive frameworks, Mulkay shows how he was rejected by the validating community as his methods and results came into conflict with their accepted norms. More importantly, he shows how the cognitive framework of the peer group proved a barrier to recognition of Pasteur. He argues that a study of external social factors is insufficient without a consideration of the processes of cognition.

This view is supported in subsequent work by Brannigan (1981). Brannigan writes of 'folk elements' in theories of science and about science. He labels as 'folk theory' ideas which appear to offer rational explanation, have wide intuitive appeal and can function at a commonsense level; and gives examples where he considers 'folk theorizing' has entered science. Taken as a whole, however, Brannigan's work invites a more radical, relativist reading. He argues that 'discovery' (including scientific discovery) is a social achievement; it is through its reception by the scientific community that a reported discovery becomes an accredited 'fact'.

The work of Collins on *replication* similarly argues that the transmission of scientific knowledge and the resolution of scientific controversy are social accomplishments. It is widely held that *replication* provides the means by which the scientific community can check the validity of reported results. Collins shows that this is less clearcut than might be imagined. In one study (Collins, 1974) he shows that publications from one group describing how to construct a new form of laser (a TEA laser) were insufficient to enable workers at other centres to construct a working replica. For this it was necessary for someone from the originating centre to go and 'make it work'. Tacit aspects of the innovators' knowledge meant that their work was not communicable in written form only to others outside their own institution.

In a subsequent study of the search for gravity waves, Collins (1975) draws attention to the fact that demonstrating the existence of a phenomenon is coincident with agreeing that your apparatus is a viable detector. If one research group claims to have found the phenomenon, then failures to replicate their findings elsewhere may simply mean that the replica detectors are not working, and not that the phenomenon does not exist as claimed. The resolution of the dilemma is necessarily a social, rather than a logical achievement. These ideas are clearly of some relevance to a consideration of the N-ray affair.

Learning about Theory Change from Simulations

The ideas outlined briefly above are difficult ones and might be deemed too advanced for many school pupils to grasp. What then should we take as realistic expectations for learning from the N rays simulation, and what understandings or awareness should we look for in evaluating its outcomes?

In general we might hope that students would appreciate that surrounding an announcement of a knowledge-claim there are social and psychological factors which exert subtle pressures on the direction of research, its outcomes and the reception of new ideas. We might hope for some awareness of the idea that reception of a knowledge-claim involves a process of justification through testing by a peer group, and that replication is commonly seen as a key part of the testing procedure. Students might also come to appreciate that it is not easy to come to definite conclusions about knowledge-claims as replication is not always possible and consensus is not easily reached, in short, that the tactics and strategies of science do not proceed as smoothly as models and images employed by 'textbook science' would suggest.

In addition we might look for evidence that students were able to grasp the scientific background to the case study and relate this to their own science knowledge. Finally, we would hope that the simulation might promote interest in the history of science and increase awareness of science as a human endeavour.

Evaluating Simulations

How then might we judge the success of a simulation? One very obvious indicator is how long it has lasted — how long the students have been able to sustain their roles and keep the simulation going. On the two occasions when evaluation data have been collected on the N rays simulation it lasted for one hour and for two hours, showing that this simulation is viable. The ability of students to create an effective simulation of this duration implies that the supporting materials are intelligible, and provide a rich enough background to the N-ray affair to stimulate and support a variety of inter-actions between the participants.

Duration alone, however, is not a convincing indicator of a simu-lation's success. In addition we might want to look in more detail at some indicators of the quality of the discourse and dramatic interactions it promoted and, in the case of a *scientific* simulation, at the more specifically scientific aspects of the enactment.

Jones (1982) writes of the *functional effectiveness* of the materials used to support a simulation. He suggests that evidence of effectiveness is pro-vided by episodes of *integrated role-play*, where credible characterization has involved the use of information from the simulation materials. Secondly, he suggests that in a successful simulation it should be possible to identify interactions showing how players cooperate to keep the simulation moving. This would indicate players capable of following the mechanics of simulation sufficiently well to perceive any difficulties experienced by others, and to find solutions. Jones terms this behaviour *participant monitoring*.

These two aspects of the functional effectiveness of a simulation really represent two distinct frames of reference: the *content frame*, dealing with assimilation and reworking of information from the role cards, and the *interaction frame*, involving participant monitoring. Both of these frames relate to behaviour from within the roles. These are similar to the two frames used by Barnes and Todd (1977) to analyze and discuss small group discussion. In the case of a simulation, however, there is a third additional frame. It might be called the *organizational frame* and refers to occasions when students step out of role (and become themselves) in order to manage aspects of the 'real' situation they are in.

Let us now look at some excerpts from the simulation transcripts and see all these aspects in action. The excerpts are long enough to give some idea of the sustained and absorbed nature of much of the role-play, but still represent only a very small amount of the total discourse recorded.

Excerpt 1

In excerpt 1 we see how the content frame is maintained as six different players discuss the effects of N rays on the retina. The scene is Blondlot's laboratory in the University of Nancy. The situation is, of course, contrived in bringing all Blondlot's critics to one place. The dialogue is shown in the left-hand column with a commentary on the right.

Lummer: Scottish researchers too have discovered that they think the variability of results from observation by eye is due to focusing muscles...

Content frame: using simulation materials.

Charpentier: [interrupting]: With reference to experiments where the eye is used to make observations, I suggest that in fact effects in the eye are due to an effect that the N rays have on the eye and not to an effect that they have on the screen. That it is the eye and not the screen which is being affected. The screen does not become more phosphorescent, but that N rays reflected from it affect the eye directly.

Participant monitoring as Charpentier anticipates and interrupts. Charpentier responds to criticism by a clear restating of his case, emphasizing physiological explanation.

Wood: But how can you be sure that these rays are N rays? In what way are they different from X rays?

Using a natural conversational strategy, by picking up on Charpentier's repetition of 'N rays' to change subject back to the physical properties.

Becquerel: Well, they are *refracted*. They can be refracted, as Blondlot's experiments have shown.

Developing content frame by logical argument.

Schenck [tentatively): But I worked back from his experimental results on refraction and I have found out that refraction is so small that it is impossible to work out the refractive index for these N rays.

In character but less than positive. She is unsure about content frame.

Blondlot: You will agree with me that they are refracted, whereas X rays are not. So this refraction is clearly different from X rays....

Good participant monitoring as Blondlot's opening phrase supports Schenck and seeks to maintain her involvement. Pursues logical argument.

Schenck: But they are refracted by such a small amount and you...

Schenck, encouraged, returns to her theme, but cannot sustain it.

Blondot [interrupting]: But they are still refracted, that is the scientific evidence.

Content frame takes priority over interaction frame. Blondlot's comment shuts Schenck out. Uses the term 'scientific' to denote 'reliable'.

Wood [gesturing towards Schenck to include her]: Your measuring equipment is so crude though and it is just not accurate enough to measure this refraction.

Good participant monitoring. Wood wants to use Schenck's point but realizes Schenck is too tentative. Gesture shows desire to keep Schenck involved.

[This discussion continued for another ten minutes, ending with Wood triumphantly producing a metal prism from her pocket!]

Excerpt 2

The second excerpt involves just three players, with one only very briefly involved. It shows particularly clearly how well the two main players have assimilated the content frame of the simulation. Both speak confidently and develop information presented in the briefing materials into a fluent passage of role-play.

[Schenck and Wood are looking at the spectrometer experiment]

Schenck: Will you explain what the screens are please?

Blondlot: Yes, well, the screen behind the aluminium is a phosphorescent screen which as the N-rays fall on it . . . as they pass through the prism . . . whether they are refracted or not to some degree . . . and we hope they are . . . when they strike the phosphorescent screen, it will produce a glow. When this experiment was carried out into X rays they fell directly in line with the source. When we did *this* experiment we found that the rays were refracted.

Not only does Blondlot have a good grasp of the information from the simulation materials here, he is also acting the part of a scientist demonstrating an experiment.

With the new source of radiation, N rays, we found that the rays were refracted and using this table we were able to measure the degree and angles of refraction from the actual source. Now here is the Nernst lamp producing N rays and we also have passing heat and light and other forms of radiation . . . we hope to stop these.

[There is now an exposition of how black paper will block visible light, wood will absorb heat, aluminium will filter out 'other' electromagnetic radiation and finally, a slit in wet cardboard will allow a 3 mm beam of N rays to pass through to the prism.]

Confident use of other science ideas: refraction, heat and light as electromagnetic radiation, absorption and transmission of radiation.

Blondlot: Finally, we've got wet cardboard. It does absorb N rays. This wet card should allow a 3 mm beam of N rays to pass through, so hopefully we've got a 3 mm collimated beam of N rays passing through to the aluminium prism.

Wood: Wouldn't it be better to have the whole experiment in the darkness because you've got light rays coming in from all around it?

Wood here may be seeking to engineer a situation where he can remove the prism, as described in the briefing materials.

Blondlot: No. Because you've got to have N rays incident at a specific point on the prism to pass through.

Blondlot may be using participant monitoring in the organizational frame here to block Wood, making it harder for him to remove the prism.

Wood: Yes, but still I'd say there's light rays coming in from the window and all around the room.

Wood persists.

[This exchange persisted for a few minutes but ends in Blondlot's dismissal of any need to darken the room since the beam from the

Despite Wood's persistent challenge, Blondlot marshals enough arguments to deny Wood for the moment. He does this by skilful use

Nernst lamp is strong enough to overcome any effects from daylight. He refers to the phophorescent screen saying that there will be a glow when the concentrated beam of N rays hits the screen. The concentration of light rays is not on a specific point in this experiment, whereas the collimated beam of N rays will be.]

of the content frame, arguing credibly against darkening the room.

One example of the artificiality of simulations is evident here. The student playing Blondlot knows from his background reading of the story of Wood's removal of the prism. He may, therefore, object to the darkening of the room, not because he believes this is what Blondlot would actually have done, but to make it more difficult for Wood to trick him. To that extent he may be operating in the organizational frame of the simulation here.

Excerpt 3

In the third excerpt we again see six players interacting. The context is the debate over the use of a narrow phosphorescent strip to detect N rays in the spectrometer experiment. Becquerel is retreating in the face of criticism from Lummer, Rubens, Schenck and Wood. The exchange shows good elaboration and development of the content frame by several of the students as they draw on their background science understanding of electromagnetic radiation to argue their case.

[To clarify the detector arrangement in the same experiment, Becquerel sets up an OHP with a sectional view of a screen with two eyelines leading to its centre, one vertically above and one oblique. Rubens and Lummer watch closely.]

Becquerel: You have a light source . . . for illumination and we've got a phosphorescent screen and what we found out was that when the N rays fell on it it improved the phosphorescence and if we looked at it along a normal the screen was brighter, but if we

Content frame. Direct use of simulation materials.

looked at an oblique angle it was much the same as before.

Lummer: This can also be done by heat though, if the screen gets hot, it glows.

Making direct use of briefing materials.

Becquerel: It doesn't show on this... it's just N rays that are coming through.

Becquerel tends towards organizational frame, but manages to stay in role.

Blondlot: I believe that Monsieur Becquerel used the same equipment as this and so the diagram is for N rays.

Blondlot's intervention shows good participant monitoring. By naming Becquerel, he pushes him back into the content frame. His intervention also clarifies the diagram, again within the content frame.

Wood: And did *you* have specialized eyesight?

Becquerel: No... and also I found N rays as we call them came off at oblique angles at times, but we haven't got far in this field.

This refers to an earlier exchange about the need for specialized (or trained) eyesight to see N-ray effects.

Lummer and Rubens: Oh yes, very convincing!

Weaker players. Language used suggests they are having difficulty remaining in role.

Becquerel: N rays fall on to this phosphorescent screen and have got short wavelengths... are re-emitted at longer wavelengths — nearer to microwaves and gives the impression it's of longer wavelength. It gives the impression you can see better. And even when we put a paper object in front of the screen and it looks like normal you can still see the screen through it, as the longer length rays can still pass through there (pointing).

Spirited defence. Becquerel draws on his school science to make his case, thus developing the content frame of the simulation. Microwaves would not have been known at this time.

[After a pause, Schenck responds.]

Schenck: Wouldn't the wavelength have to change a great deal for you to be able to see?

Schenck uses his knowledge of the electromagnetic spectrum to counter Becquerel.

Becquerel: No, there is only a short range of wavelengths you see and most of them are concentrated in the short waves and when they are re-emitted they come out as longer wavelengths.

Becquerel uses his knowledge of the 'greenhouse effect' to provide a good counter to this attack.

Rubens: When you look at the electromagnetic waveform, you can see that visible light is a long way from where you say N rays are . . . .

Rubens probably means the electromagnetic 'spectrum' (not 'waveform') here.

Becquerel: Yes, it is the effect it gives, it makes the screen more phosphorescent.

Rubens: Yes, but look where N rays . . . it's near to heat waves. Heat rays make it glow so it could be heat rays.

As on the previous occasion, Rubens develops the content frame using his physics knowledge.

Lummer: Yes, it could.

Becquerel: No, it's like when you shine UV rays on to a phosphorescent screen, it increases brightness, so we've excluded other types of electromagnetism. There's only N rays coming into it, nothing else.

Becquerel again draws on his experience of UV radiation.

Rubens: Yes, but when you said N rays, did you not say you were getting rid of all type of rays, like X rays?

[Becquerel stops and says that his pen doesn't draw all types of rays. Blondlot steps in to announce that new supplies of photographic paper have arrived. Lummer and Rubens suggest that the photographic paper be used to identify a hidden N-ray source. Two boxes are to be used, but only one contains the source.]

The argument and counter-argument have nowhere else to go at this point. Becquerel is on the verge of moving into the organizational frame. Blondlot's participant monitoring allows him to intervene immediately, keeping the simulation going. Although it lets Becquerel off the hook, Lummer and Rubens accept the change of direction to keep the simulation alive, and respond within the content frame, using information from the briefing cards.

The general impression in all these extracts, and in the transcripts more generally, is of lengthy periods of coherence and structure, with players co-operating to change direction and emphasis when a particular point is exhausted, in order to keep the simulation going. The transcripts, not surprisingly, show different degrees of competence in role-play. One player (see Excerpt 1) could not develop her role fully, largely because she did not entirely understand the briefing information. This showed in the relatively rapid failure of functional effectiveness where she relied on direct exposition in role-play. Other players, however, tried to help by involving her and using her role information 'on her behalf'. So participant monitoring can bridge some gaps.

Both simulations led to lengthy debriefings, both informal and formal. One of the debriefing sessions was recorded and it is to this that we now turn to evaluate the other aims of the simulation, to develop students' understanding of ideas about theory change.

Students' Ideas about Science and Scientific Theory

The debriefing was conducted rather like a semi-structured interview, using a small number of key questions to channel discussion and ensure coverage of the key points. In the extracts presented below the names of the characters are shown in brackets to indicate that the students are now speaking as themselves and not in role. As there were more students than roles, some students acted as 'assistants'; they are indicated by S. The discussant who led the debriefing is shown as D. Again these excerpts represent only a very small sample of the whole debriefing discussion.

There was much discussion of how Blondlot could have come to promote a theoretical idea which turned out to be so misguided, and why he defended it so strongly against criticism. Students were divided in their assessment of Blondlot, some thinking that he believed in N rays throughout, others that he had become trapped after his initial publications. Comments indicated an awareness of the influence of prior expectations:

> [*Blondlot*]: You think sometimes when . . . if you're trying to do an experiment in school, and you can deliberately rig it to work. But if you're looking for something, you're expecting something, you haven't been told the correct answer, and you're looking for something to happen, you start believing it. You know, you say, Yeah, I can see it happening, and perhaps it isn't, you believe it if you want to believe it.

> S: If you're not neutral about it and you've got a view of — you know — you're saying, 'this is right' and you don't really want to change it. You're going to not

<table>
<tr><td></td><td>really look at it fairly and you're not going to see things that you don't want to . . . .</td></tr>
</table>

D: How do you think people react when they get the evidence to oppose their theory, how do you think that they actually . . . .

[*Wood*]   [interrupting]: They react against it, they don't want to accept it if they're so enmeshed in their own theory, determined to think it's right then if someone says 'No I've got evidence to say it's wrong', they're not going to listen, they're just going to say, 'It depends on that' . . . or they can take it as a challenge.

[*Blondlot*]: I think, in Blondlot's case, he'd got so set on the idea of these things actually in existence, that in his sub-conscious he'll have either rigged the results, or whatever, or turned a blind eye to inconsistencies. And so it did seem to him in his own mind that these things were true.

[*Schenck*]: It's like the intensity of a spark. They could have sub-consciously thought it was brighter, yet to a normal neutral person it maybe appeared the same.

[*Blondlot*]: Well, I don't think Blondlot really believed it.
[*Schenck*]: Oh I think he did, I think he believed it.

Some thought that Blondlot should have been more tentative in making his claims. It is difficult to assess, however, how far this represents the wisdom of hindsight, a point to which we will return later. Repeatability of results and replicability by other workers were mentioned several times as indicators that findings could be trusted.

S: I'd say the first point when you start to question is when you can't get the experiment to work. It's when the experiment [is unreliable] and there's too much error, or too much chance.

[*Schenck*]: It's down to inaccurate equipment like the spark gap . . . he wasn't using sophisticated enough equipment, detectors like, which give a really fair un-questionable result . . . I think he had to use more soph-isticated . . . he had to spend time designing it . . . and he could have said, right there's the equipment, it's un-questionable that they're the results.

[*Wood*]:   You need to present your own results on a neutral basis, you're now able to say 'well no, I'm wrong'.

[*Schenk*]: Yeah, he should himself have been sceptical, he shouldn't have jumped to conclusions.

[*Wood*]: You've got to question what you're doing as you go along.

Another area of discussion concerned the external pressures on Blondlot and his co-workers. Recognition was generally appreciated by the students as a motivation for doing science. Practical application of results was also seen as something which would lead to recognition. This pressure was perceived by several students as having pushed the N-ray researchers to promote their findings overvigorously and with unwise haste.

[*Wood*]: They tried to make it [the N-ray research programme] grow, with sort of trying to see what it did health-wise and things. And because they weren't sure of the basic facts, it couldn't really . . . .

[*Blondlot*]: I think the fact that he was trying to apply medical uses to it before it had even been properly proved . . . .

[*Wood*]: Trying too early.

[*Blondlot*]: . . . it would . . . you know, he pushed it too much, was actually trying to use it for medical purposes.

S: That shows the pressure he's under.

The discussion also touched on the nature of scientific theory. In the next extract, which followed some comments by students about how theories they had been taught in school were later seen to be 'untrue', or at best partial, the discussant puts the question of the provisional nature of scientific theory. This stimulates some interesting comments about theory and evidence in general and then as applied to the N-ray affair. Although the views expressed suggest that few have thought through ideas such as verification versus falsification, the exchange does reveal an awareness of these issues, and suggests a readiness to develop and explore these ideas more formally.

D: Are you saying that, say, a model or a theory can stand still until someone disproves it?

[*Blondlot*]: If it's satisfactory to answer questions and proves the properties of things at the time and it's sufficient to do that, then it's a viable model. As soon as it doesn't do that, or someone comes along and proves otherwise then they can get rid of it and get a new one.

[*Le Brun*]: Generally if an experiment sort of backs up a theory than it's accepted until an experiment comes along that shows different . . . .

[*Schenck*]: It seems if you are looking at, like, in Justice here. We say, 'You're innocent until proven guilty', but elsewhere you're guilty until proven innocent. It's just various ways of looking at it isn't it?

[*Wood*]: I think it's . . . if lots of experiments are being done and, you know, you think it's right, well then you take it; but if they just suddenly make a theory and it's not really been looked into, then I think you've got to look into it . . . . You need evidence to back up that theory.

[*Rubens*]: It's no good just assuming it's right until it's proven wrong.

[*Schenck*]: Yes, I think Blondlot wanted it to be right, so he just went straight on and he wouldn't take any opposition or criticism.

[*Wood*]: You've got to be able to look at your own theories and think, 'Well maybe that's wrong' and not mind if it's wrong.

[*Schenck*]: And test other people's information.

This final comment introduces the idea of *replication* as a means of testing reported scientific information. Students seemed to appreciate, however, that replication might not provide an entirely straightforward test, as the following extract shows.

[*Le Brun*]: If [the experiments] didn't work for anyone else, then there's a doubt . . . .

D: But maybe if you've worked with some equipment for months and really know it inside out, maybe *you* can get it to work, and other people just coming new to it can't get it to work. Is that acceptable or not acceptable, what do you think?

[*Wood*]: Yes . . . up to a point . . . .

S: [interrupting]: I would say it was acceptable . . . because . . . if you look at people, some can get better results out of some forms of equipment than others . . . .

[*Wood*]: But I think other people should study it and use it . . . .

[*Schenck*]: But we're talking about experts in . . . people who are all experts in that field and knew how to use that equipment. And they were saying that their ability to use the equipment wasn't as good as theirs . . . .

[*Blondlot*]: That's the problem really. It's not open to the rest of us to make decisions on that .... You need to have knowledge to be able to form your own opinions.

Finally, it may be worth mentioning one problematic aspect of a simulation of a historical case study. As with other uses of historical material, it is always easy to be wise with hindsight. The following exchange, however, shows that at least this problem was recognized by the students in relation to their interpretation of the N-ray affair.

D: ... when it was first put to you, did it [the discovery of N rays] seem to ring true?

SS: No.

[*Schenck*]: I think that's where with hindsight now it's ... we now know more about the electromagnetic spectrum, it didn't seem to fit in with that.

[*Wood*]:   Then they wouldn't have known so much .... But now we know so much about everything else, we can see it in a different light.

[*Schenck*]: I said about hindsight, looking back ... but actually looking at it then, you can see how he possibly made the mistake.

[*Wood*]:   He didn't know as much as we do now.

[*Blondlot*]: Precisely, if it had been true, like you said before, it would be today a bit of accepted science. It becomes an accepted fact of science. And we've never been taught about N rays, so it can't be right, it's an unaccepted fact of science ...

This final comment looks like a straightforward assertion that things which are in the textbooks 'must be right'. As it was said rather ironically, it might, however, be interpreted rather differently — as implying that the ideas and concepts which we regard as 'right' are those which have been accepted into the textbooks.

Conclusions

Experiences with the N-ray simulation show that students with a general background in science can take the role descriptions and background briefing information provided and use them to reproduce in spirit a controversy from the past. Evaluation of simulations shows an ability to manage the content and interaction frames, often using quite sophisticated participant monitoring to help colleagues over difficult patches and to keep the simulation going. In addition to any science learning that has taken place these are valuable lessons in cooperation and collaboration within a group. Students have also been made more aware of the human face of science, by seeing a controversial episode through the ideas, passions and interests of the main protagonists.

The students' ability to identify and discuss aspects of philosophy and sociology of science in the debriefing discussion is encouraging, as these matters are often thought too difficult for schoolwork. The evidence is that many key ideas can be appreciated and that we do have a basis for stimulating students to think harder about the nature of science, and to develop more powerful ideas and theoretical perspectives on science as they study it. In living and discussing the lifetime of a deviant theory these students may have become sensitive to aspects of science that are usually only tacitly assumed in 'normal' school science. Whether their approach to the rest of their studies has changed remains a matter for speculation, but we may have some reason to hope that experiential learning of this sort *can* bring about a small paradigm shift from reception to enquiry.

Acknowledgments

I should like to thank the staff at North London Collegiate School and Garforth Comprehensive School, Leeds for helping me to set up the N-ray simulation as part of a sixth form induction course. In particular, I should like to thank the students in both schools who made both simulations so successful and enjoyable.

The simulation has been used on a number of other occasions, including one enactment by a group of sociologists and historians of science at the British Society for the History of Science/British Sociological Association Science Studies Group Conference on 'The Uses of Experiment' at Newton Park College, Bath in 1985.

References

BARNES, B. and EDGE, D. (Eds) (1982) *Science in Context: Readings in the Sociology of Science*, Milton Keynes, Open University Press.
BARNES, D. and TODD, F. (1977) *Communication and Learning in Small Groups*, London, Routledge and Kegan Paul.
BRANNIGAN, A. (1981) *The Social Basis of Scientific Discoveries*, Cambridge, Cambridge University Press.
BROAD, W. and WADE, N. (1985) *Betrayers of the Truth*, Oxford, Oxford University Press.
BRUNER, J. S. (1957) 'On perceptual readiness', *Psychological Review*, 64, pp. 123–52.

Patricia Burdett

BURDETT, P. (1982) *Misconceptions, Mistakes and Misunderstandings. Learning about the Tactics and Strategy of Science by Simulation*, MA dissertation, University of London Institute of Education.

COLLINS, H. M. (1974) 'The TEA set: Tacit knowledge and scientific networks', *Science Studies*, 4, pp. 165–86. (Reprinted in Barnes and Edge (1982), *op. cit.*, pp. 44–64.)

COLLINS, H. M. (1975) 'The seven sexes: A study in the sociology of a phenomenon, or the replication of experiments in physics', *Sociology*, 9, pp. 205–24. (Reprinted in Barnes and Edge (1982), *op. cit.*, pp. 94–116.)

DEPARTMENT OF EDUCATION AND SCIENCE, (1985) *General Certificate of Secondary Education: The National Criteria. Science*, London, HMSO.

DEPARTMENT OF EDUCATION AND SCIENCE, (1989) *Science in the National Curriculum*, London, HMSO.

GOULD, S. J. (1981) *The Mismeasure of Man*, New York, Norton.

HANSON, N. R. (1969) *Perception and Discovery*, New York, Freeman.

HOLTON, G. (1978) *The Scientific Imagination*, Cambridge, Cambridge University Press, Ch. 2.

JONES, K. (1982) *Simulations in Language Teaching*, Cambridge, Cambridge University Press.

KLOTZ, I. M. (1980) 'The N-ray Affair', *Scientific American*, 242, 5, pp. 122–31.

MULKAY, M. (1972) *The Social Process of Innovation*, London, Macmillan.

MULKAY, M. (1979) *Science and the Sociology of Knowledge*, London, George Allen and Unwin.

NYE, M. J. (1980) 'N-rays: An episode in the history and psychology of science', *Historical Studies in the Physical Sciences*, 11, 1, pp. 125–56.

PINCH, T. (1986) 'Controversies in science', *Physics Bulletin*, 37, 10, pp. 417–20.

POLANYI, M. (1962) *Personal Knowledge*, London, Routledge and Kegan Paul.

POPPER, K. (1972) *Objective Knowledge*, Oxford, Oxford University Press, Ch. 4.

ZIMAN, J. (1968) *Public Knowledge*, Cambridge, Cambridge University Press.

ZIMAN, J. (1978) *Reliable Knowledge*, Cambridge, Cambridge University Press.

Suggestions for Further Reading

This book draws on ideas and approaches from several different fields. Readers may, therefore, find it useful to have some general suggestions for further reading in areas with which they are less familiar. These are arranged to correspond to the sequence of chapters in the book

Introduction

A useful general introduction to philosophical ideas about science is:

CHALMERS, A. F. (1982) *What Is This Thing Called Science?*, 2nd ed., Milton Keynes, Open University Press.

More advanced treatments are likely to reflect a particular philosophical view. Two very readable texts, focusing on the issues of realism/instrumentalism and rationality/irrationality respectively, are:

HACKING, I. (1983) *Representing and Intervening*, Cambridge, Cambridge University Press.
NEWTON-SMITH, W. H. (1981) *The Rationality of Science*, London, Routledge and Kegan Paul.

The book which opened up the possibility of a sociology of scientific knowledge is:

KUHN, T. S. (1962, reprinted with additions, 1970) *The Structure of Scientific Revolutions*, Chicago, University of Chicago Press.

Unlike many classic texts, Kuhn's book is concise and readable. Two other useful accounts of the sociology of knowledge and its application to the social study of science are:

MULKAY, M. J. (1979) *Science and the Sociology of Knowledge*, London, George Allen and Unwin.
WOOLGAR, S. (1988) *Science: The Very Idea*, Chichester and London, Ellis Horwood and Tavistock.

Comprehensive reviews of the literature dealing with the relationship between philosophy of science and science education are:

HODSON, D. (1985) 'Philosophy of science, science and science education', *Studies in Science Education*, 12, pp. 25–57.
HODSON, D. (1986) 'Philosophy of science and science education', *Journal of Philosophy of Education*, 20, 2, pp. 215–25.

A very broad and general argument about the 'hidden curriculum' of science and its role in creating 'technological consciousness', based on a study of classroom discourse, is presented in:

GORDON, D. (1984) 'The image of science, technological consciousness, and the hidden curriculum', *Curriculum Inquiry*, 14, 4, pp. 367–400.

1 Accomplishing Scientific Instruction

Two accessible introductory accounts of ethnomethodology are:

BENSON, D. and HUGHES, J. A. (1983) *The Perspective of Ethnomethodology*, London, Longman.
LEITER, K. (1980) *A Primer on Ethnomethodology*, Oxford, Oxford University Press.

Research based on the analysis of classroom discourse is discussed in:

EDWARDS, A. D. and WESTGATE, D. P. G. (1987) *Investigating Classroom Talk*, Lewes, Falmer Press.

There has been relatively little sociological work on the induction of children into science as a way-of-thinking. One exception is:

DELAMONT, S., BEYNON, J. and ATKINSON, P. (1988) 'In the beginning was the bunsen: The foundations of secondary school science', *Qualitative Studies in Education*, 1, 4, pp. 315–28.

2 Bending the Evidence: The Relationship between Theory and Experiment in Science Education

Two useful books on school science laboratory work, both written by experienced practitioners, are:

WOOLNOUGH, B. and ALLSOP, T. (1985) *Practical Work in Science*, Cambridge, Cambridge University Press.
SOLOMON, J. (1980) *Teaching Children in the Laboratory*, London, Croom Helm.

The 'process' view of school science — emphasizing the methods or 'processes' of science — is explored critically in the edited collection:

WELLINGTON, J. J. (Ed.) (1989) *Skills and Processes in School Science: A Critical Analysis*, London, Routledge.

Chapter 2 draws extensively on Kuhn's description of scientific training. There is a particularly useful account of this in:

BARNES, B. (1982) *T. S. Kuhn and Social Science*, London, Macmillan, Ch. 2.

Some sociologists of science have turned their attention to the uses of experiment in scientific work. An account of some important sociological ideas about experiment is:

COLLINS, H. M. (1985) *Changing Order: Replication and Induction in Scientific Practice*, London, Sage Publications.

3 A Study of Pupils' Responses to Empirical Evidence

Research on children's ideas about electric circuits is reviewed and reported in:

SHIPSTONE, D. (1985) 'Electricity in simple circuits', in DRIVER, R, GUESNE, E. and TIBERGHIEN, A. (Eds), *Children's Ideas in Science*, Milton Keynes, Open University Press, pp. 31–51.
COSGROVE, M. and OSBORNE, R. (1985) 'A teaching sequence on electric current', in OSBORNE, R. and FREYBERG, P. (Eds), *Learning in Science: The Implications of Children's Science*, London, Heinemann.
DUIT, R., JUNG, W. and VON RHÖNECK, C. (Eds) (1985) *Aspects of Understanding Electricity*, Kiel, FRG, IPN/Schmidt and Klaunig.

Scientists' reactions to experimental results which appear not to fit with theory are discussed in:

HOLTON, G. (1978) 'Subelectrons, presuppositions and the Millikan-Ehrenhaft dispute,' in *The Scientific Imagination*, Cambridge, Cambridge University Press, pp. 25–83.
PINCH, T. J. (1985) 'Theory testing in science — the case of solar neutrinos: Do crucial experiments test theories or theorists?' *Philosophy of the Social Sciences*, 15, pp. 167–87.

4 The Construction of Scientific Knowledge in School Classrooms

The constructivist approach to learning and teaching in science is discussed in:

DRIVER, R. (1983) *The Pupil as Scientist?*, Milton Keynes, Open University Press.
OSBORNE, R. and WITTROCK, M. (1985) 'The generative learning model and its implications for science education', *Studies in Science Education*, 12, pp. 59–87.

Two useful reviews of studies in specific areas of science and of their implications for teaching are:

DRIVER, R., GUESNE, E. and TIBERGHIEN, A. (Eds) (1985) *Children's Ideas in Science*, Milton Keynes, Open University Press.
OSBORNE, R. and FREYBERG, P. (Eds) (1985) *Learning in Science: The Implications of Children's Science*, London, Heinemann.

An account of classroom practice which emphasizes the development of *shared* understandings and sees education as a process of cognitive socialization through language use is:

EDWARDS, D. and MERCER, N. (1987) *Common Knowledge*, London, Methuen.

5 Science as a Discipline, Science as Seen by Students and Teachers' Professional Knowledge

Schön's idea of 'reflection-in-action' is discussed in:

SCHÖN, D. (1983) *The Reflective Practitioner*, London, Temple Smith.

Various attempts have been made to identify different teaching styles used by science teachers. Two of the better known are:

EGGLESTON, J. F., GALTON, M. J. and JONES, M. E. (1976) *Processes and Products of Science Teaching*, London, Macmillan.
HACKER, R. G. (1984) 'A typology of approaches to science teaching in schools', *European Journal of Science Education*, 6, 2, pp. 153–67.

The idea of a link between teachers' views of science and of science teaching is explored in:

POPE, M. L. and GILBERT, J. K. (1983) 'Explanation and metaphor: Some empirical questions in science education', *European Journal of Science Education*, 5, 3, pp. 249–61.
HEWSON, P. W. and HEWSON, M. (1987) 'Identifying conceptions of teaching science', in NOVAK, J. (Ed.), *Proceedings of the Second International Seminar: Misconceptions and Educational Strategies in Science and Mathematics Education*, Vol. 2, Ithaca, N.Y., Cornell University, pp. 182–93.

There are useful discussions of the nature of teachers' professional learning in several of the chapters (for example, those by Russell and Johnston) in:

CALDERHEAD, J. (Ed.) (1988) *Teachers' Professional Learning*, Lewes, Falmer Press.

6 The Social Construction of School Science

A useful review of issues and of the literature on social influences on science learning is:

SOLOMON, J. (1987) 'Social influences on the construction of pupils' understanding of science', *Studies in Science Education*, 14, pp. 63–82.

A particularly rich source of primary data for anyone interested in exploring the influences of the social group on the meanings children ascribe to phenomena is the set of case studies documented by the Children's Learning in Science Project:

BELL, B. (1985) *The Construction of Meaning and Conceptual Change in Classroom Settings: Case Studies on Plant Nutrition*, Children's Learning in Science Project, Centre for Studies in Science and Mathematics Education, University of Leeds.

WIGHTMAN, T. (1986) *The Construction of Meaning and Conceptual Change in Classroom Settings: Case Studies on the Particulate Nature of Matter*, Children's Learning in Science Project, Centre for Studies in Science and Mathematics Education, University of Leeds.

BROOK, A. and DRIVER, R. (1986) *The Construction of Meaning and Conceptual Change in Classroom Settings: Case Studies on Energy*, Children's Learning in Science Project, Centre for Studies in Science and Mathematics Education, University of Leeds.

7 Writing and Reading in Science: The Hidden Messages

Many books have appeared in recent years on the uses of reading and writing in the development of scientific understanding. Two important ones are:

SUTTON, C. (1981) *Communicating in the Classroom*, London, Hodder and Stoughton.

CARRÉ, C. (1981) *Language Teaching and Learning: Science*, London, Ward Lock.

Analyses of science textbooks which draw attention to their 'hidden messages' include:

FACTOR, R. L. and KOOSER, R. G. (1981) *Value Presuppositions in Science Textbooks: A Critical Bibliography*, Galesburg, Ill., Knox College.

KILBOURN, B. (1984) 'World views and science teaching', in MUNBY, H., ORPWOOD, G. and RUSSELL, T. (Eds), *Seeing Curriculum in a New Light: Essays from Science Education*, Lanham, Md, University Press of America, pp. 34–43.

8 Waves or Particles? The Cathode Ray Debate in the Classroom

and

9 Adventures with N Rays: An Approach to Teaching about Scientific Theory and Theory Evaluation

These two chapters deal with specific attempts to modify the image of science presented to children through science education using historical case studies.

Accessible accounts of the background to the cathode ray debate and the N-ray affair respectively can be found in:

HARRÉ, R. (1981) 'J. J. Thomson: The discovery of the electron', in *Great Scientific Experiments*, Oxford, Oxford University Press, pp. 157–65.

KLOTZ, I. M. (1980) 'The N-ray affair', *Scientific American*, **242**, 5, pp. 122–31.

The proposal that some history of science be included within science education in order to teach about the nature of science is a recurrent one. L. E. Klopfer's (1964–66) pioneering *History of Science Cases* (Chicago, Science Research Associates) was a school version of J. B. Conant's (1957) university-level *Harvard Case Histories in Experimental Science* (Cambridge, Mass., Harvard University Press). Historical materials were prominent in *The Project Physics Course* (F. J. Rutherford, G. Holton and F. G. Watson, 1970, New York, Holt, Rinehart and Winston) and were one of many strategies used in G. S. Aikenhead and R. G. Fleming's (1975) *Science: A Way of Knowing* (Saskatoon, University of Saskatchewan, Department of Curriculum Studies).

General issues regarding the use of historical materials in school science are discussed by:

BRUSH, S. G. (1974) 'Should the history of science be rated X?' *Science*, 183, pp. 1164–72.
RUSSELL, T. L. (1983) 'What history of science, how much, and why?' *Science Education*, 65, 1, pp. 51–64.

Notes on Contributors

Robin Millar is a Lecturer in Education at the University of York, where he is involved in the initial and in-service education of science teachers and in science curriculum development. He previously taught physics and science in several comprehensive schools. His research interests are in science concept learning and in social studies of science in the context of science education. He is co-editor (with Rosalind Driver) of *Energy Matters* (Centre for Studies in Science and Mathematics Education, University of Leeds, 1986).

Patricia Burdett teaches science at Thornes House School, Wakefield. She is interested in active learning methods in school science and in introducing ideas from history and philosophy of science in school science. She developed her ideas on using simulations of historical controversies in science as part of her MA studies at University of London Institute of Education. More recently she was a co-author of *Science Skills: Problems in GCSE Science* (London, Hodder and Stoughton, 1988).

Rosalind Driver is Reader in Science Education at the University of Leeds, and is the Director of the Children's Learning In Science (CLIS) Project. Her research interests are children's conceptions of natural phenomena and the way these develop during schooling. Recently through the CLIS Project she has been investigating ways in which teaching can take account of students' conceptions to promote conceptual development in science. Her publications include *The Pupil as Scientist?* (Milton Keynes, Open University Press, 1983) and *Children's Ideas in Science* (Milton Keynes, Open University Press, 1985).

Jane French worked as a teacher before taking up postgraduate studies at the Universities of Bristol and Manchester. With a basic interest in teacher–pupil interaction, she has studied aspects of the social construction of gender as well as of science in the classroom. She taught sociology of education at New College, Durham before co-directing a classroom research project funded by the Equal Opportunities Commission at the College of Ripon and York St John. She continues to do some teaching for the University of York, but now devotes much of her time to writing.

Colin Gauld is a Senior Lecturer in Education at the University of New South Wales in Sydney, Australia, where he is involved in the education of science and mathematics teachers. After graduating from Sydney University, he taught science and mathematics in state and private schools in Australia and England for a number of years. He has particular interest in the role of history and philosophy of science in science education, in cognitive and affective aspects of teaching and learning science and in the interactions between science and religion.

Hugh Munby is Professor in the Faculty of Education, Queen's University, Kingston, Ontario, Canada. His research interests are in teachers' professional knowledge and science education, with a special interest in teachers' language. His publications include *What Is Scientific Thinking?* (Ottawa, Science Council of Canada, 1982) and *Seeing Curriculum in a New Light* (Lanham, Md., University Press of America, 1984).

Tom Russell is Associate Professor in the Faculty of Education, Queen's University, Kingston, Ontario, Canada. He teaches in the areas of science education and curriculum studies, with special interests in the analysis of teaching as well as teachers' professional knowledge. He has published articles in all these areas, and is co-editor of *Seeing Curriculum in a New Light* (Lanham, Md., University Press of America, 1984).

Joan Solomon is Research Fellow and Tutor in the Department of Educational Studies, University of Oxford. She has many years' school teaching experience. She was Coordinator for the Science In a Social Context (SISCON) in Schools Project, and of the Science Teachers In Research (STIR) Group. She has written widely on science education, with specific interests in teaching and learning about energy, science and society, and the social context of science learning. Her publications include *Teaching Children in the Laboratory* (London, Croom Helm, 1980). She is currently Director of the Discussion of Issues in School Science (DISS) Project.

Clive Sutton lectures in the School of Education at the University of Leicester. He co-directed the Science Teacher Education Project. He was amongst those who began in the 1970s to express dissatisfaction with an overreliance on practical work to promote science learning, and who started to focus instead on the language used by learners in their struggle to comprehend. He first expressed these views as contributor to and editor of *The Art of the Science Teacher* (London, McGraw-Hill, 1974) and later in

Communicating in the Classroom (London, Hodder and Stoughton, 1981). His chapter in this book is an extension of that concern.

Ton van der Valk is a senior researcher in physics education at the Centre for Science and Mathematics Education at Utrecht University, The Netherlands. From 1967 to 1972 he studied theoretical physics at Leiden University. He then taught physics in secondary school. From 1980 to 1986 he was a member of the PLON team, coordinating the pre-university (A level) part of the project. During that period he was co-author of the unit *Around 1900* and author of the *Teachers' Guide* for the unit. He is now doing research and development work on a thematic/theory unit about energy and work.

Index

Index

plant: food, 88, 100–2, nutrition, 87–8, 100–2, tropism, 45–7
PLON (Physics Curriculum Development Project), 160
Polanyi, M, 187–8
Popper, KR, 42, 58, 187, 189
potassium permanganate lesson, 17–21
potential energy, 95
practical work, 38–43, writing about, 138–42
principled understanding, 97–100
process science, 39, 119–20
public understanding of science, 1
Pupil as Scientist? The (Driver), 120
'pupil-as-scientist' metaphor, 38, 66
pupil: groups, 127–33, talk in groups, 128–33

radiation, 93–4, intensity of, 94
radioactivity, 93–4, 100, 163, 165, 174–5, 183
random, 93, 98
reciprocity of perspectives, 14, 32
reflection-in-action, 113–4, 124
reflexivity, 13
reframing, 113–4, 120, 123–4
replication, 41, 189–90, 201
restructuring ideas, 84, 86, 89–100, 103
ritual knowledge, 97–100
Roger (case study), 119–23
Röntgen, W, 163, 181–3

SATIS (Science and Technology in Society project), 155
'scaffolding', 96
Schön, DA, 112–3, 118–9, 123–4
Schutz, A, 84, 131
science: as craft, 34, as masculine, 6, as a method, 39, and gender, 5–7, processes, 39, 119–20, question in feminism, 7
Science in Process, 142, 148, 157
scientific: argument, 111, fraud, 188–9, papers, 142
second-hand knowledge, 53–4, 58
simulations, 181, 185–6, 190–1

social construction of meaning, 84–5, 127, 133, factors in learning, 84–5, 127, 133
sociology: of knowledge, 131, of scientific knowledge, 40
sought-after outcomes, 17–19, 31
standard science education (SSE) view, 39, 43, 48–51
STIR (Science Teachers in Research) group, 127
STS (Science, Technology, Society), 133–5
Students' Intuitions and Scientific Instruction (SI)^2 Project, 86

tacit knowledge, 55
theory: change, 187–90, testing, 51–2
theory-laden observation, 40, 147, 157
thermometer, use of, 25
tropism, 45–7, experiments to demonstrate, 45–51
two-component model of electricity, 69–81
teachers' professional knowledge, 112–4
temperature, 22–31, 90
textbooks, analysis of, 112, 124, 152–4, 158
Thomson, JJ, 165, 168, 176
transmission of knowledge (view of teaching), 114–9

'unconscious finagling', 188

Vygotsky, LS, 96

warrant, 111
Warwick Process Science, 142, 157
water circuit analogy (for electricity), 79
wave-particle duality, 171, 177
weight, 86–7, 95, of air, 88
Wendy (case study), 114–9
women question in science, 7
Wood, RW, 183–5
Woolnough, B and Allsop, T, 42–3, 57
World 3 (Popper), 187
writing about practical work, 138, 42

Ziman, J, 41, 189

216